Mary Magdalene

NEW TESTAMENT EVE

my thought process and spiritual exposure was Dr. Joseph Hopkins, as well as roommates, the Rev. Craig Schaffer and Mr. Jeffrey Yeager. It was during my time in New Wilmington, PA that I began my serious quest searching for the truth of the Christian faith and universal world view. Throughout my life numerous authors and their works, many listed in this book, influenced and helped to shape my Christian and Biblical outlook. The author who had the first great impact on me was Josh McDowell and his academic insight on the Resurrection of Jesus. Rich was my experience at Pittsburgh Theological Seminary with instruction from many wise and capable professors, including, but not exclusive to, Dr. Robert E. Kelley and Dr. John H. Gerstner. One of the most valuable connections for me during my ministry was meeting and sharing a plethora of ideas with Laurence E. Weed, a school teacher in our area, a lay pastor, and an elder at Natrona Heights Presbyterian Church. Mr. Weed has always possessed a keen and intelligent mind with tremendous critical thinking skills. Interaction with him was always mentally challenging and had a profound impact on expanding my thought processes. It was also Mr. Weed who introduced me to the late Dr. Kenneth E. Bailey, both his person and his works, from which the genesis of this book derives.

At the outset of composing this book, I was met with the fact that I had learned much over a 36 ½ year career, 3 ½ years in seminary, and 4 years of college. Many books had been read and much knowledge had been gained over this time. The issue I had to address is where, when, and to whom I had to thank for the development of my understanding of Biblical theology. I am indebted to individuals such as Josh McDowell, Sean McDowell, Hugh Ross, John Warwick Montgomery, Paul Little, R. C. Sproul, Walter Martin, Lee Strobel, C. S. Lewis, Gresham Machen, Jonathan Edwards, D. James Kennedy, John Stott, Gleason Archer, Norman Geisler, Philip Yancey, Randy Alcorn, the late Dr. Kenneth Bailey, in particular, and many others whose words, ideas, and thoughts permeate this book. Much of faith and spiritual apprehension is a communal affair. Their words and ideas became the words and ideas I employed and shared with my congregations and youth groups. I desire and have attempted to give proper credit to those who have influenced me and whose ideas and words I have shared in many sermons and classes during my career. The only real novel ideas I have in this book are those surrounding the history and what I perceive as the symbolism in the great encounter of Jesus and Mary Magdalene on Easter morning in Joseph's garden at the tomb. If I have failed in any way to make proper approbation I sincerely apologize. The individuals listed above are my heroes and members of my spiritual hall of fame. Their influence upon my life and this book is incalculable.

I am most appreciative and extremely grateful for those who have assisted me during my work on this book. I am indebted to my editor, Phil Grove, whose insight and creative input have enhanced this project. I am grateful to Mr. Douglas Deemer, Mrs. Marcy Korb, and the late Diane Edinger for their critical contribution to this work. I am also thankful for the help I received from my cousin, Douglas Malcolm in terms of his encouragement and advice leading to the publishing of this book. Thanks goes out to Richard Keener for this thoughts, insight, and Biblical contribution.

Most of all I am thankful for the motivation I received from God's most precious Holy Spirit to engage and complete this work. This project is something I came to believe spiritually was a significant part of God's agenda for me during this time period in my life. As such, I am also most thankful for my wife's patience and understanding throughout the time commitment necessary to engage and complete this book. Laurie's support and help with computer assistance was most important in moving toward completion.

This book shares a four-fold dedication. First of all, this book is dedicated to "all the saints who from their labors rest." Particularly, all those hundreds whose funerals I have officiated throughout my career and life. This includes those individuals for whom I long and hope have shared in the fullness of the "Mary Magdalene Moment":

Heather Ann Ehrman
Carl Kotchman
Bradley Raymond Kerr

Alexander Shane
Nico Dargenzio
Lee Ann Schultz Negley
Jody Lee Bonatesta
Diane Stevenson Edinger
Karen Humphrey
Caleb Cole
Marissa Mrozinski
Julia Bond
Derek P. Eckman.

Secondly, I wish to dedicate this book to the youth groups I left behind as I announced my retirement and ended my leadership of the groups amid many tears on our final retreats in May, 2017, held at the Guyasuta Boy Scout Reservation in Pittsburgh. I retired a couple years early, in part, to write this book. It was a wrenching experience to leave behind the groups I had developed and led for 30 years, as well as my 38-year youth group ministry which was much the joy and happiness of my service to Christ. This book, in part, is dedicated, as promised, to them:

Olivia Ahr	Cole Bergquist
Jaci Bowser	Sarah Burkett
Ava Bollinger	Matthew Conrad
Dominic Chifulini	Danielle Guthrie
Caroline Johnson	Sarah Klingensmith
Nathan Lehew	Emma Mann
Taylor Pavshak	Ava Rea
Mickey Jo Richards	Julia DeSanto
Kaitlyn Gardone	Ryleigh Hendrickson
Kiley Karolkoski	Tyrus Kerr
Lillian King	Anthony Lehew
Olivia Lumsden	Justine Miller
Emma Pomaybo	Joslyn Schrag
Robyn Schreiber	Haley Sweetland
Cade Teribery	Jaylynn Sobotka
Alexa Schrag	Caleb Uhrinek
Erin Collins	Emily Crawford
Braden Goldberg	Jillian Guthrie

Madalyne Heinle	Makayla Heinle
Mekenzie Heinle	Alexia Morrow
Keith Nikolaevich	Scott Polly
Larkin Richards	Tyler Slezak
Tyler Spencer	James Vance
Josephine Vance	Jacob Wendt
Caitlin Misejka	Kira Lester
Hadley Collins	Aaron Korb
Alli Love	Eve Johnson
Jenna Nold	Hannah McGinnis
Brett Campbell	Braden Campbell
Joy Snow	Lysle Reichenbaugh
Megan Artman	Michael Anuszek
Carolin Eberle	John Lehew

Thirdly, I wish to dedicate this book to my late great uncle, George D. Stuart who was the former editor-in-chief of the Valley Daily News in Tarentum, PA, a veteran of both World Wars, a former Pennsylvania State House Representative, and the wisest man I have ever met. It was he who taught and demonstrated through his actions at "Journey's End", Canadohta Lake, Crawford County, PA, what it means when "coming alongside to help" through life's "gloomy valleys"!

Finally, I also wish to dedicate this book to my lovely wife, Laurie Ann Wright Malcolm whose great affection has inspired me my entire married life!

CONTENTS

Preface
Mary Magdalene: New Testament Eve

The Bible is first and foremost a thematic compilation of 66 books into two great testaments. Many of the great themes of the Bible are set out within its first three chapters and conclude, roughly, in the final three chapters of John's Revelation. As some have noticed, the Bible does have a beginning and an ending which serve as "bookends" to the great drama worked out and through the course of the text. These themes begin in Genesis and rake through the sacred Writ from start to finish. Biblical and theological education is often so focused on exegesis and wrestling with the nuances of word, verse, and chapter that people rarely step back and take in the grand view and totality of the drama the Bible portrays.

The greatest theme of the Bible, in my opinion, is that of the "with-me God." It appears in the first two verses of Genesis chapter 1 with the God who "hovers" over the chaos of the earth. In great symbolic style, the reader is alerted to a God who is present and near us in the chaos and maelstrom of our lives. Here we get the first indication that God not only cares for us and is watching our person and the events of our lives but has the creative energy and resources to do something about that which plagues us. Our God is not a "stand-off" deity as in deist machinations[1] but a God who is involved with us personally, actively, and intimately. The Bible clearly speaks of a God who "paracletes"[2] with us on life's journey as portrayed in Psalm 23. Here we have the portrayal of God not only as our leader and principle Head but as a true comforter. The 23rd Psalm portrays a God who comes along side of us as we walk through the gloomy valleys of life. Our God is also a militant God who is ready to defend God's own. As our "good shepherd", God makes sure God's own reach "journey's end." God not only walks along side of us as we deal with the rigors of this life, but takes us all the way to the "forever zone" of God's company. The theme of the "with me God" is found throughout the Bible. The incarnation of God in the person of Jesus Christ ("Immanuel – God with us", Matthew 1:23), who took on human flesh and lived life as we live it is the biggest illustration of the "with me God" theme. Of course, besides the 23rd Psalm, John, in his writings, expounds on this theme highlighted by chapter 14, verse 3 of his Gospel and chapter 21, verse 3 of his Revelation. Within the theme of the "with me God" two thoughts jump out to help me define and clarify what life in this God is all about, and what God is doing in our world since our creation. The two thoughts are actually two words: love and eternity.

Love and eternity are two themes of the Bible wrapped up in the over-arching "with me God" portrayal of God's Self. Love and eternity speak Biblically of a reality in life and a destination of life at the same time. The two are meant to go hand in hand, but sin has not only broken the bond between the two but separated humankind from the reality

---

1   Deism affirms a Creator God (the Latin "deus" translated "god") who has established the existence of the universe. This Deity, however, does not intervene or interfere in the order that has been created. Deism was a movement of the 17th and 18th century intellectual thought which denied divine interaction with humanity. God was understood to be completely transcendent and not imminent.

2   The Latin "paraclete" comes from the Greek "parakletos". "Para" refers to coming "alongside" and "kletos" to "help, assist, relieve, and aid". Together the word can be understood (in Christian theology referencing God or the Holy Spirit [John 14:16, 26]) as "one coming alongside to help." This is well illustrated in the action of rescue and defense of the Good Shepherd in Psalm 23:4.

and experience of both. The purpose of the Christ event was not only to bring the two back together but to grant us the living reality of the possession of these two forever. This book is about the one moment in human history wherein God, in the person of Jesus the Christ, restored us to the magnificence of both love and eternity together, forever, again.

I became personally aware of the combination of love and eternity together in one of the richest, most fulfilling moments of my life. My wife, Laurie, and I had travelled to the Upper Peninsula of Michigan to a small village on the shores of Lake Superior known as Grand Marais. This harbor town is at the eastern entrance of Pictured Rocks National Seashore, and sports two squat lighthouses in its quaint harbor. These lighthouses mark both the beginning and end of the access to both the harbor and the lake. During the evening, Laurie and I walked out the long and rocky harbor breakwater to the light which juts out into Superior. We sat down at the base of the lighthouse to watch the setting sun over the lake to the west. I sat there holding my wife as the setting sun illuminated her face and the wind played with her hair, causing it to dance about and brush back and forth over my face. The lake was alive with motion as the breeze rustled the water into what appeared to me to be a joyous dance of its own. The colors of the setting sun above the waters were rich and sharp in its yellows, oranges, reds, pinks, purples, and blues – a mosaic of color as if painted by a master artist. As we sat there, it came to my mind that we were gazing at the waters, of what appeared to me to be, the "journey's end" of life. In that moment, my love for my wife and for God reached a point that can only be described as ecstasy. Never had I, up to that moment, been more in love with them or felt more love from them in an intensely spiritual way. In this very soulish time and experience in my life, both eternity and love came together, becoming one, in such a dramatic way that peace and joy filled my heart. More than that, however, was the surety that both love and eternity were to intermingle with each other as part of God's plan for us now and in God's ultimate expression of our humanity in relationship with deity. Looking out from the base of that lighthouse, safe and secure, the chaotic description of the world at the beginning of the Genesis account scurried away and faded before me. In this transcendent moment, it was replaced by a new divine reality, testifying to me, of God's willingness to bring about an astounding transformative change to this sin-plagued and rebellious world. The wind, the motion of the waters, and the atmospherics took on a new character in my physical vision and in my mind's eye as if we were gazing upon the waters of eternity. The intense beauty and the magnificence of the moment appeared to be otherworldly. What played out before me was both comforting and joyous. It was from this time on that I began to look for some similar story in the Bible which might effectively combine both love and eternity. It was not long until I found it.

1

"In the Garden"

"Imagine me and you, I do – I think about you day and night, it's only right – to think about the one you love and hold on tight – so happy together. Me and you and you and me no matter how they toss the dice, it has to be – the only one for me is you, and you for me – so happy together. I can't see me lovin' nobody but you for all my life – when you're with me, baby the skies'll be blue for all my life."

(Garry Bonner & Alan Gordon/The Turtles)

The Bible really does have a beginning and an end. The beginning of the Bible deals with creation, the establishment of a relationship between God and humankind, the development of a very serious breech in that relationship, and the announcement by God that He has a plan to heal the breakup. As the first three chapters of Genesis walks us into the divine-human dilemma, the last three chapters of Revelation walks us out of that dilemma into a complete newness in the divine-human relationship. At the end of John's Revelation, we discover the results of

God's action to heal the breech. In so doing, we witness the destruction of all that which plagues us, the permanence of the "with-me God", and the reality of the eternal life that God had originally intended for us in the first place. Paradise lost is now paradise found. Paradise squandered is now paradise restored (but far more glorious). We move from the Creation to the finality of the Re-creation. The drama of the whole scope of the Bible of the working out of God's plan now comes full circle. This thematic and symbolic understanding of the course and scope of the Bible is a better argument in terms of the "closing of the canon" (66 authoritative books for the Christian faith) than any other exegetical argument that has been offered. The Bible truly has a beginning and an end! The glorious news for God's own is that the end is "only just the beginning".

Thematically, in the opinion of this writer, the story of the Bible revolves around five people. The five do not include Moses, Elijah, Peter, and Paul. The five do include God's incarnation in the person of Jesus the Christ, Adam, Eve, Jesus' earthly mother, Mary, and Mary Magdalene. Of these five, of key importance at the beginning and at the end are Adam, Eve, Jesus, and Mary Magdalene. Mary, the mother of Jesus appears, in my opinion, to play the role of a connecting personage between the beginning and the end. If one were to break things down to the least common denominator in terms of the completion of the intersection of love and eternity, it would come down to Jesus and Mary of Magdala.

It is also interesting to note that among the many gardens portrayed for us in the Bible, the story of salvation history revolves around 4 of them: Eden, Gethsemane, the garden tomb of Joseph of Arimathea, and the garden of the "New Heaven and New Earth" (the Eschaton).[3] Of these four gardens, the primary two for our consideration are Eden and that of Joseph of Arimathea. It is amazing the parallelism between Eden and the garden tomb. In this story we have two gardens, two people (a

---

3   In Christian theology, "the Eschaton" means the completed and final era or age of salvation history. The term was coined by Charles Harold Dodd in 1935 as the "divinely ordained climax of history." Eschaton comes from the Greek *eschaton*, the neuter of *eskhatos* meaning "last." It is frequently employed to describe "end times", "end of days", "last or final days."

man and a woman), two Adams, two Eves, two lights, two callings, two messages, two relationships represented, two states of loneliness, two periods of waiting, two adversaries, two conditions, two movements, two flights, two dispositions, two placements, two states of excitement, two notions of sleep, two acts of clothing, two settings of time, and perhaps there are more. The first garden and its events establish the genesis of the divine-human relationship and its severing. The second garden reverses the ill circumstances of the first and restores the relationship that has been so strained and severed.

Genesis chapters 1 and 2 chronicle the creation, not of the whole universe, but planet Earth. As Hebrews 11:3 indicates, all that which is material comes from something invisible. In Genesis 1:1 we learn that God has created the basic inorganic components of the universe which are often considered as time, space, energy and mass, or matter. The "days" that follow reference God's creative activity on planet Earth alone. As such, three specific acts of special creation (the Hebrew "bara", which implies a creation out of nothing) are referenced for us: Genesis 1:1, Genesis 1:21 and the creation of the life principle which some have termed "consciousness", and Genesis 1:27, which is the creation of humankind in the image of God. Regardless of all the theories of origin and the debate over the time frame reference of God's creative activity, specifically the origin of the first human being, the fact of the matter Biblically is that God created an original man and, out of the genetic material of that man, an original woman. From this first pair all human life, regardless of race or ethnicity, has developed. Scientific and genetic studies have theorized that all human life comes from one original woman (known as the Mitochondrial Eve,[4] defined as "the matrilineal most recent common ancestor – MRCA – of all currently living humans"), though such findings are not yet considered conclusive[5] As I have stated and written in the past, there is only one race, and that is

---

4   Rebecca L. Cann, Mark Stoneking, and Allan Wilson, "Mitochondrial DNA and Human Evolution." *Nature* (January 1987).

5   While the name "Mitochondrial Eve" is a journalistic representation given to the research by Cann, Stoneking, and Wilson, challenges to their research and findings remain. The subject is fascinating but a firm conclusion may not be reached until sometime in the future.

the human race. While there are some different traits and distinctions among the human family (perhaps evidence of some micro-evolution within a "kind"), it appears that all the genetic information and combinations were already present in Adam and Eve. Let us remember that we know nothing of their skin tone and personal physical traits. What we do know is that they were perfect human specimens, and that Adam, upon first sight of Eve (Genesis 2:23), was ecstatic!

It is, however, not the purpose of this book to delve into the science of creation but to examine the circumstances of the first man and woman, their relationship between each other, and also their relationship with God. Many people have often heard it said, or seen it written, that there are two creation stories in Genesis. Much of this has been theorized in the Documentary Hypothesis (J, E, D, P – Jehovist or Yahwist, Elohist, Deuteronomist, Priestly source material) of Julius Wellhausen and taught in seminaries for decades.[6] It appears to many others, that what seems to be two accounts of creation in Genesis, is the Bible's first appearance of the Hebrew Parallelism writing style.[7] While this style is very evident throughout the Old Testament (particularly in the Psalms) and is prevalent in many various types (Standard Parallelism, Step Parallelism, and Inverted Parallelism), it also occurs in the New Testament, particularly in Paul's writing of First Corinthians, according to the late Dr. Kenneth Bailey.[8] Genesis 1:1 through 2:3 is the general account and overview of God's creation on planet Earth. Genesis 2:4-25 is a more specific look and focuses upon the creation and circumstances of the first man and woman along with their Creator.[9] Here we learn much. We cannot, however, proceed with what we learn about the orig-

---

6   The Documentary (Wellhausen) Hypothesis theorizes that the first 5 books of the Bible (known as the Pentateuch or Torah) is a collection of independent writings which were gathered and combined into one narrative by editors and redactors.

7   Parallelism is a literary device. It is a significant component of Hebrew poetry and Biblical literature wherein one phrase is repeated, expanded, amplified, or contrasted with another. There are many forms of parallelism which are identified by a number of terms by various scholars and authors.

8   Dr. Kenneth E. Bailey, ThD, "Leadership in the New Testament" (lecture, Pittsburgh Theological Seminary, Pittsburgh, PA, June 8-12, 1998).

9   Gleason L. Archer, *Encyclopedia of Bible Difficulties* (Grand Rapids, Michigan: Zondervan Publishing House, 1982), 68-69.

inal man and woman in chapter 2 without examining chapter 1 of the creation story. In the 6th day of creation, as the third act of creating something out of nothing takes place, God declares, "Let us make man in our image, in our likeness . . ." (Gen. 1:26). What may surprise the reader here are the words, "Let us". "Let us" represents plurality. What options are open to us here for interpretation? "Let us" cannot represent God and other created beings, such as angels. "Let us", representing the "royal we", also does not make much sense to me. "Let us" must represent some other sort of plurality. What it informs us is the Creator represents plurality in reference to the composition of the divine self. We have here a glimpse into the foundational doctrine of God that continues to unfold throughout the Bible. The word "trinity" is the term devised to convey this picture of God. God's singular essence is manifested in three persons: Father, Son, and Holy Spirit. The triunity of God remains mysterious and mentally challenging exceeding our human capacity to fully comprehend. The transcendent nature of Being who has created everything, however, is completely plausible. God is, and God does exhibit three distinct, yet interrelated personalities and personal expressions of divine Self. In my estimation and that of others, the three persons explain the origin of relationship, love, and compassion in terms of God's creative intent. If God were just one, and only one, could God possess love? The various names for God, particularly in the Old Testament, are profound.[10] Each one gives us more revelatory information about God's person and being. Our God is certainly a "big God". The name for God in our text is "Elohim". Elohim is a plural noun found only with a singular verb or adjective. Elohim represents plurality in singularity. Elohim is one who stands in covenant relationship. Elohim represents unchanging love. Elohim represents God as love. As pointed out by the many who have written books on the names of God, love is triune. For God to be love there must be a lover, a beloved, and a spirit of love. As triune, God can express and exhibit within the divine Self affection and compassion. Before God created anything in this

---

10   Andrew Jukes, *The Names of God in Holy Scripture* (Grand Rapids, Michigan: Kregel Publications, 1986), 6.

universe or multiverse,[11] God possessed the capacity to create and express love. Love explains much of the divine plan (God's set of purposes and destinies for creation). God in three persons has great bearing on what it means to be created in the image of God. God is a "relational" Spirit who has created beings to be "relational" as well. To be "created in the image of God" means many things, which we will take up below, and is a key consideration for us in that God created us for relationship. Before we continue in our discussion of being created in the image of God, let us consider the word or name "Adam". "Adam" represents "mankind" or "humankind". Much is communicated about us in Genesis 1:26, 27. As humans, we are both made and created. There is a difference between the Hebrew words "make" and "create". To "make" something is to employ the materials that are already at one's disposal. To "create" means to speak into being that which did not exist before as is already noted above. That God formed "man" from the dust of the earth means that God used the tools and materials already created and available to form the first human. This material predates Adam. It is not novel. What is novel, is the creation of spirit. No earthly creature prior to the first human has spirit. While there is some debate on the subject of whether human beings combine 2 things or 3 things, it appears that God does combine in the first human the physical (the body or "asa"), the soulish like that of some of the animals in terms of the exercise of the will, emotions, yearnings, passions, and self-awareness (nephesh), and the spiritual. Humans, in this conception, have three parts: the physical, the soulish, and the spiritual. While we, in one sense, have three parts, we do not bear the image of God physically (God is Spirit and has no physicality), though we are like God's incarnation in the person of Jesus. Only Jesus, however, is the exact representative or likeness of God in human flesh. We are material and spiritual with the soul operating as the interface between the material body and the (postulated) nonmaterial spirit that Paul seems to describe in Romans 7 and 8.

---

11   Hugh Ross, *Why the Universe is the Way it is* (Grand Rapids, Michigan: Baker Books, 2008), 105.

The human can exist apart from the physical body (though to be human means a corporeal existence). A soulless or spiritless human is not a human at all. A soulless or spiritless human cannot exist. So, what does it mean to be created in the image of God? The answer is the same as Jacob Marley's to Ebenezer Scrooge, "Much!" To be created in the image of God means (and this list is not exhaustive): we have the capacity for abstract thought including a drive to discover truth and absolutes; we can appreciate beauty and aesthetics; we can form, understand, and exercise ethics – a moral code – an innate awareness of right and wrong (conscience); we have personality; we have a consciousness of self; we have language capacity – the ability to communicate that includes complex symbol cognition and expression; it means that we have "eternity in our hearts" (Ecclesiastes 3:11) concerning matters of death and the afterlife (being made for eternity, we are not immortal in and of ourselves, but only through the decision of the One who created us and chooses to sustain us); we have a propensity for worship and the desire to communicate with a higher being; we have the capacity for personal fellowship with God if we so choose (capable of a loving communion and intimate relationship with God); and, like God, we possess a spiritual nature that is the ultimate unique element of humanity (while God is Spirit, we, each of us, are a spirit). Note the language in Genesis 1:27, "So God created man in his own image, in the image of God he created him; male and female he created them." What is critical for our understanding of this verse is that God, who is neither a man or a woman physically (or any other way), has both male and female characteristics. Both genders are made in the image of God. There is, however, something unique here in terms of the Hebrew language. In Hebrew the letters of the word for "man" are "aleph", "yood", and "shin". It is interesting to note that the letters of the word for "woman" are "aleph", "shin", and "hey". The Hebrew letters "yood" and "hey" form the divine name (Yahweh). "Together" (according to Dr. Frank T. Seekins, an expert on ancient Hebrew word pictures), God's image is formed." The divine name, in other words, is formed by the composite unity of a man and a woman. This means that "the male-female relationship" is "extremely important" as we see played out in Genesis chapter 2[12]. This is also very telling when it comes to the concept of marriage and ultimately why the divinely instituted covenant of marriage, Biblically, can only be between a man and a woman. Also note that after the creation of the human species on the sixth day, God refers to God's work as not just "good", but "very good".

What does this mean for you and me? What is the sacred text telling us? Right from the beginning verses of the Bible we learn that we were created to receive, experience, express, exercise, abide in, and enjoy a relationship with God Almighty. Truly, it is all about relationship and those who think and teach otherwise are just flat out wrong! Our creation in God's image makes relationship possible. It is something God desires, and God desires to have it with those whom God chooses. Have you ever stopped to think how wondrous, amazing, and marvelous this is? Think about it! We, you and I, can know the Creator God, be with God, and experience the works and marvels of God forever! Thinking that God wants a relationship with each one of us, no matter how poor and pathetic we might be, is simply mind blowing! No matter how we might cower and hide from such an occurrence, it does not change the fact of God's desire. I very much like the song sung by the Turtles back in the 60's. It was also very popular with my youth group as many of us would request it repeatedly during karaoke. The song is "Happy Together", as attested above. "Happy Together", to me, pretty much sums the original attitude, and the attitude that I feel not only throughout the Bible but particularly in the book of Revelation. The door of the house church at Laodicea in Revelation 3:20 I think is instructive. The door of the house church represents the door to the hearts of each individual member of that declarative and worshipping body. Jesus arrives at the door of our corporate and individual hearts. He knocks on the door seeking entry into our persons and lives. He wants to share fellowship with us. In that, the house church is like the common Palestinian house in the birth narratives of Jesus; our Lord comes to where we live. If we open the door to Him and let Him in,

---

12   Frank T. Seekins, *A Mighty Warrior* (Phoenix, Arizona: Living Word Pictures Inc., 2004), 22.

His presence with us carries with it two promises: the promise of location and the promise of communication. Sitting down and sharing in a meal together is a sacred aspect of hospitality in Hebrew antiquity. It tells us that He, the with-me God, wants to be present (on location) with us, and share in the intercourse (communication) of our lives with us. He knocks in hope of a response. Reminiscent of the question that remains and hangs in the air both at the end of the book of Jonah and the parable of the elder son in Luke 15 (examined in chapter 26), will we – will we open the door and let him in?

Please be advised, as we proceed, that much of the information in the next two paragraphs reflects the work of Hugh Ross, a member of the *Reasons To Believe* ministry based in California whose totality of writings, messages, recordings, and books are extraordinary and worth adding to your library! There are a good number of things that the casual reader misses when it comes to reading the creation narrative in Genesis (please note that there are other creation narratives in the Bible including Psalm 104, Job 38-42, among others). This is not only true of the first chapter of Genesis, but particularly important when it comes to the second chapter in this book of origins. Verse 8 of chapter 2 needs to be carefully rendered. Notice here that Eden does not cover the entire planet. This has been a great misconception by many a Church School instructor. (Recently, Eden has been identified, by some respected researchers, as a small location that is now at the bottom of the Persian Gulf to the southwest of the strategic straits of Hormuz.)[13] Also notice that Adam is created outside the garden of Eden and placed inside the garden by God. This may indicate, perhaps, that Adam may know something about the circumstances of life outside the Garden. This garden of God is a special place, unlike the rest of the sphere, and Adam has the task of being the steward of God's garden. A steward is someone who tends to and takes care of the property of another. In this case, Adam is instructed with the oversight and maintenance of that which belongs, in a special way, to the Creator God. Verse 15 must also

---

13   Hugh Ross, *Navigating Genesis: A Scientist's Journey Through Genesis 1-11* (Covina, California: Reasons to Believe Press, 2014) 96-100.

be noted in this regard. Some of Adam's duties are described in verses 19 and 20. According to Hugh Ross, Adam is responsible to observe the animals, get to know their tendencies, and give them names. This, in Ross' estimation, would take some time. It takes time for Adam to get to know the flora and the fauna of God's special preserve. He is introduced to the "nephesh" animals – the birds, mammals, and higher reptiles. In process of studying them and making identification with them, Ross notes that Adam discovers that he can experience relationships with them that is impossible with plant life, trees, and vegetation. These creatures can communicate with each other and with him. He discovers that he can communicate with them as well. In the process, Ross notes that Adam learns that the creatures of Eden possess a sense of feeling, reasoning, and relational qualities. Adam may have become intrigued by them and learns that even a sense of mutuality exists between him and them. They are pleasing to him and can serve him, as he is pleasing to them and can serve them. The creatures of Eden, Ross imagines, are not frightened by Adam. They trust the care-taker. In time Adam learns their needs and how he can help them and serve them better.[14] Eden must have become a joyful situation in which to live. All this time, however, I think that God was setting Adam up for something even more joyful. A great amount of time could have passed. The usual understanding of the casual reader or student is that Eve was created immediately after Adam. Once again, the time frame reference is important here. It appears to me, as it has appeared to Hugh Ross and others, that such a job of observation and interaction with the creatures of Eden would require a substantial amount of time. I cannot help think that Adam was alone as a human being in the Garden for a long time. There are two things one might consider here: Adam, in spite of his fellowship with God and the creatures of the Garden, might develop a sense of loneliness, and the task of steward of the garden requires help. It may be reasonable to assume in the language of Genesis that God wanted to extend God's special preserve to the entire planet. In Genesis 1:28, we learn of God's desire and command to expand Eden (which

---

14   Ibid., 101, 103-105.

means "delight") throughout the sphere. Adam and his progeny are to expand, move out, and care take of the whole planet. This task is a mighty one and requires human fruitfulness and reproduction. The problem, Ross observes, is that Adam lacks one thing, a complement in order to achieve all this. Adam would notice that every creature, including God, has a complement, but him. Of course, when it comes to God, we are not talking about a goddess as in the mythology of the Greco-Roman world or other cultures. Being triune, within God's singularity is the plurality of a lover, a beloved, and a spirit of love. He observes that the animals live together as male and female. God is self-complementary as Father, Son, and Holy Spirit so that relationship exists, is exercised, and exhibited, among the persons of the godhead. I cannot help but believe that God did this on purpose. Adam comes to learn much, but the key thing he comes to know is that only he is alone in this way.[15]

Among the many things I note in Scripture are, what I call, "the great delays." In my estimation the first "great delay" in the Bible is the creation, coming to, and gifting of the woman to the man. We might also understand the time of Noah as God's delay in the punishment of wicked and violent humankind. There is the delay in the lifting out of Jacob's son, Joseph, from the ill circumstances he was treated to in Canaan and Egypt. There is a great delay in the rescue of the Israelites from their captivity in Egypt. Ezekiel and others prophesy about a delay in the return from the Babylonian captivity. The coming of the Messiah can be understood as a "great delay" in the "fullness of time." Similarly, there is what we are living through now – the great delay in the expected second physical coming of the Christ to planet Earth. I also think there is another "delay" of God in terms of the resurrection accounts of which I will speak later. Great delays should not be unanticipated when it comes to God and salvation history. We should also understand that God often employs "great delays" in our lives when it comes to our circumstances and the working out of our prayer requests. I think that Adam is alone, in terms of being a solitary human being, in God's paradise for quite some time. How long this time might have been, we

---

15   Ibid., 105.

cannot speculate. In the opinion of this writer, I think God wanted to purposely heighten Adam's sense of loneliness and sense that he acutely needed help. After purposely maximizing these things, God is ready to bestow God's great gift to Adam, and it comes in the form of a woman who becomes known as Eve. God really does something marvelous here. As time passes God allows Adam to feel an acute awareness that something is missing. God gives him sufficient time to feel his need for a complement. God heightens Adam's sense of expectation for the reception of the revelation and gift of Eve.

The text indicates in verse 18 that, "It is not good for the man to be alone. I will maker a helper suitable for him." Understanding the word "helper" here is critical. There are two Hebrew words for "help." The Hebrew word, "obed" means "servant". The Hebrew word, "ezer" means "ally". The word employed here is "ezer". Eve is created to be an ally to and for Adam. What I have read from others during my career is that the letters of the word "ezer", Ayin and Zar, form Hebrew word pictures. Ayin means "an eye to see", and Zar means "a weapon man" or an enemy. Eve is created not as some lowly servant or slave of the man. Rather, she is created as an ally. Her spoken purpose (but not her only purpose) is to watch Adam's back and engage with him together in the stewardship responsibilities of the garden caretaking.[16]

It has been often commented on through history that Adam, who came first, is the superior created human by God. Others see Eve, as the last and pinnacle subject of creation, as superior. Neither of the suppositions is true in my evaluation of the text. A correct view negates both. Commentators and expositors have long noted that Eve was taken from Adam's side. Eve was not taken from his head, they say, to rule over the man. Nor was she taken from Adam's foot to be trounced and stepped upon by the man. The taking of Eve from Adam's side (the translation "rib" may be an inaccurate rendering of the text), in my estimation, not only denotes that Eve's make-up is of the DNA of the man, but that Eve is to walk together with the man, side by side. This reminds me of the Macedonian Phalanx imagery employed by Paul in Philippians 1:27

---

16   Seekins, 23-24.

and 28. Adam is put into a deep sleep from which God removes a "sela" or portion of the man. This biopsy, or tissue sample, taken from Adam is employed in crafting Eve. God employs the sample to generate one who is both similar and dissimilar. What we are to understand that God has accomplished here is the creation of a complement for the man. God has created a woman. Her role is to walk through life beside him. Together, they form a new God-ordained entity. She is his ally to keep "an eye to see the weapon man." I like the Celtic concept of marriage. Some in Celtic studies have commented that the ancient Celts viewed the symbolism of marriage between a man and a woman as the couple standing back to back. This reminds me of "radar". Together, standing back to back, the couple has a 360-degree view. As a composite unity, they "strive with one another" to fend off any challenges to their persons and marital unity. This speaks much to me in terms of the concept of Biblical marriage. In marriage we are to form a composite unity where two become one emotionally, mentally, relationally, psychologically and spiritually. Together, they are to mirror something of the depth of love and unity evident among the persons of the triune God. Together, they are to plumb the depths of love. Biblical marriage is all about complementarianism. Man and woman are to strive to form a perfect relational union wherein the man and woman complete each other while reflecting the image of God as male and female. God has created men and women as interdependent beings. 1 Corinthians 11:11-12a says, "In the Lord, however, woman is not independent of man, nor is man independent of woman. For as woman came from man, so also man is born of woman." Adam, as Genesis 1 through 3 reveals and indicates, faces a daunting task and a destructive force bent on frustrating God. By himself, Adam lacks the resources to face the task and challenges that lie ahead. Together, Adam and Eve, men and women, can overcome the difficulties and surmount the obstacles to achieve great ends together as Proverbs 31 testifies. Adam needs an ally for the completion of the planetary assignment. This is an assignment that requires a multiplying population of which Eve is the first and the origin of the rest. Adam also needs someone like himself in whom to relate. In Eve, God fills the void and completes the picture. Together, the man and the woman form a composite unity. Together, they form a bond so close that they cannot imagine life without the other. Together, they form something of the image and essence of God plumbing not only the depths of intimacy and relationship with each other, but with God as well.[17]

One year, on our wedding anniversary, my wife, Laurie, presented me with a card in which she inscribed the words, "We are two very different people, but somehow it works!" It works if God is always at the center of the marriage. God is and must be the motivating dynamic undergirding any and every marriage. It works if God's people would wrestle to understand God's purpose and meaning in marriage which is much more than our temporal happiness. There is an eternal lesson in marriage that helps us to understand and relate to God as well as making us fit for eternity; an even deeper relationship with each other in the coming eschaton. On another date of our wedding anniversary, my wife presented me with a card in which she thanked me for "taking such good care" of her. Husband and wife are to have each other's back in marriage and serve one another. Like Adam, we are all stewards of God's property (Psalm 24:1, Matthew 25:14-30, and Luke 19:11-27). A right rendering and understanding of Ephesians 5:21-33 teaches us that ours is to be a "mutuality" - a mutual submission and servanthood one to the other.

What we also need to note in the text, as we leave our survey of chapter 2, is that Adam was thrilled with God's gift of Eve. This moment in the history of humankind is what I call the "Great Presentation", which I believe is repeated in the New Testament. God makes Eve and brings her to the man. The translation of the Hebrew into English, "This is now bone of my bones and flesh of my flesh; she shall be called 'woman', for she was taken out of man" does not do justice to the expression of excitement and sheer delight Adam experiences in God's gift. In God's perfect timing and at the moment of the delivery of God's gift of woman, Adam awakens and declares what we can only call the "wow" factor. Here, introduced by God, is a physical, soulish, and spiritual

---

17   Ross, *Navigating Genesis*, 107.

creature just like him, but different in all the ways God's plan requires. Adam exclaims his ecstasy in the Hebrew by saying, "At last now!" Here was a creature he could relate to on all levels of the human experience and one with whom he could explore the height, depth, and breadth of relationship intimately and spiritually. He is completely delighted and enthralled as if to say, "Wow, what a gift from God!" Here is the gift of another person to help him. Here is the gift of another person to save him. Here is the gift of another person to complete him. Here is the gift of another person, together with whom, to forge something of the image of God. Imagine the moment when he first sets eyes on her, and she him! It is a powerful moment whose intent is to change everything and to complete everything God has in mind. It is one of the great encounters of history, and one in which, we will see, will need, of necessity, to be repeated. Of course, what I have heard some comment upon during my career is what appears to be the complete failure of Eve in her mission to "keep an eye on the weapon man."[18] We will continue the story in the next chapter.

---

18   Seekins, 24

2

"All About Eve":
Eve Almost Makes Paradise Complete

"MacArthur's Park is melting in the dark. All the sweet, green icing flowing down...."

(Jimmy Webb/Richard Harris)

"All About Eve" is a 1950 movie starring Bette Davis as Margo Channing and Anne Baxter as Eve Harrington. The movie was based on a 1946 short story by Mary Orr entitled, "The Wisdom of Eve." The film was nominated for 14 Academy Awards, winning six, including Best Picture. It is the story of how one woman befriends and then tries to supplant another, ruining life for both.

Eve was created by God not to supplant Adam, but to help bring God's creation around to perfection. I guess one could say that things went terribly wrong. The rest of the story of the Bible details how God moved to redeem the situation and make things marvelously right again, and this time, for all time.

It might be fun to imagine the life that Adam and Eve lived. Certainly, it was not a lazy carefree environment. As stewards, they had many responsibilities. Eden, though, appears to be the picture of the perfect place and the perfect condition. It was good and God pronounced it "very good". It was not perfect. It was not the ideal. It was, however, part of the plan and the way to secure the ultimate circumstances and condition God had in mind. The gift of Eve almost makes paradise complete. All that remains is to choose wisely. Choice is the one thing that makes love real. Choice is the one thing that gives meaning to life and relationships. Choice is the one thing that qualifies compassion. Choice is the one thing that gives meaning to worship, praise, and adoration. Choice is the one thing that defines friendship and virtue. Choice is the one thing that makes paradise, paradise. A number of years ago my wife asked me the question, "Why do you love me?" I think she expected me to respond with a list of her qualities and some glad moments in the history of our time together. Instead I responded by saying, "I love you because I chose to love you!" This reply did not sit too well with her. What I explained to her was that I believe that love is very much a choice. I choose to love her. I choose to do, as Tony Campolo often comments, "the things that a lover is supposed to do."[19] From choice comes the acts of love. Love for me is both choice and action. What I was attempting to communicate to my wife was that she need not worry about the ravages of time and age. I had made a choice and I was determined to stick with it – loving her and her alone. Likewise, paradise, it seems to me, comes down to choice. This may be odd for a person with some "predestinarian" views to affirm.[20] I am one

---

19   Tony Campolo, *Who Switched the Price Tags?* (Dallas: Word Publishing, 1986), 148.

20   Predestination is a complicated and controversial term employed in Christian theology. It is drawn from the doctrines of God's omniscience and sovereignty. Omniscience means "all knowing." Sovereignty means "in control or having authority over." Historically, many Christians affirm that God knows the past, present, and future. Primarily, the doctrine is the belief that God has predetermined who will receive salvation. Some theologians apply the term not only to salvation, but also God's control over even small details in life. Predestination is often viewed as the opposite of free will. While there are many views concerning predestination (infralapsarianism,

who believes that God knows and plans beforehand. Yet I still affirm the necessity for some sort of concept of choice and free will. I may not know how to systematize it, but in reading and studying the Bible, it appears to me that the Scriptures hold the two in tension. Adam and Eve, up to this point in our story, had not been challenged on their exercise of free choice. In particular, the overarching choice in the garden God had established. Until they did, the picture would not, and could not, be complete.

In the story of the creation of Eve, as we move through the second chapter, it becomes apparent that God is attempting to form a "perfect unity" between the man and the woman. The Greek word, "telios" talks about the "end game." Love's "end game" is to make the choice of abiding with another and following through on that commitment, accomplishing acts that are based on the decision to love. The Biblical marital union begins through the free choice of entering into a covenant agreement. In this agreement not just two people are involved, but three. There is the man. There is the woman. The third person is God. Entering into the marriage covenant speaks to the very person, presence, and character of God. It is an intense relational union as depicted in the final three verses (Genesis 2:23-25) of the second chapter. "'This is now bone of my bones and flesh of my flesh; she shall be called 'woman,' for she was taken out of man. For this reason, a man will leave his father and mother and be united to his wife, and they will become one flesh.' The man and his wife were both naked, and they felt no shame." Together, the man and woman are to form a composite unity. As two independent beings, they are to form a bond so close that they cannot imagine life without the other. As two independent beings they are also to form the image of God (who, once again, possesses both male and female characteristics). Two becoming "one flesh" is highly charged spiritually and

---

sublapsarianism, supralapsarianism or antelapsarianism) and variant understandings of its meaning and extent, what this writer acknowledges, is before the creation of the universe God knew what would play out in the aftermath of God's creation and established the cosmos as a reflection of the salvific drama that would play out on planet Earth. In other words, God knew, planned for, and established what would take place in salvation history according to God's great purposes for humankind in relationship to God.

is meant to delve into deep areas of personal and spiritual integration. The intimacy that we are supposed to share in marriage between a man and a woman informs the depth of intimacy and relationship we can have forever with God. While this can be difficult to express as language is limiting, it is apparent that the ultimate purpose of marriage is in the knowing completely of another in the marriage covenant, which leads to an ultimate knowing of God and God's operation as three in one!

Over the years, I have heard some refer to the drama of Genesis chapters 1 through 3 as "the divine comedy". While I do not find anything humorous about it at all, it is interesting to note that the tempter launched his assault directly upon the one who was given to have and watch Adam's back. The divine covenant, with its test of refraining from eating of "the tree of knowledge of good and evil", was an agreement God made with Adam alone. Adam, who was created outside the garden of Eden and placed by God within its confines, would have observed the major differences of life in the world both outside and inside the garden. Outside Eden was death and decay. Inside the garden was "the tree of life", which would keep him alive forever. Upon the advent of Eve, it would have been Adam's responsibility to explain these things to her. It is apparent that he did just that, for Eve seems to have understood the warning and the consequences of disobedience. One can only wonder, since the covenant was given by God to Adam, and Eve did not have first hand experience of life outside the garden, just how sharp was her understanding. The tempter, perhaps, saw a weak spot that he might be able to exploit here. A direct assault on Adam probably would not have been successful, but the right kind of attack on Adam's ally might prove to be fortuitous.

While discussion of a personal Satan in the form of a serpent strike many as purely mythological, the content of the attack is both revealing and quite deep intellectually. Here you have the basis of true Satanism, the foundation of all false religion. In this story we have one of the great confrontations of all time. A confrontation that will have to be replicated due to human miscalculation and loss in this story. The tempter begins the assault (Genesis 3:1) by questioning God ("Did God really say...?")

and fostering doubt in the mind of Eve as to God's intent in terms of not eating (Eve adds the notion of "not touching" – Gen. 3:3) from "the tree that is in the middle of the garden." The tempter counters Eve's correct response learned from Adam by declaring (Gen. 3:4), "You will not surely die, for God knows that when you eat of it your eyes will be opened, and you will be like God, knowing good and evil." This is really a loaded statement for evident here are three or four lies and certainly a variant world view from that which Eve had received. "You will be like God" must have been enticing to Eve from everything she knew about God from Adam and on her own firsthand basis in relationship with God. The concept that godhood is possible casts doubt on God, who appears to be holding something good back from her and her husband. Death is the penalty for eating of the tree of knowledge, but the tempter counters with the declaration that death will not result, "You will not surely die." Was the tempter trying to get her to believe that death is only an illusion? It appears that the key to godhood and immortality is the possession of the knowledge that the tree can give. God is made to appear here, once more, as if God is holding something back from them. Once enlightened, they can ascend to a new status alongside of God so, in reality, that which was deemed to be bad, in this new way of thinking, is actually good. I find, along with other scholars and writers here, a sense not only of the diminishing of the concept of a personal God who decrees moral absolutes, but the hint of the universe being a self-existent unity. The unstated question might be here, "how could any tree produce death which grows out of the same soil as the good trees?" The argument that the tempter employs reveals much about the belief system which launched Lucifer's rebellion, and the trap that all of humankind has found itself ensnared in ever since. A fuller discussion of this is, however, not the purpose of this book.

Eve takes of the fruit and eats it. Instantaneous negative results do not occur. She hands Adam some of the fruit of the tree, and he, who should have known better, eats it as well. Their awareness of their nakedness implies, among other things, that a confrontation with God concerning their actions is inevitable. They come to their senses that

God may not be too thrilled with their choice, however appealing it seemed to them at the time.

The reality that the whole world has been turned upside down begins in verse 8. What does it mean that the Lord God "was walking in the garden in the cool of the day...?" Many have taken this statement to indicate something of the closeness of the fellowship of Adam and Eve with God in these days of Eden; that God was present in some form and that this was a common regular action on the part of God with his creatures. That may be so, but the language seems to indicate something other than blessed fellowship and hide-and-go-seek game playing. Exacting how God is present with them has been questioned as well. Is God's appearance here a theophany, wherein God appears in some tangible human form? Is what is described here an invisible, symbolic, and incorporeal appearance of God? Or does God make God's presence known through the actions of the wind coming in the form of a storm? The phrase "cool of the day" could be translated "the wind of the day." The word for wind here is "ruah". Could this refer to evening being the breezy time of day? Might this refer to the evening breeze and the time approaching the setting sun and the rising wind? While "walking" does suggest a certain closeness, intimacy, and fellowship, could it not also depict righteous conduct of which the two offenders are now hiding in fear? Might this wind be a strong, terrible wind that lashes through the vegetation of the garden? We know that God makes God's presence known in windstorms such as Job 38:1 and the circumstances of Pentecost in Acts 2. Whatever is the case, God is not playing some cute game with Adam and Eve! God comes in judgment. God announces God's presence through some physical production of sound. God is present in the garden as God moves audibly among the trees and plants. God's approach is meant to summon God's cowering creatures who mistakenly believe that they might be able to hide from Him. In that they hid from God, might their action indicate a coming of the Lord in a way they had never experienced before?

God calls out Adam alone. Adam is the one who is ultimately responsible. The failure is primarily his due to the fact that the covenant was made with him. Immediately, however, the blame game begins. It is almost comical that Adam says to God (Gen. 3:12), "the woman you put here with me – she gave me some fruit from the tree, and I ate it." Adam is attempting to get out of trouble by placing the responsibility for the situation upon both Eve and the one who brought Eve to him. God immediately addresses the one God gave to Adam to watch his back and she, failing to take responsibility for her action, says (Gen. 3:13), "the serpent deceived me, and so I ate it." God then pronounces judgment on the three of them by addressing the serpent first, then Eve, and finally Adam. There is much here concerning the impact of human "fallenness" affecting both humanity and nature which have been much detailed by others. What is important here is twofold: Humanity's relationship with God has been, in all reality, severed; and we have the first hint that the results of "the fall" of humanity from a state of "original righteousness" to one of "original sinfulness" will be overcome in a time in the future. Adam and Eve are expelled and banished from the Garden of Eden. Human decay, aging, and death and dying now become vital parts of the human experience and God's continuing plan for humankind. While I know that some have seen a parallel in the expulsion of Adam and Eve from the Garden and the birth process from a mother's body, Eve, who becomes mother of all in the current world, is also the co-creator of the way the world currently is today.

God now has, what appears to be, a monumental problem with which God must deal. God has created humankind, not because God has a need for humankind, but out of the overflow of love which lives in the three persons of the Trinity. Early in my ministry on a retreat with my youth group predecessor at Natrona Heights Presbyterian Church, a youth group member spoke reminding those on this large multi-group retreat that "God needs us!" This is a totally false misconception coming from our egocentric and narcissistic culture. God does not need us to be God! God created us not out of need, but to share God's goodness and magnificence with creatures who could understand and appreciate the Divine One. Truly, humankind was created because of God's desire to share benevolently with others. Our creation was not based on divine need, but a cosmic desire by the Designer to share what has been designed.

What now is God going to do? God is much concerned about divine holiness and veracity. When God declares something, God must keep God's word! We must know at-all-times that God is truthful and trustworthy. God must be completely true to God's Word or else God's Word is greatly diminished, challenging, in my way of thinking, God's very Deity. How can we trust a God who declares and promises great things if God is a vacillating deity? In Eden, God had gone very far in terms of stacking the deck in favor of Adam and Eve obeying and achieving, at an unknown appointed time in the future, a glorified body (as we learn about in the New Testament), and life everlasting. Even the fact that failure to keep the covenant would have an impact on their progeny played into the reasons to keep the covenant. God had told them that the penalty for failure in keeping the covenant was death. God knows, that to be true to God's Word, judgment must be exercised! Yet, God loves Adam and Eve, and does not want to destroy the termination of the sixth day of creation or the relationship with them that has previously been forged. It is my opinion that God really did highly regard and favor both Adam and Eve. I believe that God's depth of love for them was infinite. In particular, it is my opinion, that God deeply loved the woman God created and did not want to see her, or her husband, destroyed. God knows the necessity of being true to God's Word and exercise the death penalty. Yet, out of God's great love and regard for God's creation, God desires to exercise grace to save them from themselves and the ill affects of their transgression. Of course, God has a plan. God knew what would happen and from the beginning of creation. God wrote it in the stars (the original understanding of the ancient zodiac). As God creates, God sets God's plan into motion. God's initial unveiling of the plan is found in Genesis 3:15, the first Messianic prophecy. Please note that the plan is first spoken, not to Adam (though he was present), but to Eve.

Many people have speculated and pondered God's rationale and plan throughout millennia. While I do affirm that the Bible teaches us that God chooses those whom God loves, I also affirm that the very notion of love implies choice – a certain freedom of the will. Adam and Eve chose poorly. It appears that they have wrecked God's plan and ruined Paradise. By their sin, Paradise has been lost. By their sin, the Paradise that was to expand throughout and cover the planet was forfeited. That does not mean, however, that God is frustrated in God's work and ultimate desire. Dr. Norman Geisler's book, "The Roots of Evil" describe the good Doctor's thought of what God just may be doing here. Dr. Geisler writes that we can image a better world than the one in which we currently live. He forwards a profound thought that what God might just be doing with humankind is providing us with the "best way to the best world."[21] I agree with Dr. Geisler. It appears to me that what God has done in reaction to Eden, from our perspective, is to let us go ahead and be the "gods" of this planet. I can just imagine God speaking to humankind and saying, "OK, so you folks think that you can run this planet better than I can! You have chosen to be gods of this sphere, and I am going to let you be just that! Let's see just how well you do and what kind of world your choices render!" On Earth, we have experienced what billions of little gods running around and exercising a certain prerogative of deity has brought us. We have brought upon ourselves only violence, death, and destruction. All our efforts to create the "perfect world" have failed in fire and fury or died in a whimper. We have failed and failed miserably. At some time in the future, God will call a "time-out" to this current era of human history and intervene when I think it becomes obvious to us that there is a God, and God is not us, personally and corporately. God has not abandoned God's intent and purpose to cover the earth with God's gift of Paradise. What God wants to make sure of is that we, still exercising choice, remembering what human governance (including our own history, experiences, and observations while living this life) wrought on the earth, will now and forever choose God's way, never again turning a paradise that God has given us into something more akin to hell. God has not abandoned

---

21   Norman L. Geisler, *The Roots of Evil*. (Grand Rapids, Michigan and Dallas, Texas: Zondervan Publishing House and Probe Ministries International, 1978), 45, 59-63.

Eden. Paradise lost is the Paradise God wants to restore only millions of times more glorious than the original. I think that this life has great meaning and purpose. Part of that meaning and purpose is to experience what I like to call, "the school of God", which prepares us experientially for the "New Heaven and New Earth" (the Eschaton) that God is preparing to give us. Please note that Biblically, especially as revealed in Revelation, that we do not create the "City of God" or restore Eden ourselves. It is strictly a gift of God. In the coming eschaton, I believe that we will continue to exercise choice, but this time looking back at the continuous tragedy and violence of human history, the lessons we learned in living our own lives, a succinct understanding of the Passion of the Christ and his glorified bodily presence with us, the magnificence of God's New Jerusalem and a more direct and instantaneous communication with God, the absence of the tempter, and a fuller reality of the grace, love, and joy we now share, we will, individually, and most importantly, corporately, respond with a resounding and forever "no" to the world in which we came, and "yes" to God's plan and ways. We will, forever, let God be God! This life is to prepare us for the next life. The good news is that God has not left us to our own devices, but God has intervened in human history to save both Adam and Eve and to do it in a way that saves us, God's chosen, as well.

Eve almost made paradise complete! However, banishment from Eden and her ultimate physical demise is not the end of the story!

3

Chaos, the Fall, and the Relationship of One

"Holy, Holy, Holy! Lord God, Almighty!... Merciful and mighty! God in three persons, blessed Trinity!

(Reginald Heber)

The banishment of Adam and Eve from the Garden of Eden is not only a significant event in salvation history but also speaks a great deal about the nature and character of God. The culture of North American Christianity today, in my opinion, seems to have produced a God more in the image of the way we think God should be in order to satisfy the narcissism of persons and our time, rather than the characteristics of the God revealed in the Bible. One of the most beloved passages in the Bible is the 23rd Psalm. In the Shepherd's Psalm several significant themes of the Bible are present, including an often-missed statement about one of the leading characteristics of our God.

David's Psalm picks up the "chaos" of the earth which is first described in the initial two verses of Genesis 1. In this Psalm of David, a corridor of gloom confronts humanity. In various descriptions this thoroughfare of life's journey is translated as the "gloomy valley", "valley of dark shadows", "valley of deep darkness", "dark valley", "dark ravine", "darkest valley", "valley as dark as death", and the common rendering "valley of the shadow of death." This passage refers to a time of stress, anxiety, and crisis in our lives while on journey through this life. It is a crisis that comes to a person even in an area of lush vegetation and ample provision such as the hill country or a mountain valley would provide. Granted, there is much difference between valleys in Europe and many parts of North America and those in Palestine, but the reason to travel such valleys is for water and the vegetation that the water provides. This crisis has often been interpreted as one with life threatening challenges, particularly one that imperils our very existence. The Psalm seems to refer to a time of high anxiety which threatens not only our peace and enjoyment of life but our very survival. I have always agreed with the late author and prelate John Stott that in a crisis we have two very specific questions: the "why God" question ("why am I experiencing this trying or evil circumstance") which is a question which frequently goes unanswered; and the "where is God and does God care" question, which according to Stott is far more critical to us.[22] So according to the Psalm, in the time of crisis and distress in our lives, where is God and does God care?

The Psalm begins with God leading the flock. Let us call it the shepherd's position. God, who is amplified by Jesus as "good shepherd" in the Gospel accounts, leads us and restores us. The phrase "He makes me lie down in green pastures, he leads me beside quiet waters (necessary for the sheep to drink), he restores my soul", all testify to the great love and care of the shepherd for his sheep. "Restoring our soul" carries both the sense of spiritual as well as physical renewal. Restoring our soul is a reviving of one's inner resources, spirit, and

---

22   John R. W. Stott, *The Cross of Christ*, (Downers Grove, Illinois: InterVarsity Press, 1986), 329-336.

perspective. It is a breathing in of new life whose purpose it is to help us renew our pilgrimage through life. Our life, accordingly, is to be characterized by movement not stagnation. Once energy is gained it is to be employed. The shepherd takes us to green pastures and blesses us with food, water, and repose. While this makes us happy, it is no permanent dwelling place.

In the first three verses of the Psalm, God as shepherd leads us. As we begin the second of the Psalm's three sections in verse 4, a dramatic shift occurs. In this verse, we find ourselves having left the green pastures and quiet waters. We are back on journey. We enter the "valley of dark shadows." My experience hiking and mountaineering in the western United States speaks to me of these types of valleys. Canyons in mountainous terrain are often narrow with high walls and cliffs impinging upon us and limiting the direct sunshine through much of the day. The trees, rocks, and vegetation can take on eerie shapes during lengthy periods of the day. The valley can hide many things, including predators which lurk in the shadows ready to pounce. It is at this moment in the Psalm that we need to note the position and location of the shepherd. Where is the shepherd? He is no longer leading at or near the head of the flock but comes and takes up position beside us. "Yea though I walk through the valley of the shadow of death I will fear no evil for thou art with me." (King James Version, Psalm 23:4). This is one of the most significant statements in the whole Bible! During the moment of our greatest danger, the shepherd comes alongside of us. He escorts us personally. In challenging times and times of need, our God draws alongside God's own. God becomes our "paraclete." God becomes our companion at our side to help! God is our ally to personally preserve us and ensure that we complete our journey. God is our escort. God is not just any ordinary escort. God escorts us as a militant personage. I have always likened this image to a certain class of warship that was employed by the United States in World War II. The DE, or Destroyer-Escort, was a light destroyer classification well fitted for convoy duty. The task of the destroyer escort was to steam alongside the merchant vessels and transports to fend off attacks from the air and sea, particularly submarines. Their assignment was to defend the unarmed ships and also to provide rescue if the situation called for it. God, as the paraclete in verse 4, is armed and dangerous. On His belt God carries a club strictly designed to defend the sheep from predators should they attack. In God's hand is a crooked staff employed to discipline, control and rescue members of the flock from precarious positions through the perilous journey. The "thou art with me" God testifies that God, our eternal traveler, will see us through all the rough parts of our travels right to journey's end. The "thou art with me" God means that we do not travel alone. It is this image of God as a militant personage that few people, I think, consider. Our God is a tough customer! God is not one to be "messed with." I was in seminary in the post-Vietnam era when any reference to military imagery was frowned upon. I remember that I was chastised by some for discussing the Macedonian Phalanx to which Paul refers in Philippian 1:27. These military-type images are present in the Bible, and they are most meaningful.

There are those today who envision a major difference from, what appears to be, the vengeful God of portions of the Old Testament to the loving God portrayed in the New Testament. To make any kind of division like this is doing disservice to the text and to the character and nature of God. I find it interesting how much the tough language of Jesus in the "woes" of Matthew 23 are ignored today. How great in this era is our elimination from consideration of passages we find problematic that do not fit our pre-conceptions?

As I stated in chapter two, when humanity sinned, we opted to become "gods" of this world, desiring a life operation without the Biblical Creator God. That is still very true today. "We want what we want when we want it, and we want it now" often regardless of the dire consequences for us and others. Josh McDowell says it best, "Behind every negative commandment that God give us, there are two positives: to protect you and to provide (something better) for you."[23] We act as if we are smarter than God. We truncate the Word by our pick-and-choose approach to the Scriptures. We excuse ourselves of much of the Word, reciting to

---

23   Josh McDowell, "'No' The Positive Answer." *(Video lecture published January 22, 2010).*

ourselves and others (and there are plenty of people who gladly take up the mantra and agree) that the Bible is culturally outdated and a relic of the ancient past. Many who emphasize the gift of grace in Jesus Christ have become functional antinomians.[24] I have had several people tell me that they can "sin up a storm" personally, for it matters not because they "believe" and will still inherit eternal life. Such a theological and personal position is not only antithetical to Reformed Theology, it is not Scripturally sound as well! Judges 21:25 seems to sum up the human situation since our banishment from Eden nicely, "In those days Israel had no king; everyone did as he saw fit." Most people take this phrase to refer to the lack of a monarchy in Israel during the time of the Judges. What if this declaratory statement includes the concept of the Kingship of God as well? What do you get if everyone is running around as little deities? Do you not get a sense of anarchy and chaos throughout the world? Sadly, that is exactly what we have!

Where is God then in the world we have chosen? God's initial position is set out for us in Genesis 1:2. Our God is hovering over the chaos, but also desires to "paraclete" with God's own. In some ways God appears in the Bible to be a "stand-off" God, and in other ways God appears to be an interventionist God. God stands off to let us rule God's world, but God also intervenes to save God's own. God has poured out judgement on the world in many situations of sin and violence. Have you ever noticed, that in every case, especially from Noah onward, God intervenes in judgment to preserve God's people, to save a remnant, and keep from harm those loyal to Him? In so many of these stories in the Bible God acts as the militant personage described in David's Psalm.

During my career I have witnessed a great devaluation of two prime doctrines derived from the Bible: the doctrine of "Original Sin"[25] and

---

24   Antinomianism is a position held by some Christian theists that Christ's salvation by grace alone through faith no longer necessitates one to follow Biblical moral laws. This position asserts that Christians are free from the moral law due to the Gospel of grace as a free gift of Christ. This term comes from the Greek meaning "against law." In this author's experience many advocates have shared the viewpoint that all they have to do to be saved is to "believe." Grace gives them, in their opinion, license to do anything and everything they desire to engage. How one lives and conducts one's life matters not!

25   "Original Sin" or "Ancestral Sin", is the theological term employed to describe the state of sin

the doctrine of "Total Depravity."[26] These two doctrines barely exist anymore in North American Christianity, and most church goers would have a hard time recognizing them let alone defining them. It is my opinion that much of the progressive movement in the 20th and 21st centuries in the United States has abandoned the concepts of Original Sin and Total Depravity. Government policy has been based, especially during and since the Lyndon Baines Johnson administration, on the concept of environmental change. In other words, if you change the environment, you can change the heart. How has this worked out since the mid-1960's? The Bible, on the other hand, indicates that the only way to change the environment is to first change the heart. The total governmental premise of the United States has been in error for decades. Is it any wonder that nothing ever gets solved? R. C. Sproul, J. I. Packer, John MacArthur, among others, have written much in the modern day about the "Holiness of God." Dr. Sproul sets out the case and characteristics of a Holy God quite well in his writings.[27] A Holy God cannot tolerate sin. A morally and ethically perfect God demands the same moral and ethical perfection from those whom God has created. Two other very important books, concerning the subject of evil and sin, are Karl Menninger's 1973 work, "Whatever Became of Sin", and J. Keith Miller's 1987 work, "Sin: Overcoming the Ultimate Deadly Addiction." My career from 1981 through 2017 was marked by a great many people seeking personal counselling. I remember one individual

---

in which humanity finds itself since the sin of disobedience and rebellion of Eden. Original Sin is a condition into which the children of Adam and Eve are born outside of a relationship with God and a proclivity toward evil and unrighteous thoughts and actions. Original sin is often referred to as humanity's "sin nature". Original sin is the opposite of the state of "original righteousness" in which Adam and Eve were created enjoying close relational intimacy with their Creator.

26   "Total Depravity" is a theological doctrine closely associated with and deduced from the tenet of original sin. It is the consequence of the sin and fall of Adam and Eve. The doctrine states that every person is born into this world with a fallen nature, a proclivity to sin, apart from a relationship with God, and unable to experience God's saving grace without the intervention and action of the Divine. Total Depravity is also known as "Pervasive Depravity" and "Radical Corruption". Distinctions in the doctrine exist within Christian circles, theological positions, and denominations. Total Depravity is one of the Five Articles of Remonstrance (1610) and the first point of Calvinism's 5 points known by the acronym: TULIP.

27   R. C. Sproul, *The Holiness of God* (Wheaton, Illinois: Tyndale House Publishers, Inc., 1987), 40.

who sought my counsel claiming he had numerous addictions, which he would count off and name almost impersonally, blaming them for his ill behavior and transgressions. Many were the office visits wherein I just wanted to scream that he was dealing with his sin nature and behavior and stop excusing himself by claiming nearly a dozen addictions. Romans chapter 3 is most instructive. We learn here that all humankind is guilty of sin. We learn here that everyone is morally bankrupt. We learn here that all of us are short of the ideal God originally had in mind. In verse 9, Paul asserts that no one is righteous.

"We have already made the charge that Jews and Gentiles alike are all under sin. As it is written: 'There is no one righteous, not even one; there is no one who understands, no one who seeks God. All have turned away, they have together become worthless; there is no one who does good, not even one. Their throats are open graves; their tongues practice deceit. The poison of vipers is on their lips. Their mouths are full of cursing and bitterness. Their feet are swift to shed blood; ruin and misery mark their ways, and the way of peace they do not know. There is no fear of God before their eyes.' Now we know that whatever the law says, it says to those who are under the law, so that every mouth may be silenced and the whole world held accountable to God. Therefore no one will be declared righteous in his sight by observing the law; rather, through the law we become conscious of sin…. For all have sinned and fall short of the glory of God…." (Romans 3:9c – 20, 23)

The miracle of it all is that God loves and saves many. Throughout my life I have often wondered just how God can save us who are, as a former physician of mine stated, "filthy and dirty creatures." During my career I have been blessed to lead three youth group ministries over an expanse of 38 years. I have led small, medium-sized, and large youth groups. During those four decades I have dealt much with the foibles, follies, and sins of the youth. The relationships that developed with the pre-teens and teenagers became much like a loving father with his children. I learned to love them despite their sin, and often were the times that I found myself attempting to bail them out of terrible situations. Often were the times that my heart ached for them, and I shed tears for and with them. They were, in a sense, my children, and I would do almost anything to help them turn around and resolve their situations. Some of those I loved the most were those who sinned the most. I remember one situation where God became very involved with me, leading to one of the most significant spiritual encounters I have had with the Almighty. One individual in the youth group basically did what David attempted to do in the Bathsheba story of 2 Samuel, chapters 11 and 12. The first transgression leads to another which leads to another and so forth. I was called into the situation twice, and sadly, was devastated for the individual by the continuance of poor choice making. I have never wept more bitterly for a youth group member than this situation. After a few months passed, the individual desired to talk with me about the choices that were made and where to go from here in the person's relationship with God. In my preparatory prayers for this coming encounter, God dealt with me, shall we say, in a very direct way. I have always affirmed, even from my childhood, that God desires and can communicate with God's own. The letter in Revelation to the Church at Laodicea (chapter 3:14-22) speaks to me in verses 19 and 20 of two promises God makes to His Church and individuals thereof: the promise of location and the promise of communication. Jesus, in verse 20, knocks on the door of the Laodicean house church. He desires entry. He wants us to open the door of our heart(s) to him come in and share table fellowship with us. This is both an active fellowship and a continuous fellowship. The Greek wording here implies the main meal of the day which was a time consuming, leisurely affair signifying relationship. Here we have Jesus coming to our house and desiring to abide with us right where we live. This is both a significant passage in the "with-me" God theme and speaks of two-way communication in relationship with our God. Of course, from verse 19 we also learn that God chastens those whom God loves. The situation presented to me implied both. However, the first person who had to be chastened was me. The Spirit of the Lord began by asking me the question, "Who is the greatest sinner here, you or her?" I hesitated and reasoned that I was the greater sinner due to my age, having the time to rack up more sins. God's response indicated that I had answered correctly. Then God said to me, "I want you to go and talk to her as one sinner to another. I love her, and I want her fully restored to me." The conversation that the guilty party and I shared was long and most meaningful. The individual in question repented of her sins and adopted a totally new outlook on the situation and its implications becoming, in the aftermath, a solid proponent of God's love, mercy, grace, and dictates. Not only did this situation instruct me greatly, but it led to one of the dearest relationships of my life. Due to all that we shared, my bond with this individual is very strong.

One of the things this situation has taught me, as I pursue salvation history and the themes of the Bible, is how critical is, what I call, "the relationship of one" (from a binary perspective). It is my impression from the story of Adam and Eve that God was not only very upset and angry with them, but very hurt as well. God loved Adam and Eve dearly and would not let them go, despite their sin. In fact, it appears to me that God ends up taking the role of Adam in order to save one individual, Eve. In one way of looking at and reflecting on this story, I think one could say that Jesus came to save one – the person of Eve, who becomes the mother of all humanity, and through whom, humanity is blessed, due to God's rescue operation to save her (yes, Adam is included in God's salvation as well, as God takes Adam's role in a new way as steward of creation in the person of Jesus). To me the Bible is all about relationship(s). Eve becomes an archetype throughout the Bible of God's plan and action of salvation. To me the Bible speaks loudly concerning God's loving plan to rescue and restore Eve. Indeed, it may just be that it is truly "all about Eve." God loves Eve, personally! Through loving Eve, God also loves the extended fruit of her womb. Person by person, God loves us, the children of Eve. God desires our salvation. God moves to enact our salvation. Is there any evidence in the Bible that this theory of "the relationship of one" has any validity? I certainly think there is!

4

The Need for The Perfect Adam

"My hope is built on nothing less than Jesus' blood and righteousness;
I dare not trust the sweetest frame, but wholly lean on Jesus' name. On
Christ, the solid rock, I stand; all other ground in sinking sand."

(Edward Mote)

The Bible portrays a great drama with five primary actors and actresses
revolving around four gardens. A further declension reveals four essential personages and two gardens. The two essential gardens in the
drama are Eden and that of Joseph of Arimathea. The absolutely four
essential personages are Adam, Eve, Jesus, and, the person I refer to
as "The New Testament Eve." The great drama of salvation history is
much about our need for the perfect man. We have an essential need,
according to God's working of the plan, for the perfect Adam. The most
important question that a person must answer in their life is this one:
"Who is Jesus, known as the Christ?" If Jesus is who the Bible pur-
ports him to be, life and eternity hang in the balance! The Bible is not

some mystery book of secret codes and numerology, as some believe and attempt to teach it to be. It is rather a book of many intertwined and interwoven themes, some of which one must mine the depths of language, symbolism, and culture. The main message of salvation in the person of Jesus Christ is quite simple in the 66-book compilation, while the book itself is complex and deep. Everything simple and deep within its pages revolves around the one revelation of God in the person of God's incarnate Son who is revealed as Jesus, entitled "the Christ." The Bible shouts that Jesus is, in fact, God in human flesh. This is especially true in the prophecy of Isaiah in chapter 9:1-7. Isaiah records that given to us a child is born. It is God's Son who is given. This Son is entitled "Wonderful Counselor". He is not only the source of all divine wisdom, but supreme in divine wisdom as well. He is both the source and embodiment of the stuff of wisdom. The Son is also the "Mighty God". The Son is God Himself. The Son is all divinity and all power. The Son is also the "Everlasting Father". The Son is the Father forever. The Son is also known as the "Prince of Peace". He is the prince beneficent. In him and with him he brings a condition of positive well-being and the wealth of harmony. He is the personification of total "shalom." Peace is more than a condition or state of being. Peace, Biblically, is personified. Peace is a person. Peace is the person of God's Son, Jesus the Christ!

One of the overarching themes of the Bible that rakes through its pages is the theme of the Adams. There is the Adam of Genesis, creation, and Eden. There is the Adam of the New Testament, re-creation, and the gardens of Gethsemane, Joseph of Arimathea, and the Eschaton (the New Heaven and the New Earth, including the New Jerusalem). There is the first Adam. There is the second Adam, also known, appropriately, as the last Adam (Romans 5:12-21 & 1 Corinthian 15:20-22, 45-49). Jesus the Christ is portrayed in the Bible as the second and last Adam. He is the counterpart of the first Adam. When the Adam of Eden fails to accomplish God's purpose and work, another Adam is raised up. The second Adam is the only one competent in the story of the Bible to undo the effects of the first Adam's sin and inaugurate a new humanity. Through the Adam of Eden, death came and reigned. The sin of the first

Adam involves his posterity resulting in death. Through the second or last Adam, righteousness is now available to all, but only credited to some of the first Adam's posterity granting new life reversing death.

Paul embraces the concept of "corporate personality."[28] The whole of humankind is viewed Biblically to have existed in Adam. Adam's life is re-enacted in all subsequent events of human history. The Old Testament Law reveals that there is no permanent sign in history of redemption outside of a divine act of God. The issue becomes whether sin is spread by a genetic or biological link to the first Adam or by imitation of the disobedience of the first Adam. Paul, in my estimation, reveals that it is both. There is a vital link (Romans 5:12) among all of Adam's posterity to Adam, himself. Imitation of Adam is also rife as Romans 3:23 indicates, "for all have sinned and fall short of the glory of God" (see also Romans 5:14). Biblically, Adam is humankind in its totality. His sin, in other words, stands for all.

Salvation is really a "works" thing. In the divine/human covenant in which God made with Adam, it appears that if Adam obeyed God in everything for a prescribed time period, glorification into a spiritual body (which is still physical) granting a God-sustaining immortality would have resulted. This would be a forever life relationship with God. Adam, along with Eve, fell for the tempter's lies. They chose poorly. Since the covenant, I believe, was weighted in their favor included the consideration of their posterity, the outcome meant that they and we would all share in their success, or conversely in their malady and sentence. The Bible declares that all human life on the planet comes from one original woman regardless of ethnicity, color, or what many refer to as race. A genetic link to Adam carries Adam's covenantal failure to

---

28   The concept of "Corporate Personality" in terms of Biblical scholarship and theology was advanced by H. Wheeler Robinson (1872-1945 – *Corporate Personality in Ancient Israel*, rev. edn., Edinburgh: T & T Clark, 1981). Robinson identified areas of the Old Testament where individuals and the relational grouping to which they belonged were treated equally. This is especially true in terms of collective punishment (see Achan's sin in Joshua 7:1-26). Paul employs the concept of corporate personality by the use of the Greek word, "en" for "in Christ" and "in ("through" or "with") Abraham" (Galatians 3). Note Paul's argument in Romans 5:12-21; 1 Corinthians 15:20-22. Paul's conception and employment of corporate personality in terms of Adam and Christ is descriptive of the groups of people each represents. Adam represents all of fallen humanity. Christ represents all of redeemed humanity.

us, in which we theologically term "original sin." Human life is, to put it one way, in the blood. We all come from and share the blood of Adam. Among other things, "original sin" indicates that we are born outside of an "original righteousness" in which Adam and Eve were created. Original righteousness indicates that Adam and Eve were created with a relationship, from the start, with God. The Bible, however, reveals that there is a third person who is born with original righteousness. We know him as the human Jesus. The prophecy of His coming and God's great rescue operation begins in the words of Genesis 3:15 concerning the "seed of the woman."(the term "seed" as translated by the KJV). From "the woman" would come one who would overcome, in the future, the results of "the Fall" of Adam from the grace of God ushering in a new human reality and era. The forces of Satan would be aligned against him, striking him and killing him. In the confrontation, however, he would crush Satan and his evil empire completely. The Bible reveals that the "seed of the woman" cannot come from the blood of Adam. The "seed of the woman" comes from the Holy Spirit. The "seed of the woman" is an indwelt seed. Concerning the "seed", God the Father speaks the creative Word. What does all this mean? It means that there is coming a "second Adam". The second Adam comes from heaven. His origin is of God and is God. He comes on a mission. He is on the mission of and for God. Christ is known as the second Adam or the last Adam.[29] As such, he comes with two tasks to perform. He has two works in which to engage. In this respect, our salvation is of "works", though His work from His passion comes to us solely as a gift of grace. This work cannot be accomplished by anyone in the bloodline of Adam. The bloodline of Adam possesses the original taint of sin. What we have in Jesus, who is as fully human as He is fully divine, is a second line of humanity. He is, in and of himself, a human line of one. He is completely human, but not of the line of Adam. He is genetically human but shares not the specific genetic lineage of Adam. Possessing "original righteousness", as the first Adam once had, he can, being divine, accomplish the "work of obedience" Adam failed to do. Adam was to live a pure ethical, moral,

---

29   1 Corinthians 15:45-49.

and obedient life. Adam was to be, in every aspect of person and personal expression, perfect. Adam's test of faithfulness, it is believed, was for a specified amount of time though we know not how long this was to be. It was, it is believed, not a forever test. Perhaps we get a hint of its possible duration in that Jesus, most likely according to Rick Larson, was born on June 17, 2 BC,[30] and was crucified on April 5, 33 AD,[31] was 34 (almost 35) years old.[32] Jesus accomplished this work of perfection. In so doing Jesus becomes the only one who can be the substitute for us to take the penalty for our sin upon himself. Taking the penalty of our sin upon himself is the second task Jesus is to perform. Fulfilling the themes of the tabernacle and temple sacrificial system, Jesus becomes both the sacrifice and the High Priest who presides over the sacrifice (Hebrews 7-10). Jesus, who is morally perfect and untainted by sin, ends our indebtedness to God. As second or last Adam, Jesus sets us at liberty. The book of Hebrews is the high priestly book that explains the person, mission, and nature of the Christ to the Jewish culture at the time of its writing. The author of Hebrews indicates that the Son is the Creator. The author of Hebrews indicates that the Son was sent by the Father into the world to save creation and to rescue us from our earthly calamity. The Son is not a messenger, but the one who occupies the eternal throne. The Son is invested with universal sovereignty and dominion. The Son is unchangeable and morally perfect. He shares three differences from the rest of humanity. These three differences are:

---

30   This date is derived from Rick Larson's DVD documentary on the Star of Bethlehem. Please note that Ernest L. Martin's book, *The Star of Bethlehem: The Star that Astonished the World*, on which Larson's work is partially based, sets the date of Jesus' birth as September 11, 3 BC. Larsen views this as the day of Jesus' conception. These dates are worth considering, but significant objections to the theories of both Martin and Larson remain.

31   Jesus' death on this date is ascribed to by many researchers who purport solid evidence to support their claim. Among the many articles, on-line articles, and books concerning this matter of dating see *The Final Days of Jesus: The Most Important Week of the Most Important Person Who Ever Lived* by Andreas J. Kastenberger, by Crossway Books, April 3, 2014. Please note that objections to this dating of the crucifixion exist including the suggestion of a Thursday crucifixion.

32   Note that Rick Larson's theory concerning the star of Bethlehem has been challenged by Colin R. Nicholl in his book, *The Great Christ Comet: Revealing the True Star of Bethlehem* (Crossway Books, September 30, 2015) and his on-line article "What is Wrong with Rick Larson's 'Star of Bethelehem'" DVD documentary. It is interesting to note that objections to Nicholl's theory exist and can be visited currently on-line.

the origin and birth of the Son is a miraculous work of God; the life of the Son is sinless; and the purpose of the Son is to perform the work we cannot do and then die for our sins as both High Priest and sacrifice. This Son is our Savior and King. He is the second person of the Trinity. He is both merciful to humanity and faithful to the Godhead.

This writer is, and always has been, a firm advocate of the doctrine of the Virgin Birth. Machen wrote a marvelous defense of the virgin birth which I found helpful in my defense of the doctrine throughout my career.[33] Machen's 1930 book is must reading for any Christian serious about the importance of this doctrine. It is also must reading for anyone who doubts or questions this doctrine! In terms of the Christian Church I affirm seven primary doctrines. I have always re-ferred to them as "The Big Seven": the Bible as the authoritative Word of God, the Trinity, the Incarnation/Virgin Birth, the Substitutionary Atonement (Jesus' work on the cross), The Bodily Resurrection, the Deity of Christ, and Justification by Grace through Faith. Notice that I have included the word "Incarnation" alongside of the "Virgin Birth." To me, the most significant part of the concept of the Virgin Birth is the "front-end" of the doctrine, that of the Incarnation. The real miracle of the doctrine is not the Virgin Birth itself, but the fact that God created in the womb of Mary the fertilized embryo that became the person of Jesus. Notice the language of Matthew 1:20 and Luke 1:28-37. What God performs in the womb of Mary is the creation of a fertilized egg. God speaks the human Jesus into being as a new cre-ative act. It is the Holy Spirit who is the agent of this action alone. No one needs to think that Mary, or anyone else for that matter, provided genetic material. The reason for this is clear. Jesus, who is fully human, cannot share in the genetic line of the actors of the Fall. He who is fully human is a second line of humanity. He is a line of "one." He is conceived by the Holy Spirit with "original righteousness" coming wholly from the Holy Spirit with no linkage to the line of humanity's

---

33   J. Gresham Machen, *The Virgin Birth of Christ* (Grand Rapids, Michigan: Reprinted by Baker Book House Company, 1982, with permission by Harper & Row Publishers, Incorporated, 1930), 1.

original parentage. I remember arguing this point in seminary when everyone, including the class professor, still somehow affirmed a genetic link to Mary (remember that this was a time when the idea of "test-tube babies" and artificial insemination was approaching on the horizon). This concept of a genetic link has led some to the doctrine of the "immaculate conception"[34] of Mary in an attempt to deal with the contradiction that such a position causes in terms of "original sin". Jesus, as the second Adam, means exacting what it meant. Jesus begins a new line of humanity into which God's own are spiritually born and adopted (Romans 8). Mary, as marvelous as a person as she was, was not free of sin (Luke 1:47). During my years in the ministry I always found it humorous to hear the song, "Mary Did You Know" come from the lips of those whose parent church body affirms the sinlessness of Mary. The words of the song make it clear that Jesus came to save her as well. I also found it interesting that many people who affirmed the bodily resurrection of Jesus Christ had trouble "swallowing" the idea of a virgin birth. If God has the power to raise the dead, God certainly has the power to speak the creative Word and, through this method, implant a fertilized egg in the womb of a chosen woman. If God can speak into being space, time, energy, and matter, God certainly can form a baby, in like manner, in the womb of Mary. In fact, to affirm any other idea of the origin of Jesus presents the Biblical reader with all sorts of difficulties of which church history can certainly testify.

The biggest challenge of the Biblical doctrine of the Incarnation/ Virgin Birth comes from those, and there are many, who embrace the Adoption Theory[35] of the Christ or something similar to it. When we talk adoption concerning Biblical matters, we must recognize that there are three things that come to mind: two are accurate and one is not. If

---

34   The "Immaculate Conception" of Mary is the doctrine wherein Mary is conceived without original sin in order that Jesus may be conceived without original sin. While this concept has long existed in parts of the Christian Church for many centuries, it only became the official position of the Roman Catholic Church in 1854 by the ex cathedra declaration of Pope Pius IX in his papal bull Ineffabilis Deus.

35   Mike Gascoigne. "Virgin Birth, Jewish Adoption and Genealogy of Yeshua," *Anno Mundi Books*" (1997 and updated in December 1999), www.annomundi.com/bible/virgin_birth.htm. (accessed April 1, 2019).

you are talking about, as Paul does, being adopted into the family of the Christ, this is all about the spiritual adoption of believers in Jesus. While we are not of the physical line of Jesus, we are engrafted or adopted by Christ as children of God the Father. We become part of the line of Jesus through this spiritual adoption. A second notion of adoption that is Biblical is the notion of adoption in Jewish culture. This is important when rendering the right relationship between Jesus, Joseph, and Mary. According to the Hebrew rules at that time for adoption, if a child was adopted, it was then affirmed as if that adopted child was of the lineage and bloodline of the adopting parents. The baby or child was considered by all to be the actual child of the parents as if they conceived and birthed the child.[36] In this way we can say that Mary was truly the mother of Jesus. In this way, we can say that Jesus was of the lineage of King David. It is the third notion of adoption that becomes problematic. There are those who reject the doctrine of the Incarnation/Virgin Birth as being mythical, legendary, and a product of latter development of Christological thought. The Gospel of Mark, which contains no Nativity story, unlike Matthew and Luke, and John's opening theological rendering of origin, is pointed to in support of the theory that Jesus was "adopted" by God as His Son and the Messiah at the time of his baptism of repentance (act of identification with fallen and sinful humanity) by the Baptist, John.[37] Some affirm that Jesus lived an ethically pure and sinless life growing up and was, therefore, a candidate for adoption as theorized in the 2nd century, non-canonical writing known as the *Shepherd of Hermas*.[38] Others affirm that the baptism of repentance by John removed Jesus' sin so that he could become

---

36   Machen, 128-131, 135, 186.

37   The Adoption theory pertaining to Jesus by God is also known as "Adoptionism" and "Dynamic Monarchianism". It is a nontrinitarian doctrine that maintains that Jesus was adopted as God's Son. This most likely occurred at Jesus' baptism. Variant viewpoints maintain that the adoption took place at Jesus' birth, resurrection, or ascension. Adoptionism rejects any idea of a pre-existent and eternal Christ. Adoptionism maintains that Jesus has been divine since his adoption (though he is not equal to the Father). Adoptionism is often employed by those who deny Jesus' virgin birth by Mary. It was declared heretical in the 2nd century by both the Synods of Antioch and the First Council of Nicaea.

38   James L. Papandrea, *The Earliest Christologies: Five Images of Christ in the Postapostolic Age* (Downers Grove, Illinois: InterVaristy Press, 2016), 29.

the sinless adopted child of the Father.[39] Accordingly, the idea then follows that through baptism, transfiguration, and resurrection Jesus gains a progressive exaltation, or that he displayed his adoption at his transfiguration and through his resurrection. This theory of the gradual deification of a mere mortal is hard to justify on the grounds of the early writing of the New Testament (this author affirms the arguments of many[40] that all the books of the New Testament, including Revelation, were written prior to the destruction of Jerusalem in 70 AD),[41] the clear message of New Testament itself concerning Jesus, and the grounds of the themes of both Testaments. Sadly, the effort here, in the opinion of this writer, is to lessen the authority of the Christ and Scripture so that people are not as bound to it as its words indicate to us that we are to be. A degraded Christ then degrades the Word, which opens up all kinds of possibilities for those who desire a different kind of Christ in a different kind of world.

The "two-Adam" reality is a necessity for the salvation of humankind from the blight of sin. The first Adam failed in the performance of the work of obedience and perfection he was called by God to accomplish. His failure necessitates the second Adam who must accomplish this work of obedience and perfection and then, and only then, can he become the sacrificial substitute to reverse the sin of Adam which has condemned us all. Only by being born with original righteousness can he possibly perform this work. Only by being God incarnate can Jesus succeed. Humanity has a need for a perfect Adam and Jesus is He. Humanity, however, has a need for a perfect woman as well. A rescue of Eve must take place and be demonstrated for all the world to see.

---

39   Vexen Crabtree, "Christian Adoptionism and the Baptism of Jesus Christ: Centuries of Belief Before the Trinity," *The Human Truth Foundation* (January 11, 2011). www.vexan.co.uk/religion/christianity_adoptionism.html (accessed April 1, 2019).
40   R. C. Sproul, *The Last Days According to Jesus*. (Grand Rapids, Michigan: Baker Books, 1998), 13.
41   Josh McDowell and Sean McDowell, *Evidence for the Resurrection: What it Means for Your Relationship with God* (Ventura, California: Regal, 2009), 141.

5

The Adams' Family

"Let's give Adam and Eve another chance, to bring their children back together…. To show us how to love one another."

(Red West and Richard Mainegra/Gary Puckett and the Union Gap)

Before moving forward in this writing, I think it is worth taking the time to amplify the previous chapters, especially chapter 4, with an in-depth review and closer examination of the Incarnation and Virgin Birth. The Bible's "Adams' Family" primarily concerns the households of Adam and Eve, and Joseph and Mary, along with their first-born son, Jesus. Many people, particularly during Advent and Christmastide, entertain the question, "Why did Jesus have to be born?" This question is really an open-ended one as people inquire about the Christ event. Critical to any kind of answer to this question is a return to the source of the issue which raises the question in the first place. We must return to Eden and inquire about its primary inhabitant, Adam. Maybe the initial question ought to be, "Why did God create Adam and initiate with Eve the line

Reverend Robert Cameron Malcom IV

of the human race?" While we have given an answer to this question in the previous pages, let us reflect a little more on the subject.

While we may never know the complete set of reasons or the logical basis God employed as to God's thinking behind our creation, we must be willing to reflect upon a very frank assessment concerning our God. God is God, but so often we encrust God with high theological ascriptions such as omnipotence, omniscience, transcendence, omnipresence, beneficence, sovereignty, and universality. Let's face it, this kind of concept of God, while I affirm the ascriptions listed above, do not necessarily engender warmth in terms of knowing God and sharing in a relationship with God. I think, at times, we have to get beyond the elevated language we employ when we think and speak of God and the accompanying concepts we entertain when we use such language, and remember that first and foremost God is a person. Personhood, especially as we see portrayed in the interaction of the "persons" of the Trinity, reveals a God with an intense desire. God's desire is the very same one we have, for haven't we been created in God's image? What is this desire? God's desire is to know and be known by others. God's desire is to share God's intense goodness with beings who have the capacity to experience and appreciate that goodness. God, I guess you can say, possesses a good feeling! God's good feeling is about Godself and God's ability to replicate goodness in others. While God's essence can be described in many ways, one of the leading self-descriptions of God is that of love. God is love (I also believe that God is just as much joy and peace, among other personified traits as well – please note the "fruit of the Spirit" in Galatians 5 and the repeated employment of love, joy, and peace that Jesus employs in John's "Farewell Discourse."). True love necessitates a lover, a beloved, and a spirit of love. We have that in our trinitarian concept of God. God's love, in my estimation, is the overflow of goodness from the essence of one being (person) to another. Let's just say that God is so packed full of love that God desires to share this God-perceived overabundance with others. God's love and goodness is something that God desires not to retain within the three persons of the Trinity.

God created us, I believe, for fellowship. God created us so that we might share God's goodness, appreciate God's goodness, and enter into a loving relationship with God, not only for the blessings God is able to bestow but for God's very personhood (for who God is in and of God's Self). We were created in this relationship to enjoy and reflect God's glory in both a deeply personal and communal way. God wants what God created us to want, to love and be loved.

As presented previously in this writing, God's human experiment represents God's grand experiment. Love, according to my definition, implies freedom. Freedom, it seems to me, implies choice. Choice implies risk. To create creatures like God's Self, who have the capacity to choose to love or not to love, is taking a real gamble. It seems to me that God is limitless, and yet through God's creative choices God imposes upon God's Self some limits by exercising God's freedom to create this and not that. It seems to me that if God had created robots, computer programmed to love God, that would not be love at all. God desires love. And so, God created willful personages like God's Being who were emotionally, mentally, psychologically, and spiritually similar to God's Self. In so doing, God chose to strictly limit God's Self in relationship to us, God's new creatures. We could say, that looking at it strictly from the human point of view, that God took a big risk.[42] Of course, looking at it from the divine perspective may represent another matter entirely. Our knowledge of such things is imperfect!

As we have discussed, God created a wonderful paradise and made what theologians call, "the divine constitution." As I understand it, the divine constitution provided for life or death for Adam depending upon his obedience to the test God initiated. If Adam has not sinned, he would not have died. He would have been granted the gift of immortality by the God who forever sustains our eternality. The test appears to be simple if one accepts its historicity, which this writer affirms. It all boils down to the concept of trusting completely in God to always obey God, acknowledging that God's way, as our "Manufacturer", as one person

---

42   Philip Yancey, *Disappointment with God* (Grand Rapids, Michigan: Zondervan Publishing House, 1988), 60.

put it, are the best ways to protect us and provide prosperity for us, both individually and communally.

Human idolatry begins when, in our freedom, we think that we can do some of this better than God or totally on our own without God. One of the big lessons, I think, we have to learn in life is that we are not, in any way, smarter than God. In so doing, we substitute or replace God with a new deity, ourselves! The Bible calls it sin and addresses it in the first several of the Ten Commandments. While Adam initially receives the blame as the representative head of the human race, we all have the choice between obedience to God and doing "our own thing." Sadly, humanity, has an intense proclivity for FUBAR (Fouled Up Beyond All Recognition). That talent has never left us!

It is not difficult for me to see how easy it was for Adam to fail. While Adam knew something of life outside of Eden, living in the shelter of paradise did he even begin to know what the consequences of an errant choice would be? Today we have far more knowledge of the terrible consequences our ill choices produce, yet that does not seem to have any impact to keep us from sinning for one minute.

Gary Puckett and the Union Gap band once sang a song entitled, "Let's Give Adam and Eve Another Chance." Essentially that is what God decided God wanted to do. But how? Once again looking at this from the human perspective, it appears that God has a real problem in which to deal. God's problem was that God loved Adam and Eve and their coming family and desired to extend mercy. Yet, at the same time, a holy and perfect God expects holy and perfect behavior. There is no possible way for Adam to make up for his sin. Even if it were possible for Adam never to sin again throughout his whole life, he could not make up for that one error. God does not give extra credit assignments. Nor does God give "brownie points." When perfection is the expected norm, then all goodness is required leaving nothing that can be done to atone for even one small sin. Adam initially fell one point below perfection, but perfection – absolute perfection – is what is required by a holy God. If God requires all goodness anyway, then there is no work Adam could perform to make it up. Of course, what goes for

Adam goes for us as well. Perhaps one might think that God was being a bit unrealistic here. There are two ways, I think, of looking at this. Dr. Joseph Hopkins of Westminster College taught that while God does not change his expectations for us, it certainly does appear, as the Bible unfolds, that God is training us up as a parent would a small child.[43] Philip Yancey, in his book, "Disappointment with God", says, "the record of the Bible shows God learning how to be a parent."[44] Yancey is correct that one could certainly draw such a theme out of the text and come to this kind of conclusion. Certainly, it appears in the Bible that God, who is deeply hurt by our rejection of Him and who at times appears to be confused by our rejection of God's person, is trying to do everything God can to discover what works and what does not work when it comes to the divine/human relationship.[45] You might come to the conclusion that this whole thing, with creatures who can resist God's will, is a new circumstance for God. Or is it? I deeply respect Philip Yancey as he is most insightful and one of my favorite authors. His perspective on this is most interesting and valuable to note, but there might be more to consider than what he has written.

Another problem we entertained earlier in this work is the dilemma God faced concerning Adam's sin. It is the circumstances surrounding God's veracity. God, in the agreement with Adam, had pronounced the death penalty for failure to obey God's Word. The one thing of which God appears to be extremely jealous concerns God's Word. God is adamant about keeping God's Word. If God had not passed the death penalty on Adam, God would have violated God's own veracity and sense of justice. When God says that He is going to do something, God wants us to know God's sincerity about keeping God's Word. How will we, God's creatures in fellowship with God, know that God means what God says unless God means it and keeps it every single time? As the late Dr. John Gerstner stated often in lecture, "God is very jealous about

---

43   This idea of the late Dr. Joseph M. Hopkins is remembered from classroom lectures in 1973 and 1974, particularly in the Old Testament Studies course.
44   Yancey, 63.
45   Ibid., 64.

His Word!"[46] God had set out from the beginning the parameters or boundaries of relationship mutuality with Adam. God had rendered a death sentence for disobedience. God had to be true to God's Word and execute the sentence of capital punishment on Adam; otherwise, God's Word would be devalued, and God would not be found to be totally reliable, not only on this situation, but in many other situations, including the good and blessed things as well!

God had to be true to God's Self, yet God loves His creatures and does not want them to perish. There had to be another way. Of course, God knew this and planned this other way, in the opinion of this author, prior to the creation of the universe itself! The answer to what appears to be God's dilemma was to exercise the law of substitution. The crime had to be paid. It had to be paid in full. It had to be paid in a way though that gave humanity another chance. In order to do this, God had to substitute another human being for Adam to do the work of obedience that Adam failed to perform while keeping the divine constitution. This human being had to remain sinless. At this point in the story he now had to remain sinless, not in the environment of paradise, but in the poisonous brew that is this current world. This human being had to remain perfectly obedient, refraining from giving in to temptation. This human being also had to pay the penalty for Adam's sin. This person would have to perform both Adam's work of righteous obedience, and pay to satisfy the penalty for Adam's sin. What human being could possibly do both? This concept of substitution has not totally been lost on society. I remember my late father telling us that during his school days of the 1930's and 1940's teachers and administrators in grammar school and in the higher grades would permit another person to be substituted for the individual due punishment. My father indicated that he volunteered on occasion to receive corporal punishment to spare one of his friends. This is the concept of substitution in action in our real-life setting, though of yesteryear!

---

46   This quote is taken from the memories of Dr. Gerstner's year-long classroom series (3 courses) on the person and works of Jonathan Edwards from 1979-1980 at Pittsburgh Theological Seminary.

Of course, another human being in and of him or herself could not do it! Only God could possibly accomplish this effort. Only God could fulfill the agreement God made with Adam and be perfectly obedient. Only God could pay the penalty of Adam's sin and now the sins of the whole species, without executing all of us to eternal death! And so, God's plan was to send God's Son, in essence of God Self, and through the Son both our work of obedience could be secured as well as paying the penalty for our sin. Jesus is the second Adam. He is the new Adam. He is the last and final Adam in this Adams' family affair.[47] Jesus is the new head if the human race. Jesus is the new father of humanity. His fatherhood is not biological or genetic. His fatherhood is spiritual and substitutionary. To accept Jesus is to embrace God. If we embrace Jesus' work of obedience on our behalf, and if we accept his work of substitutionary death to be our own, then through Christ, God considers that the work of perfection is secure and the death sentence against us has been carried out. In this way, God has fulfilled all of God's concerns. God has been true to God's Word, and God has given us the opportunity for close and lasting fellowship again. In short, God has saved us for eternal life by rescuing us from eternal death. Through Jesus, we are made clean and pure as if we had never sinned, thus earning, as a gift, eternal life.

There is another very crucial factor here that may not mean as much theologically, but certainly means a great deal to this author personally and spiritually. Through Jesus, we come to understand and appreciate the personhood of God. If, as Tony Campolo and others have stated, "Jesus is the best picture we have of God, and Jesus is the best picture God has of us!",[48] then through the incarnation and virgin birth, we get a very earthly perspective on God. It may be too much to say, but the humanity of God in Jesus also gives God an experiential perspective on all things earthly and human as well. I am not an advocate of Process Theology,[49] but I think it is one thing to view this earth from

---

47   1 Corinthians 15:22, 45-48; Romans 5:12-14.
48   Tony Campolo made this statement in his video recordings which were noted by this author over the decades.
49   The Process Theological system was advanced by Alfred North Whitehead and Charles

a divine perspective (from heaven looking down), and quite another to view things from a human perspective (from earth looking up). I am not taking anything away from God here, but I cannot help think that knowing something because you lived it, experienced it, breathed it, struggled with it, and walked with it (like the expression "walking in someone else's shoes") is something quite meaningful even for God living from the human or earthly perspective. As we know, it is one thing to know something from secondary sources but quite another thing to know something because you lived it. In Jesus, God made a full and complete identification with us. By becoming one of us, God, in the person of Jesus experienced personhood from an earthly perspective to add to God's experience of personhood from the divine perspective. Jesus lived life as we live it right from our very beginning. Jesus lived life with all its ambiguities, problems, difficulties, travail, tragedies, sorrows, successes, and joys. Jesus lived life experiencing the shortcomings and failures of others. He experienced human lies, denials, and betrayals. Jesus experienced how the poor choices of human-beings impact others individually and corporately. He experienced the limitations of communication. He lived through mockery and rejection. Jesus experienced just how hard life can be. Jesus learned what it means to set aside divine power and to humble himself. He learned what it means to be cut off from the love of the Father. He experienced what it means to suffer, bleed, and die. He demonstrated what it means to sacrifice oneself for another. Jesus also experienced what it means to love another from the human, earthly perspective (what the omniscient God knew from the divine perspective is now observed and lived out in the incarnation). The concepts of his various roles, especially that of deliverer and friend, took on, perhaps, a new and added meaning as he loved and befriended many people in his 34-year earthly life. I appreciate the historical fact that God decided to take on human flesh and to live

---

Hartshorne. The main feature is the idea that reality is always in the process of becoming. This theological position is complicated with further expansion in thought made by John Cobb, David R. Griffin, Lewis Ford, Schubert Ogden, Norman Pittenger, and Daniel Day Williams. For a more complete sketch of the theology, reference Sinclair B. Ferguson, David F. Wright, and J. I. Packer, eds., *New Dictionary of Theology* (Downers Grove, Illinois: InterVarsity Press, 1988), 534-536.

life as we experience it. Whatever impact this had on God, it certainly permitted us to better relate to God. Many years ago, a popular song asked the question, "What if God were one of us?"[50] When I would hear the song playing through the car radio, I would find myself answering that question by shouting, "God was and is, in the person of Jesus!" The song, however, paints the personhood of God as a "slob like one of us." Jesus was certainly no slob, and that means all the world to me. God came and lived life as we live it. Through Jesus, what is being testified to us is that God can really relate and understand our human dilemmas and strivings. Jesus feels many of the things we feel. He perceives things in many of the same ways we perceive times, situations, and events. He becomes someone with whom we can really relate. Jesus is our perfect intercessor and advocate before the Father. His incarnation permits us to see this aspect of the Trinity in this way. He has, for us, made more tender and approachable our gracious and loving heavenly Father ("Abba", which speaks of intimacy, interest, and care as the word can be translated "Daddy"). He has accomplished, if such is possible, a deeper understanding of experiential perfection for an already perfect God. He has accomplished the relational work to help us see, feel, embrace, and understand in a most tangible way the perfect love God has for us. To understand the Biblical story, we must appreciate what God has done in taking on human form to further God's relationship with us and we with God. It is huge! It means a lot. In fact, it should mean the whole world to us. And it helps me to know that the entire Christ story of the second and last Adam means a great deal to God as well.

The incarnation and virgin birth are the vehicles of God's justice and self-identification with God's people. As I have stated before, the real miracle here is not the virgin birth but the incarnation. And the real controversy is not whether Joseph, or someone else, was Jesus' biological father, but was Mary Jesus' biological mother? We must

---

50   The song, *One of Us* was written by Eric Bazilian and released in February/March 1995 as part of the album "Relish". The song was recorded by Joan Osborne. It was produced by Rick Chertoff on the Blue Gorilla Records label.

take up the issue of parentage. Let us now look at the background to the virgin birth.

The Apostles' Creed contains for many three controversial statements: "He descended into hell"; "I believe in the holy catholic church"; and the phrase, "born of the Virgin Mary." With a little bit of research and understanding, the first two are readily solved and dispatched. The phrase "born of the Virgin Mary" is often thought of the stuff of legend, alternative religious cultural baggage, a cover-up for a mysterious happening, or worse, sin. Was Jesus really born of a virgin? Was the virgin birth a necessity? How was it accomplished? Is it important, and, if so, why? And how did we get this story and come to affirm it as an integral, albeit controversial, tenet of our faith?

I want to open our reflection on the virgin birth by concentrating on one phrase from Matthew 1:23 which reads, "the virgin will be with child and will give birth to a son, and they will call him 'Immanuel' which means, 'God with us.'" For some strange reason, every time I hear or read that phrase, I think of the 1960's horror film, "The Creature Walks Among Us". The purpose of God walking among us, in this case, is not to strike terror in our hearts, but to grant us God's peace, healing, and the recovery of fellowship. This is, of course, a significant reference to the "With-Me God" theme which runs throughout the Bible. The prophetic phrase which Matthew quotes[51] implies that God will be walking among us. This "God with us" is not some metaphysical apparition but an abiding in a very literal concrete anatomical way. Am I correct on this?

To affirm or negate this personal article of belief of mine (and many others), one must analyze the context of this passage and refer to at least two others. First, we travel to the Old Testament to Isaiah 7:14 from which the words in Matthew originate. Isaiah 7:14 reads: "Therefore the Lord himself shall give you a sign: Behold, a virgin shall conceive, and bear a son, and shall call his name Immanuel." (KJV). Let us investigate the word "virgin" found here. In Hebrew, the word is "almah", which correctly translated means "young woman" or "maiden".

---

51   Isaiah 7:14; Isaiah 8:8,10.

The word implies a young woman of marriageable age.[52] When the writers of the Septuagint (the Greek translation of the Old Testament Hebrew) translated this word they used the Greek word "parthenos", meaning "virgin", which does not correspond to the Hebrew word "almah" or "young woman." "Parthenos" corresponds, rather, to the Hebrew word, "bethulah", meaning "virgin". A better Greek rendering would have translated "almah" by employing the Greek word, "neanis (youth or young person)".[53] The quotation in Matthew 1:23 is taken from the Septuagint (the primary Greek translation of 70 or 72 scholars into Koine Greek during the 3rd and 2nd centuries BC in Alexandria, Egypt. It represents a time when the Greeks ruled Palestine and Greek, not Hebrew, became the primary language of the region) and not the Hebrew. It is one of a number of quotations Matthew employs to show that the Old Testament foreshadows the life of Jesus Christ. Matthew, it appears, uses these quotations rather loosely without particular regard to their original meaning or context. I believe that we may use Matthew's "messianic interpretation" of Old Testament quotes only in a secondary sense, while acknowledging that his use of Isaiah 7:14 in Matthew 1:23 is based on an inaccurate translation of the Hebrew text. "Almah" could possibly refer to a virgin, but if Isaiah had wished to make clear that he had in mind a miraculous virgin conception, he would have had to use the specific term, "bethulah."

The birth forecast in Isaiah 7:14 was meant to be a sign to King Ahaz from God. The conception and/or birth was not in and of itself a special miracle. The miracle was that a certain woman representative of all women of that precise time period would be bearing any children at all! This sign of birth was born in the political crisis of 734-733 BC. Pekah, king of Israel, and Rezin, king of Syria has formed an anti-Assyrian coalition and wanted Ahaz of Judah to join them. When Ahaz refused, Pekah and Rezin had to secure their southern flank before

---

52   Sherman E. Johnson, *The Gospel According to St. Matthew, The Interpreter's Bible*, vol. 7, ed. George Arthur Buttrick (Nashville: Abingdon, 1980), 255.

53   Albert Barnes, "Barnes' Notes on the New Testament, Commentary on Isaiah 7:14," *StudyLight.org verse-by-verse Bible Commentary* (2001-2019), https:https://www.studylight.org/commentaries/bnb/Isaiah-7.html. 1870 (accessed April 23, 2019).

attacking Tiglath-pilesar, king of Assyria, and so they made prepa-
rations to invade Judah, depose Ahaz, and replace him with a more
friendly, dependent "puppet government". Ahaz, who was seized with
panic, even offered up his own son in sacrifice, much to the disdain
of God, and sent a substantial gift to Tiglath-pilesar in an appeal for
help against the coalition to the north, much to the disdain of Isaiah.
God then dispatched Isaiah to engage an audience with King Ahaz to
basically overcome his anxiety and fear and exercise confidence in God.
Ahaz was told that God would not allow the invasion to occur. Ahaz
was unable to rally his faith in God, so Isaiah was sent once again to
him with a proposal designed to fortify his faith. Ahaz, in somewhat
of a hypocritical display of piety, declines God's offer of a sign on the
grounds that it is not a right thing to test God. Isaiah responds with
indignation and indicates that God would give a sign anyway. The
promise, first and foremost, would stand that Judah would be spared an
attack by the coalition to the north. Somewhere in Judah, a son would
be born, and his mother, who will find great joy in the deliverance of the
nation, will call him, "Immanuel, God with us." The salvation offered
and refused, despite the king's doubt and unbelief, will become a fact.
Before the child reaches the age of discrimination, the nations of the
two northern kings, now threatening Judah, would be destroyed. The
sign of deliverance, however, would also be a sign of woe for Ahaz due
to his unbelief and lack of trust in God. Assyria, as a consequence, will
now conquer Judah.[54]

Technically, this verse quoted by Matthew has nothing to do with
Jesus in a primary sense. It must be noted, however, that there are those
who disagree. Their arguments must be properly and carefully considered in terms of the concept of Biblical inspiration and the overall
thrust of messaging in the Holy Writ. The perspective rendered above
says a great deal, however, about humanity, the human condition, and
God's interaction with God's people in a secondary sense. "Immanuel,
God with us" was not to be understood in the physical sense of God
(at that time) walking among us, but that God was present with the

---

54   Stephen Winward, *A Guide to the Prophets* (Atlanta: John Knox Press. 1977), 73-84.

nation Judah and exercised power to deliver them from their enemies. In terms of this secondary sense, is not that what God did in Jesus? "God with us" means deliverance. In this way Matthew's quotation has great meaning for us! There is another thing to consider here before we move on. Due to unbelief, the sign of the birth was not only a sign of deliverance but also a sign of disaster. Is not Jesus both a sign of deliverance to those who affirm him, but also a sign of woe to those who refuse and reject his offer of salvation?

A second passage that is significant in our understanding of "Immanuel, God with us" is John 1:14, "the Word became man and lived for a time among us." (Modern Language Bible). "Lived for a time" comes from the Greek translation of the word, "egeneto". This word can be translated as "to dwell", "to tabernacle", "to tent", and "to camp." The word occurs several times in the Bible and in all instances in John and Revelation does not refer to dwelling in a real tent, but God dwelling or living physically among the redeemed. In the Old Testament, the concept of God "tabernacling" with God's people refers to God's abiding and gracious presence, most notably in reference to the strange appearances of God's "shekinah glory"[55] associated with the wilderness worship and sacrifice center known as the tabernacle and later, Solomon's Temple in Jerusalem. The use of this term in John refers to both God's abiding eternal presence, but now, more specifically, to the incarnation of God in the person of Jesus Christ. The context also can carry the idea that this physical tenting with us remains both a spiritual reality after Christ's ascension through the coming and presence of the Holy Spirit, and a future permanent reality in the eschaton. The main focus is that Jesus is God who came and lived with us. God became one of us and lived like we live.[56]

---

55   The word "shekinah" does not appear in the Bible but signifies divine presence or visitation. The word means "he caused to dwell" or a "settling" or "dwelling". The word in Hebrew, which is feminine, represents the female attributes of God's presence. Moses and Israel experienced God's "shekinah glory" in the Exodus. It was said to be resident in Jesus as well.

56   Leon Morris, *The Gospel According to St. John, Tyndale New Testament Commentaries* (Grand Rapids, Michigan: Wm. B. Eerdmans Publishing Co., 1980), 102-107.

Another passage for our consideration is Matthew 1:18-25. This text suggests several things to us. In the first place, it reflects the controversy surrounding the birth of Jesus. Many of the Jewish people were not anticipating that the Messiah would be virgin born. One of the slanders early Christians had to answer was that Jesus was born out of wedlock. Christians never deny that Mary became pregnant before Joseph and Mary consummated their union. Before Joseph enacted what was possible to him according to law in culture in terms of divorce, he was divinely instructed to take Mary into his house as his wife. She was with child not by any human agency, but through the power and will of the Creator God. Joseph, though not physically the child's biological father, would be the child's father in the Jewish legal sense.[57]

The text also suggests the all creative power of God. The Old Testament knows of many births which took place through divine intervention. The Nativity story of Jesus differs when one considers that Jesus had no human biological father. Both Matthew and Luke presuppose a virgin birth. Pagan mythology had many tales of children born from intercourse between a god and a woman or a goddess and a man. Most of the "heroes" of antiquity were thought to have had their origins in this way. Jesus' story, however, is of a very different sort. Jesus' story of origin arises out of a totally different context than pagan mythology. It is based upon a very limited revelation, of which we will examine shortly, and upon a faith in the unlimited power of the one Creator God.[58]

The text indicates that the name to be given to the one virgin born was "Jesus". Jesus means, "The Lord is salvation." The name was fairly common in Palestine at that time. The name affirms God's work in procuring salvation for God's people, rescuing us from the guilt and power of sin. While we can forgive injury performed against us, we cannot forgive sin. Our sins are ultimately not against ourselves and others, but against our Maker. Only God can forgive sin. Only God can perform

---

57   R. V. G. Tasker, *The Gospel According to St. Matthew, Tyndale New Testament Commentaries* (Grand Rapids, Michigan: Wm. B. Eerdmans Publishing Co., 1977), 33-34.
58   Johnson, 254.

the work to remove our transgressions. Only God can forgive the evil performed in life before God's divine and holy presence.[59]

This brings us back to the concept of "Immanuel" in our text. There is some thought among scholars, even though it is inconclusive, that the maiden of Isaiah 7:14 was Ahaz's wife, who gave birth to Hezekiah who succeeded his father as king. Hezekiah, unlike his father, had righteous tendencies and expressed them in his actions. Hezekiah observed the Mosaic Law, removed much of the idolatrous expressions of the people at that time, and gave God his undivided allegiance. During Hezekiah's day there was something of the expression of "tabernacling" of God among God's people. When Jesus was born of Mary, nothing less than the revealed presence of God, now in human flesh, dwelt among God's people and through Jesus God made "common cause with us."[60]

Immanuel means "God with us."[61] What we have here in this designation is the reality of the Creator God, the "I am who I am" and the "I will be what I will be" (Exodus 3:14). The only one who has real being and from whom all being flows, is now here, on earth, in human form and with us. In old Shakespearian thought this is God "mingling democratic with us" (as an English king or queen out amid his or her subjects, and is a line employed in the Roanoke Island outdoor drama, "The Lost Colony"). It is, however, far more than just that! This act was more than just a political stroll. God, in Christ, did not just mingle among us. He became one of us, a commoner amid commoners. If you miss this point in the infancy narratives you have missed the whole point about the person of God and God's great desire. Look at and consider the record for a moment. Jesus was born of the commoner, Mary. His legal father was the commoner, Joseph.[62] He was born in a common Palestinian home with the stable and feeding troughs adjacent to what we would call the family living area. He was placed in the "phatne", a common feeding trough for domestic animals. He was first visited by "unclean" ("bad company") and common shepherds during unlikely hours of the

---

59   Ibid., 253.
60   Tasker, 34.
61   Johnson, 255.
62   Tasker, 33.

night. We can also assume, based on family ties and community culture, that much of the population of tiny Bethlehem also came to visit the child and the birth family. All of these people were commoners.[63] And how did Jesus come? He came as an infant. He came into the world as we come into the world. He was, in this regard, just like us. Jesus started his mission as we start life. He started his identification with us in fellowship and solidarity with our human earthly beginnings. Jesus was a commoner. He did not begin as some super hero. God took on human flesh in the person of Jesus Christ to share and bear our sorrows, to rejoice in our joys, and to carry the burden of our sins. His identification with us starts at our very beginning. Jesus carried this identification with us throughout his life.

From a practical standpoint the consideration of the incarnation and virgin birth gives me a feeling of the approachability of God. God knows me. In the knowing, there is understanding. In the understanding, there is personal direction and the potential for self-improvement and change. God makes self-disclosure and exposure safe and gladsome. I can be known, embraced, and accepted. I can also know God. God now becomes a real, tangible personality. He has an identity of which to relate. In Jesus, the terms of relationship like father, shepherd, and friend really mean something tangible. And God also knows my environment. He knows how tough things can be in life on this sphere. Jesus was much sympathetic to our plight and individual personhood. Jesus knows not only the "dark" and "light" of life but the "grays" as well. He knows the shadows, the darkness, and the daylight. He is a commoner who cares about common folk. He walked on earth. He worked here. He struggled here. He was savaged, bled, and died here. During my undergraduate days at Westminster College in New Wilmington, PA., I had a poster plastered on the wall in my room depicting a blind man with a cane trying to make his way down city sidewalks and across city streets. In the caption in a lower corner read the cry, "I can't see the way!" In a caption in an upper corner read the caption, "Trust me, I can!" To this

---

63   Kenneth E. Bailey, *Open Hearts in Bethlehem* (Downers Grove, Illinois: InterVarsity Press, 2005), 24-25.

writer, that is one of the most demonstrative messages I take away from the doctrine of the incarnation/virgin birth. "Immanuel, God with us" communicates a powerful message both from God's physicality with us, and now God's presence in God's "precious Holy Spirit." Because Jesus is one of us, yet God; because Jesus was here, yet remains through spiritual presence; because Jesus made common cause with us, and continues to intercede for us, the concept of "God with us" makes all the difference to my life and this crazy mixed up world in which we live. The incarnation/virgin birth brings some sanity and understanding to that which is insane and utterly confusing and frustrating.

We still need more precision in our attempt to address the issue of parentage in terms of Mary and the incarnation/virgin birth. There are many doctrines in the Christian faith that make people uncomfortable. Many people, I have discovered, have difficulty with the doctrine of the Trinity. Perhaps, it is difficult for our minds to conceive of plurality in unity! The Resurrection of the dead is another doctrine with which some people struggle and/or which many questions have been raised. There is probably no doctrine currently held by the Christian community that causes more discussion and debate than the doctrine of the Virgin Birth. Many professing Christians simply do not believe it as a historical reality. Many of those who do affirm it have difficulty defending it against critics. Perhaps what makes us so uncomfortable is that on the surface it smacks too much of legend, mythology, and paganism.[64] For those of us who formerly were schooled in a classic education, it conjures up images of Zeus, the pantheon of the gods of antiquity, and their soap opera-ish type of behavior with each other and with human interaction as well. While the story in the Bible is not an act of copulation between God and Mary, for some the parallel with paganism of the gods fertilizing a human female comes frighteningly too close.

Another thing that mitigates against our acceptance of this doctrine is our contemporary rejection of the miraculous. From the time of the Enlightenment and Age of Reason, many philosophers, theologians,

---

64   Walter Martin, *Essential Christianity* (Santa Ana, CA: Vision House, 1980), 42.

scientists, and thinkers in all walks of life and in all disciplines have been re-thinking and debunking the miraculous. Many leading scholars and intellectuals postulated that everything in existence could be explained on the grounds of the laws of physics, mathematics, and biology. The view of the universe as a self-contained machine pushed God out of the realm of divine/human interaction, and eventually, to many, killed God by eliminating the necessity of postulating such a supreme intelligence. Only within recent decades have we begun to discover that there are many things in the universe we cannot explain. It appears that there are many anomalies that are the antithesis of our laws and principles of governance. The universe no longer looks like a grand machine. Some scientists and intellectuals have boldly asserted that it appears that there is some grand intelligence behind the universe or multi-verse. There has appeared speculation that there might be something else out there, somewhere within or outside of our universal, multi-verse, and interdimensional theories of reality.

Let me state, once more, that I am a firm adherent to the doctrine of the incarnation/virgin birth. To this writer, this doctrine is critical to a firm Biblical understanding of salvation history. Without it, salvation history, as portrayed in the Bible, breaks down spiritually and intellectually. If God can create something out of nothing, if God can grant new life to a lifeless body, what is so difficult to believe about the incarnation/virgin birth? There are, however, some things about the incarnation/virgin birth, at least the way it has been classically defended and explained that make it appear to be a questionable doctrine and make people, like myself, uncomfortable. Please pay attention to me on this one; I have no problem with the doctrine itself, but I do have some discomfort with the way it has been described, explained and theorized down through the centuries. There are many people, I have discovered, who share the same discomfort.

My discomfort with some of the explanations of the incarnation/virgin birth down through history are tied up with the doctrine of original sin. The doctrine of original sin states, once more, that under Adam all humanity shares in the fallen nature of the human race. Since Adam, every human being is conceived with a proclivity, or nature, to sin. Since Adam, every human being is born in a state alien to a relationship with God. The time-honored answer to how this disconnectedness and fallenness is passed has been through conception. Do you see where this presents us with a problem when it comes to Jesus? How could Jesus be of Mary and yet not contain the taint of this mysterious fallen nature? If Jesus did contain the taint of the fallen nature then he would be like one of us, needing a redeemer instead of being our redeemer! If he was born like us, a person with a proclivity to sin and disconnected from God, then how could he do the work Adam failed to do and remain perfectly sinless in order to be the substitute sacrifice for the punishment due for our sins? Somehow this original sin, transmitted like a disease through human lineage since Adam, had to be dealt with or blocked. My supposition is that if Jesus came from Mary biologically, what comes from Mary would be like Mary. Since Mary was human from the line of Adam she possessed original sin, and hence, would pass on the death sentence to Jesus. It is theologically imperative that Jesus have no innate relationship with fallen humankind, and yet, at the same time, be completely human.[65]

This issue, which is a real problem for Christian theologians, though hardly mentioned or discussed these days with the gross shrinkage in North American Christianity of Biblical theological thought, has been handled in a number of different ways, which, to me, all appear to be quite strange.

First of all, many people simply choose to ignore the issue and feign lack of interest, disregarding the dilemma or simply considering it an unimportant matter. The incarnation/virgin birth is fact to them, and they are not interested in how God accomplished it or how God did it to circumvent this notion of original sin.

Roman Catholic theologians saw the problem many centuries ago. Original sin was, quite correctly, an issue in the virgin birth. They, according to their viewpoint, wanted to maintain Mary as the biological

---

65   Sinclair B. Ferguson, David F. Wright, and J. I. Packer, eds. *New Dictionary of Theology* (Downers Grove: Illinois: InterVarsity Press, 1988), 534-536.

mother of Jesus. To do so, and yet bypass the issue of the transmission of original sin, they created another miraculous birth story known as the "Immaculate Conception." Now we have two miraculous birth stories to deal with rather than just one! Mary, it was advanced, was conceived without the taint of original sin and, therefore, could be the mother of Jesus without passing on the fallen nature. This theory, however, has no Biblical support. In fact, it puts Mary in the same status as Adam and Jesus. To this writer, it is an aberration in the divine constitution and the death penalty that has been enacted for all of Adam's lineage.[66] Furthermore, why not just say the very same thing about Jesus? Karl Barth wrestled with this issue earlier in the 20th century. His explanation advanced the concept that the sin inheritance is passed on by the male parent only. Christ, could assume, in his thought, creaturely-ness by being born of Mary, and at the same time, escape the sin inheritance by the elimination of the human father. Such an explanation is plausible, but one cannot prove or disprove Barth's thesis.[67] Louis Berkoff argued that Christ assumed his human nature from the substance of his mother. Berkoff, it appears to me, just assumed, as I think do many others, that God simply blocked out Mary's original sin nature and kept Jesus free from the pollution of the taint of humanity. Berkoff advances no theory on how God accomplished this.[68]

When I was a student at Pittsburgh Theological Seminary back in the late 1970's and early 1980's, I advanced my own theory of how God accomplished this. My theory is not brilliant at all, nor, in reality, avant-garde, but makes perfect sense upon the examination of Scripture. I remember discussing it and writing about it at the time, with classmates and a certain professor either laughing at me or getting angry with me. A few even charged me with a mild heresy.[69] People, at that time, were just not thinking deeply enough about this issue and were locked into the unsubstantiated reasoning of the past. Since my years in

---

66   Louis Berkhof, *Systematic Theology* (Grand Rapids, Michigan: Wm. B. Eerdmans Publishing Co., 1977), 335.
67   Ibid., 336.
68   Ibid., 335.
69   Ibid., 334.

seminary, advances in modern medicine and technique in the areas of fertilization and conception have helped some people understand what, I believe, the Bible is describing in terms of incarnation/virgin birth. Of course, I also discovered that the position I was advocating was also un-knowingly advocated by others without them giving it much thought.[70]

The issue basically boils down to this question, who are the parents of Jesus? Who is the biological father of Jesus? Who is the biological mother of Jesus? Proponents, as well as critics of the faith, have held three main positions. The first is that of another human being and Mary were the biological parents of Jesus. Joseph, a Roman soldier named Pantheras, or another unnamed and unknown human being have been advanced.[71] The person of God and Mary have been advanced. God, of course, providing the male substance necessary to fertilize one of Mary's eggs.[72] Thirdly, God alone. The first position is ascribed to by many atheists, non-Christians, and some liberal and neo-orthodox theologians. This position is held by those who believe that Jesus did not become the Son of God until his baptism, which is, of course, the so- called "Adoption Theory."[73] The second position is held by the Roman Catholic Church, Karl Barth, and probably many others includ-ing advocates of Reformed Theology.[74] The third position, crediting God alone as the biological father and mother of Jesus, which is the position I advance, is also held, so I am told, by many in the Anabaptist tradition.[75] The only logical and Scriptural position, according to my opinion, is that the physical substance of the one born to Mary and known as Jesus is a complete creative action on the part of God per-formed in the womb of Mary. To this writer, it seems evident and clear

---

70   The Anabaptist tradition affirms that Jesus, born of Mary, was, in reality, a new creation of God. Berkhof's critique of the Anabaptist tradition regarding the Incarnation fails due to the fact that Berkhof cannot perceive how a new human creation "not organically connected" with us could possibly mediate our salvation.

71   J. Gresham Machen, *The Virgin Birth of Christ* (Grand Rapids, Michigan: Baker Book House, 1982), 10.

72   Leon Morris, *The Gospel According to St. Luke, Tyndale New Testament Commentaries* (Grand Rapids, Michigan: Wm. B. Eerdmans Publishing Co., 1979), 73.

73   Ferguson, 6.

74   Berkhof, 336.

75   Ibid., 334.

that the action God took was to create, implant, and place a fertilized egg in the womb of Mary so that nothing of Mary's biology (genetic material) came from any other human source either male or female. In this way Jesus could be completely human but not subject to the fallen nature of humanity because he was not from the lineage of Adam. In reality, Jesus, who is completely human, is of a new human line. A line of one!

Can this line of reasoning be proved? No, it cannot! Is there some evidence that would support this thesis or line of reasoning? Yes, there is! What then is the evidence offered?

Scriptural evidence must be examined first! Matthew 1:20 reads, "because what is conceived in her is from the Holy Spirit." The key words here are "conceived" and "from". The actual Greek renders the phrase, "for the thing in her begotten of the Holy Spirit is Holy."[76] The word that is employed here is understood to mean, "the begetting of the Father and the bearing of the mother."[77] In human terms it can be compared to the creative act of God producing something out of nothing. In context, however, the phrase can be understood, not conclusively, but cannot be ruled out either, making it very plausible that what is being described here is the creation of the human Jesus by the Holy Spirit in the womb of Mary. Let us now move onto Matthew 1:18. Matthew 1:18 reads, "she was found to be with child through the Holy Spirit." A better rendering in the Greek is "she was found in womb having of/by the Holy Spirit."[78] This indicates that the child came into being through the action of the Holy Spirit. To this writer, it appears to say that the action was the Holy Spirit's alone! The verse does not indicate how this took place, but it does refer to the event of the incarnation as a God action and not an act of divine/human cooperation. In fact, the whole event is couched in the terms that this is going to happen to Mary and that she

---

76   Alfred Marshall, *The Interlinear Greek-English New Testament* (Grand Rapids, Michigan: Zondervan Publishing House, 1976), 5.

77   Walter Bauer, *A Greek-English Lexicon of the New Testament and Other Early Christian Literature*, trans. and ed. W. F. Arndt and F. W. Gingrich (Chicago: The University of Chicago Press, 1957), 154-155.

78   Marshall, 5.

really does not have a real choice in the matter! We next look at Luke 1:35a which reads, "The Holy Spirit will come upon you, and the power of the Most High will overshadow you." This passage refers to a grace imparted to Mary by the Holy Spirit. "To come upon" is a reference to imparted grace. In Scripture, these words indicate that a gift is given, and is given completely, by God without any human action taking part in the gift except its reception. God is understood here as not sharing with the human in the giving, rather God gives alone and places the gift into the womb of Mary. It is, let us say, a completed gift. Let us now turn our attention to Romans 5:14, "Adam who was a pattern of the one to come." In Romans, Adam was a type of Christ. We have seen that Paul in 1 Corinthians 15:45 and 47 refers to Christ as the second and last Adam. Jesus Christ is the Adam that came from heaven. This, to me, is highly significant. A parallel is drawn up between Christ and Adam. Christ was of the same pattern as Adam. Who was Adam's direct father and mother? The creator God, of course! If Christ was of the same type as Adam who was a direct creation of the Creator God, this supports the notion that Jesus Christ was totally human, like Adam, but of a different human line. Jesus is a new creation of God whose parents were directly of God alone. Just like Adam! Berkoff presumes this position and attempts to refute it by indicating that any new human creation not connected to Adam would not resemble us. This, to me, is nonsense! Jesus came from the same pattern as us. He came from the pattern employed to create prior to the Fall. In that Christ came from the same pattern as us, he does not merely resemble us.[79] He is created just like we are in our totality. The only exception being that as a new creation he does not share in our current fallen nature, but in the original righteousness that Adam first experienced. Berkoff's argument is weak. If you are concerned with Jesus being different than us, he is, for he is God incarnate! The conclusion of this writer from Scripture is that while it does not completely affirm the position presented here, it does not mitigate against it either. In fact, the clearest understanding of the text leads one to believe a creation by God of a fertilized egg in the

---

79   Berkhof, 334.

womb of Mary, directly from God, without any human agency, even that of Mary!

A second set of evidence supporting the idea that Jesus was completely and solely a creation of God in the womb of Mary is from the use of language. Conception refers to the action of two, an egg fertilized by sperm. Conception by the Holy Spirit implies a completed act of God, not God and Mary. God is both biologically the father and mother of Jesus. God created, similar (in some ways) to the implantation of an embryo today (looking at it in one way, and one way only), the human Jesus in the womb of Mary.

Another rational argument this writer appeals to in support of the notion that Jesus was completely and solely a creation of God in the womb of Mary is based on salvation history. When it comes to Creation, it was an act of God alone. The crucifixion, and all that is understood by the atonement, is an act of God alone. The Bodily Resurrection is wholly an act of God alone. In the Ascension, God acts alone. Pentecost is an action of God alone. In all the main events of salvation history God acts alone. Why not the same pattern when it comes to the Incarnation? Consistency in the actions of God throughout salvation history demonstrate the likelihood that here too God acts alone without any help from the human agency.

Some may raise objections to the above. What about the passages that indicate that Mary was Jesus' mother? What about the genealogies that seem to prescribe human conception? What about Genesis 3:15 that has been interpreted as a Messianic passage that proves Mary was the mother of Jesus? What about these, you ask? I have no argument with them at all! Mary was the mother of Jesus. She bore and delivered the child. Mary was the mother of Jesus, just as Joseph was the father of Jesus according to the Jewish rules of parenthood and adoption. There are passages which claim that Joseph was the father of Jesus. We already know that this is not biologically true other than Mary bore and delivered the child. The parenthood of Joseph and Mary can be understood in the adoptive sense. Joseph was the father of Jesus in the use of the term "begat" which also means adoptive as well as biological and is also used to refer to guardianship. According to the Jewish rules of adoption, if a child was adopted the child was considered as one born biologically from one's own body. This was the way it was understood in that society, even if it was not biologically true. In the adoptive sense, Joseph was every bit as much the father of Jesus. In the adoptive sense, Mary was in every sense of the word the mother of Jesus.[80]

The genealogies also prove nothing. Through Joseph Jesus was the seed of Abraham and from the throne of David, and Joseph was not the biological father of Jesus. As I have stated above, to the Jewish culture of that time, fatherhood was granted even in adoption so that it was understood that the adopted child came from one's own loins even if one did not. Adoption, you could say, was a complete ingrafting! Jesus was a gift to the seed of Abraham and to the throne of David. It does not imply a direct biological connection.[81]

The same is true of Genesis 3:15. Jewish culture held that motherhood by adoption was just as real as biological motherhood.[82] We must remember in the argument that Mary did bear and deliver the baby. She was actually the mother through carrying the fertilized egg to term and through giving birth. Even though she may have not been the genetic mother, she was the mother in every sense of the word according to Jewish thought.

Another objection comes from Luke 1:31 and reads, "And behold, you will conceive in your womb and bear a son, and you shall call his name 'Jesus.'" This is an RSV (Revised Standard Version) rendering of the text. The word translated "conceived" here is different than the word designated for "conceive" in Matthew 1:20. In Matthew 1:20 the word is really "begat." According to Gerhard Kittel, the Greek word employed in Luke 1:31 refers to a state of being pregnant and not to the act of conceiving. The word is in reference of good deeds that come directly from the agency of God. The word actually means that deeds are planted, in this case, by God into the womb.[83] The word here, instead of

---

80   Machen, 129-130.
81   Ibid., 127-129.
82   Ibid., 129.
83   Gerhard Kittel, *Theological Dictionary of the New Testament,* ed. Gerhard Friedrich, trans.

giving evidence against the theory so ascribed here, actually supports it by indicating the Jesus was planted in the womb of Mary by God. The NIV (New International Version) translation is correct when it renders the Greek that she will be pregnant rather than "you will conceive." The NIV translation is "you will be with child and give birth to a son...."

What is the point of all this, you might ask? First of all, the issue of the precise nature of the parentage was not, and is not, an issue in the Bible other than the fact that Joseph, obviously, had nothing to do with biologically fathering the child. This can be said of any other male personage as well! This is an issue that has surfaced because of our concern with the story vis-à-vis ancient mythology. The Bible tells us only the what and the why, it does not tell us, specifically, the how. The "how" has become important only because many people have rejected the whole doctrine due to the concerns I have enumerated above. The position on this subject by this author may or may not be true, but it is a viable option that is refreshing and accomplishes several things. It removes any remaining ties of paganism and mythology that people attempt, quite erroneously, to read into the story. It easily takes care of the issue of original sin that has made some of our theology appear to be rather silly (especially doctrines like the Immaculate Conception of Mary). It retains and makes complete the divine action in salvation history as an act of the divine alone. It allows Mary to be who she really was, an instrument of God, special in vocation, but not so in essence. And it allows us to relax once again with the doctrine of the incarnation/virgin birth to see the real meaning behind the story, which is God coming into our world as one of us inaugurating a new human race (spiritually through being "born from above")[84] in order to share together a promised new paradise. If you are wont to doubt the doctrine of the incarnation/virgin birth and the perspective of this author, I refer you to the best words on the subject which were spoken by the

---

Geoffrey W. Bromiley (Grand Rapids, Michigan: Wm. B. Eerdmans Publishing Company, 1980), 760-761.
84   John 3:3,5.

angel, Gabriel to Mary when Mary asked, "How can this be?" The angel responds, "For nothing is impossible with God."[85]

To complete our discussion of this subject, we must turn now to the origin of the story of the incarnation/virgin birth. The question we have to answer is, where did the story of the incarnation/virgin birth come from in the first place? Historically, we learn that a firm, well-formulated affirmation of the virgin birth extends back to the early years of the 2nd century in Christian thought. Denials of the virgin birth, which begin to appear in that century, were based more upon philosophical or dogmatic presuppositions than any genuine historical evidence. Opponents of the virgin birth have dismissed the Christian affirmation throughout time in as many as 15 ways as I catalogued many years ago. I rely heavily here on the work of J. Gresham Machen here whose thoughts and words are much represented below. Let us take a brief look at each one of these that I catalogued (once again with heavy dependence on Machen) decades ago from the thoughts and writing of others as alternative explanations to the doctrine.

The first alternative explanation is an appeal to the obvious, that the whole story is nothing but a myth. In this category of the story's origin, Hermann Weisse has an interesting take. He believes that the whole drama of the Nativity is symbolic. The genealogy in Matthew, in his view, represents Judaism. Represented by Joseph, Judaism is that of a "stepfather" to Christianity. Judaism was not able to beget a divine son. John the Baptist represents Jewish prophecy and the Jewish nation. Zacharias and Elizabeth represent the new ideas coming from the old and powerless religion. The Magi represent old world priests and their religion. Herod is a representative of worldly power. It is usually the case that myths take a good bit of time to develop, yet the doctrine of the incarnation/virgin birth was on the scene immediately after the Ascension of Jesus.[86]

A second alternative rendering of the origin of the story is that of Parthenogenesis, or that Jesus developed in the womb of Mary by

---

85   Luke 1:37.
86   Machen, 212-213.

a freak of nature. This is an appeal to an analogy with the realm of nature in which lower forms of life reproduce themselves by themselves. The objection to this explanation here is that higher forms never reproduce themselves through the development of an unfertilized ovum.[87] An example of this in popular culture was portrayed by George Lucas in Episode I of his Star Wars movies, the 1999 film, "The Phantom Menace."

A third alternative is the Rationalizing Method as I have learned some refer to it. The thinking advanced here is that many great men were thought to have originated through virgin births. Early Christians thought that Jesus, likewise was supremely great, and so it would be natural to assume that he was born this way. Also referenced under this suggestion is the attempt to avoid the shameful implications of the fact that Jesus was not the son of Joseph. Early Christians invented and came to believe in Jesus' virgin birth to scuttle this charge of shameful origin. Objections to this rationalizing way to discharge history are twofold. Great men were not thought to be virgin born. It was believed in antiquity that they were born of the act of intercourse between a god and a mortal. This is a long way from the concept of a virgin birth! Also, both the Bible and known history holds no hint of a shameful birth in regards to Mary. With the initial absence of suspicion, it is wise to cast doubt upon this explanation.[88]

Some postulate that the idea of the virgin birth comes from the Old Testament in reference to what appears to be the strange births of Old Testament characters such as Isaac, Samson, and Samuel, and the New Testament character, John (the Baptist). The objection here centers around the idea that God would take the place of a human father. Such an idea was abhorrent to the Jews. Any idea that the Holy Spirit would take the place of the male factor and enter upon creative activity of such kind was not viewed positively. Davidic descent of the Messiah would

---

87   Ibid., 390.
88   Ibid., 272-273.

also be a powerful barrier against any evolving idea of the development of the virgin birth in this story.[89]

Another idea presented to us is the prophecy given in Isaiah 7:14 that we have looked at previously. Once again, "almah" signifies a young woman of marriageable age. "Bethulah" is the word which strictly identifies a virgin. "Almah" occurs seven times in the Old Testament, and it never was employed to represent a woman who was not a virgin. Who is the "almah" Isaiah is speaking of in his prophecy? Is it the prophet's wife? Is it Ahaz' wife? Could it be some other young woman? Due to the shortness of time in the prophecy, how would this even be a sign? Was this vision of Isaiah foreshadowing a greater event? If so, how would this speak to the circumstances at hand? The fact of the matter is that the Jewish people never interpreted Isaiah 7:14 to refer to the virgin birth of the Messiah. In terms of the Messiah, they anticipated a human being coming from the lineage of David. Over the years, I have also heard others comment that every virgin at the time of Jesus in Jewish culture wondered if she would be the virgin who would bear the Messiah through a virgin birth. This is the wrong idea. Women might have wondered if they would bear the Messiah, but not through a virgin birth. This has no place in Jewish thinking. As we have learned, the Septuagint employs the Greek word for "virgin" in a loose way. It crept into the text without cause and did not reflect nor initiate a Jewish doctrine. There is no evidence in the pre-Christian period that any Jewish person believed in the virgin birth of the Messiah or any other human being as well. The interpretation of Isaiah 7:14, it seems, was an innovation of the Jewish Christian Church over and against pre-Christian Old Testament Jewish exegesis.[90]

Some have suggested that Paul's perceived notion of the pre-existence of Christ, the doctrine of Christ as the second Adam, led to the development of the doctrine of the virgin birth. The story of the virgin birth never evolved from Paul's theological thinking. It was too short a time period for the doctrine to develop from any thinking of Paul.

---

89   Ibid., 280-285.
90   Ibid., 287-293, 296-297, 307, 311-316.

In fact, the doctrine of the virgin birth, known to Paul, framed Paul's doctrine of Christ as the Second Adam.[91]

A seventh alternative explanation for the development of the virgin birth is similar to the third one presented above. This is the pagan derivation for the doctrine. In Greco-Roman paganism the idea was advanced that great men were the sons of the gods through the union of mortal women with male deities. If this is where the idea of the virgin birth originated we would have to find it in pre-Christian Judaism. In early Christianity, stories of the gods copulating with mortal women was met with horror and considered demonic. It was not the case that early Christians believed in something like "Rosemary's Baby" but due to the content of such unions being products of lust. The "gods" were considered to be slaves of pleasure who enjoyed illicit and adulterous behavior. Pagan stories are not stories of virgin births. At their heart is the notion of the carnal lust of the gods for mortal women. The story portrayed in the New Testament is a narrative of a different kind. There are, I am told, no virgin birth accounts in pagan literature. What is apparent in pagan literature is rampant lust, jealousy, hatred, and crass anthropomorphisms. Compare pagan literature to the New Testament and the lofty monotheism of the Old Testament. The Bible portrays the "awful" transcendence of God and the "awful" separateness of God from this fallen world. The lust of the gods for mortal women is the point of the pagan stories without which these stories could not possibly exist. This kind of idea in Matthew and Luke would seem to profane the whole essence and temper of their Gospel narratives.[92]

Some have appealed to Gautama, the founder of the Buddhist religion for the origin of the virgin birth idea. Some have advanced the thought that Gautama was virgin born. This is not true. The earliest records, some 200 years after his life, record not the idea that he was virgin born. The idea apparently came into fruition 800 years later, which was 500 years after Christ.[93]

---

91   Ibid., 317-318.
92   Ibid., 319-339.
93   Ibid., 339-343.

As a ninth alternative on our list is a suggestion that the origin of our notion of virgin birth came from the religion of ancient Persia, Zoroastrianism. It has been advanced that Zoroaster has a hand in the virgin birth of the Saoshyant. The Saoshyant, of which there are three according to one prophecy, are eschatological savior figures who bring about the final destruction of evil and the ultimate renovation of the earth. The prophecy speaks of the conception of these saviors by their mothers while bathing in a lake where the seed of the prophet, Zoroaster, has been miraculously preserved. There is no virgin birth evident here![94]

The religion of Babylon has been cited as a possibility in the derivation of the concept of the virgin birth. Marduk, originally a tribal sun god who became the chief deity and the Babylonian redeemer king of this ancient religion, however, is not represented as virgin born. There is no idea of virgin birth in Babylonian sources.[95]

Some have cited the ancient zodiac as giving rise to the idea of the virgin birth. While the ancient zodiac is a very intriguing study and, to some, the "gospel in the skies", the idea of the rise of the constellation of the virgin (Virgo) on December 25th at midnight somehow being connected with the birth of Jesus on December 25th has no merit. This connection between the two appeared centuries after the New Testament story proclamation. Recent studies of the ancient zodiac give evidence that the birth of Jesus came about in the early summer season. It also appears that any connection between Jesus and salvation history, with the constellations of Virgo and Leo, were identified well after the historical event of the coming of the Christ. An exception to this may be the identification of the Magi and their understanding and interpretation of the ancient zodiac.[96]

A 12th alternative explanation comes from that of Osiris in ancient Egypt. Gressmann claims that the story came from Egypt and was transported to Palestine. Gressmann points to the structure of

---

94   Ibid., 343-344.
95   Ibid., 344-345.
96   Ibid., 344.

the story and its similarities as evidence. Objections to Gressmann's theory include the carnal union between the god and the queen in the story, which is the central feature of the story without which the tale could not exist. There is no idea of a supernatural conception in this Egyptian legend.[97]

The idea of Mary being impregnated by an angel also has been suggested through the employment of the term, "overshadow". While "overshadow" is a term used in reference to the Holy Spirit, Leisegang sees a connection between the communication of spirits and human beings. Spirits, it is believed, "overshadow" women and cause the women to prophesy. Objections to Leisegang's theory includes his poor treatment of the words "spirit" and "overshadow". The Jewish people never had any idea of the communication between human beings and spirits, especially a woman in the role of prophetess. Mary was not a prophetess. As far this theory goes, never was an actual child brought forth through this connection and communication.[98]

Another idea, that has been already mentioned, is the allegation that Mary shared in an adulterous union with Pantheras, a Roman soldier, and that Mary initiated the virgin birth idea as a cover-up. Of course, this runs against all we know about the character of Mary. It runs against the whole New Testament narrative. There is nothing in the New Testament that even suggests such a thing. It is believed that the story was started by Jewish religious officials to attack the Christian faith dated to the second century.[99]

The 15th and final alternative derivation of the concept is a rather recent one held by both supporters and detractors of the Biblical assertion of the virgin birth. That idea is of alien (UFO) impregnation of Mary. There are those among the Christian community who theorize that the UFO phenomenon is demonic. Researcher David Hunt has written that alien encounters are not so much material as they are spiritual. There is, however, regardless of what one might think about

---

97   Ibid., 348-361.
98   Ibid., 363-379.
99   Ibid., 10.

the subject of aliens and UFO's, no evidence to support the supposition that Mary became impregnated by an alien creature two-millennia ago giving rise to the Biblical narrative.[100]

From whence did the story arise? Here is what we know. The author of the Lukan and Acts accounts spent a couple of years in Palestine. Luke, the physician and travelling companion of Paul, lived in the area for the two years Paul was in prison in Caesarea. During this time, Luke conducted his research for his Gospel from eyewitness sources. It is believed that he was present with James, the brother of Jesus and head of the church at Jerusalem; Mary, the mother of Jesus; Philip and his prophesying daughters; in the home of Mnason, who apparently had a great deal of information concerning Jesus' earthly life; and the oral transmissions of the sayings and events of Jesus from a multitude of people who were present contemporaries of the Christ. We also need to note from experts who claim that the narrative is a true one and could never have been made up. The characters in the book, it is claimed, do not act according to logic. The narrative itself gives rise to many questions. With only a fraction of the sayings and events of Jesus recorded, it shows a complexity of an actual life. There are also little statements and gestures included in the writing that would have been avoided if it, in fact, had been a fictitious account.

If we grant knowledge of the two points advanced above, where do we go from here to find the origin of the story? There appears to be no general knowledge of the virgin birth during the ministry of Jesus. Mary is a person who is perplexed and troubled by the trials and tribulations prophesied about her and her son that come into fruition. Jesus has not lived up to the national expectations of the awaited Messiah. Jesus had not lived up to what Mary had anticipated as well. The opposition and severe suffering he experienced was more than she ever imagined would occur. Mary apparently did as the Lukan account indicates, keeping the things of the Annunciation, Incarnation, Virgin Birth, and Nativity to herself. Mary did not broadcast the origins of Jesus and her involvement

---

100   Dave Hunt, *The Cult Explosion: An Expose of Today's Cults and Why They Prosper* (Eugene, Oregon: Harvest House Publishers, 1980), 121, 224-226.

with the divine. Who would have known the story? There are only four people who would have known the details: Mary, of course, Joseph, and her Judean relatives, Elizabeth and Zechariah. By the time of Christ's passion, Joseph, Elizabeth and Zechariah were no longer among the living. Mary would be the sole keeper of this marvelous tale. It may be the fact of the matter that she "pondered these things in her heart"[101] to keep herself from slanderous accusations and the subject of delusion and malfeasance. This leads us to another question concerning the origin of the story of the incarnation/virgin birth. If Mary becomes, after the Resurrection and Ascension of Jesus, the sole keeper of the story, why do we have two stories of origin recorded in Matthew and Luke, both of which appear to be independent of the other? This supposed contradiction, however, may demonstrate complete interdependence on the other! The two actually supplement each other. Consider that neither one is comprehensible without the other! Matthew records the story from the perspective of Joseph. Luke records the story from the perspective of Mary. Joseph, whose character and personhood is critical for Mary, the raising of Jesus, and the family, is the human protector of the young woman and her child. It is apparent that Joseph's testimony was given to Matthew by Mary. Since one of them wrote first, the "rest of the story" was taken up by the other. In both regards, it is Mary, and Mary alone, who transmitted the testimony of the origin of the Christ event. The next question has to be, when was the story recounted and delivered? It is the opinion of this writer and others, that the time for revelation and story sharing would be following Pentecost. With the Resurrection appearances and the Ascension over, the time period after Pentecost would be ideal for the true nature of the Christ event and Jesus' work to come into focus and complete understanding. It was now time for Mary to speak because the claims Jesus made for himself were now vindicated. She would now be believed! Within this little circle of believing men and sympathetic and caring women – all of whom are dear friends with whom she can trust and share the deep things treasured in her heart – she finally gives utterance to the things

---

101   Luke 2:19, 51.

that were, previously, too personal and enigmatic to be communicated to the human ear and mind. When the story was finally revealed and shared, there is no evidence that it aroused doubt, suspicion, and opposition from the disciples and leadership of the Church. Through her sharing of the marvelous genesis of the story, this amazing tale found its way into the Gospel records, the creeds, and Christian tradition. As this writer has openly stated to others, if the Christian community can accept the bodily resurrection, there should be no difficulty in accepting this marvelous work of God known to us as the incarnation/virgin birth. Those surrounding Mary in the first century, and those in the early church afterwards, came to believe it and embrace it as completely historical and factual! [102]

Before we close out this chapter on the Adams' Family, I think it is important for us to consider why the incarnation/virgin birth is important and crucial to the Christian faith and its message to the world. What follows is a rendering of seven reasons, gleaned from others (particularly Machen), as to why the incarnation/virgin birth is so vital and at the very core of salvation history. There are people who have surmised that the virgin birth is an archaic, naïve and rather silly doctrine which is an unnecessary tenet of the faith and actually harms belief in and acceptance of Jesus as the incarnate God, Savior and Lord. I disagree! This doctrine of the origin of events makes the work of God rational and understandable. It is not an obstacle to faith, but rather a great pillar of the faith.

The virgin birth is important, first of all, simply because God's authoritative Word instructs us that it is both valid and true. It is a key component of salvation history. It serves as the spectacles we look through to understand what God has done and is doing in this crazy, mixed up, and often chaotic world of ours. Too many people think that the Bible is only valid in terms of moral and spiritual matters. Even that thought today has come under increasing attack as the validity of the Word in many areas of morality, ethics, and values has come under societal clarification and matters of personal choice. Those who would

---

102   Machen, 265.

give up the doctrine claiming that the Bible it is not authoritative in matters of history and science have failed to wrestle with the Word in its cultural setting and with its cultural background, including the fact that it is not a product of the Western world, but of the near-Orient. This makes a big difference as the late Dr. Kenneth Bailey attempted to show through his writings and life's work. The Bible does contain history. It may not be the classical historical thought and progression of the West, but unless the historicity of the Bible is true, the authority of the Bible vanishes and what Christians have invested in it evaporates as well. In the end, any invalidation means we, those who profess Christ, are, in reality, without hope.[103]

A second assertion as to the importance of the incarnation/virgin birth, is that without it a "serious gap in our knowledge of the Christ would exist." Without this knowledge, our theology would be incomplete and weakened. We would not know the true identity of the Christ. We would not know Christ's role as the second Adam. We would not know the how and why of the Deity of Christ. Too many questions would go without an answer, leading to many variant theories and much speculation. The incarnation/virgin birth is the central anchor between the events of Eden and Joseph's Garden and the eschaton to come.[104]

A third reason that the incarnation/virgin birth has been advanced as important by commentators is "the consequences of a religion founded without it." While our salvation is of "works", the one work of Jesus Christ culminating in the cross, granting us the gift of grace - if we vanquish much of the miraculous and supernatural, we have a situation wherein people could claim that Jesus gained sonship with God through the expansion of consciousness and mental effort. It would lead people to speculate that all we need to do is follow Jesus' example (which is a terrible theory of the atonement). This, of course, is nothing more that the lie Eve was told in her temptation. Sin is portrayed in the Bible as something that is real, resulting in

---

103   Ibid., 382-387.
104   Ibid., 392-397.

a terrible distancing and cutting off of the relationship between the divine and the human. This chasm cannot be bridged from the human side. No infrastructure investment and endeavor can possibly link the two together again. The Bible, however, holds the key to closing the gap. The Bible is clear that this is God's work, and God's work alone in the incarnate God, the person of Jesus Christ, the second Adam. Without the historical record of redemption and its historicity, all the lofty precepts and ideals of the rest of the Bible, as well as its principled teachings and acts of goodness, are ultimately meaningless. The salvation God offers us is a matter of history and historical record. Eliminate the history and redemption vanishes![105]

A fourth assertion concerning the incarnation/virgin birth asserted by advocates of the faith is the importance for Jesus, and for us, to have lived a substantially complete life sharing our humanity. As I have asserted above, God taking on and sharing in human life right from the start speaks not only of the importance of God identifying with us, but God having this experiential point of view. The matter of the importance of this is only intensified if one understands that Jesus had to live a life without being the product of the situation in Eden (the fall and original sin). By the means of the incarnation/virgin birth, Jesus, in the pattern of the origin of Adam, could only take on the curse through a life of steadfast and sinless obedience, terminating in his fitness to become the perfect sacrifice for the sins of the world. Without the reality of the circumstances of the Nativity, the realization of Jesus' work would be impossible to bring to completion.[106]

The incarnation/virgin birth is important because "it determines whether one holds a naturalistic or super-naturalistic view of Jesus Christ." There are two views among those who espouse the concept of deity. There are those who affirm an active God who is immanent and involved with human life. For Christians, this includes the unfolding of God's one revelation of Jesus the Christ. The alternative view for theists is of a creator, transcendent God who is little involved with the

---

105   Ibid., 385-386.
106   Ibid., 394-395.

affairs of humankind. If one inquires of people if they affirm the Deity of Christ, or even the Resurrection of Jesus, the answers could possibly be wide and varied. The Deity of Christ can refer to a number of different perspectives depending on one's world and religious point of view. The same is true of the Resurrection. The idea of the Resurrection is employed today in many different senses from "continued influence", to "mystical presence", to various concepts of the transmigration and immortality of the soul. When it comes to the incarnation/virgin birth, however, the situation is different. If an individual affirms that Jesus was born without a human biological/genetic father, the conception being the work of the Holy Spirit in Mary's womb, it is problematic to see how one can escape the plain meaning of the understanding of virgin birth. Likewise, if an individual affirms that Jesus was born without any human biological/genetic parenthood, either male or female, the totality of the work being accomplished by the Holy Spirit in the womb of the virgin, those who would reject it would also probably reject a complete supernatural view of the entire Christ event. Some people today might profess an affirmation in an incarnation, but their understanding of the term does not mean to them what the New Testament means by the "Word becoming flesh." It is possible that to some, the term "incarnation" refers to a type or style of "oneness" or unity between God and humanity. This concept is way outside the understanding of the meaning in the New Testament. A precise understanding of what is being portrayed in Matthew, Luke, and John's prologue cannot be made fuzzy. The incarnation/virgin birth means one thing, and one thing only, in the New Testament. The same is true, I reason, for the other two doctrines listed above, but there is much less room for alternative explanations in terms of the incarnation/virgin birth than what has been advanced by others in terms of the deity of Christ and the bodily resurrection of Jesus.[107]

A sixth reason for the importance of the incarnation/virgin birth is that "it reinforces the Biblical teaching that nothing is 'impossible with God'". The doctrine lends more evidence to the Biblical affirmation that

---

107   Ibid., 387-392.

God is both the Creator and Sustainer of the cosmos. God is not only in charge of the universe (or multiverse), but can also work the "impossible" in our own lives as well. Many people today use the word "miracle" too loosely. "Miracle" has now been associated with magic and fantasy. To those of the mystical body of Christ, the concept of "miracle" is not of magic or fantasy, but of a work of divine reality. The blessed reality of Biblical faith is that our God and His Christ have the power to work out magnificent things for one's life, one's prayers, and one's provision in terms of our service and stewardship for our King. The Biblical God is the God of the impossible. This author can testify to that in both life and ministry and in astounding ways.[108]

The seventh and final reason the incarnation/virgin birth is important, according to those in Christian thought, is because the action and event is revelatory of God's nature and person, particularly God's characteristics and expression of love. It shows that God who created everything did not, in the words of another author, "despise the virgin's womb."[109] The incarnation/virgin birth demonstrates graphically that God really does care for God's people and God's creation. When the Magi visited the infant Jesus and his family on December 25, 2 BC, (as postulated by Larson) gifts were granted to the child and his parents in celebration of his birth announced in the stars earlier that year and in 3 BC . The reality of the birth is, however, that God celebrated it by giving us an eternal gift. Through God's gift of Jesus, the Christ, we learn that this gift of love is greater than all the Valentine Day cards, loving expressions, and romantic gestures ever rendered. God loves us! God loves us with all our sins, warts, and imperfections. The incarnation/virgin birth indicates to us that God really does care (the major concern that the late John Stott stated was crucial for human beings).[110] God really does want us to engage in relationship, get to know Him better, and forgive us fully. The hardest three things for people to ac-

---

108   D. James Kennedy, *Knowing the Whole Truth: Basic Christianity and what it Means in Your Life* (Old Tappan, New Jersey: Fleming H. Revell Company, 1985), 52-53.

109   Machen, 394.

110   John R. W. Stott, *The Cross of Christ* (Downers Grove, Illinois: InterVarsity Press, 1986), 329-336.

cept may just be that they are lovable to God, that God forgives them, and that salvation is a free gift of God's grace which cannot be worked out by ourselves (be careful of the meaning, often misunderstood of Philippians 2:12 & 13, wherein God's people work out the results of the salvation God has worked in) nor can be purchased other than by the Christ. These three things are the ultimate meaning and expression of the incarnation/virgin birth of Jesus the Christ. God did not make His coming and work difficult for us to understand. If anything, God made it very simple and easy. Regardless of our personal circumstances in life, the message of the gift of Jesus through the incarnation/virgin birth is ultimately very liberating. It is a doctrine which frees us to embrace God's love, accept God's plan of forgiveness, and place ourselves in the divine fellowship to personally share the eternal peace and joy of the God who knows no impossibility.

During my career I encountered many people who had difficulty with the concept that God could and would forgive them of a partic-ular sin or a particular set of sins. They also had difficulty forgiving themselves. In one of the most dramatic situations in my early career, I was requested by a parent to visit their adult child in the psych unit of a hospital. I had never met the individual and had much trepidation about the coming encounter. The best thing I did was to spend a little time in prayer before the encounter, and felt a very strong compulsion to take my "main" Bible with me. When I arrived at the unit, I was met by the young lady's mother and escorted into the room, where I found her curled up on the restroom floor sobbing and almost unable to move. With thoughts of "what have I gotten myself into?" coursing through my brain, we finally, amid her pleas of protest, managed to get her to a bench in the hallway, wherein she curled up beside me and I began to lovingly and carefully engage her. It did not take me too long to discover that the genesis of her current condition and state of being was due to the performance of some sort of sin and the belief that it was unforgivable by God and she was doomed to hell. I never did learn what the transgression was for it was not important for me to know in terms of the remedy that she needed. Fortunately, I had purchased a

Bible, having learned from Jonathan Edwards' example with his own personal Bible, that filling the wide margins and blank pages with notes was a wise thing to do. In one of the sections of my Bible, I had inscribed some lengthy notes, wherein I listed all the forgiveness passages in the Word. So, I turned to that section and one by one we looked them up, employing the Bible's varied images portraying the subject of the forgiveness of sin and God's love and mercy. The various portrayals of forgiveness in the Word struck a chord with the young lady's heart and mind. Little by little, her countenance lightened and the dark shadows that surrounded her evaporated. She came to understand that she was loved by God and that God's forgiveness was available to her. She embraced it, accepting Christ as her personal Savior at the end of our three hours of forgiveness discovery. Before my eyes and ears, she was transformed into a new person in Christ. The next day she was released from the hospital and declared whole and well. She has lived a joyous life in Christ ever since. How many troubled individuals are there in our society who could be healed and made whole if they only were able to know, understand, and embrace the mercy, love, and forgiveness available to them in the person of the incarnate God?

The second Adam, through the incarnation and virgin birth, is now on the scene in Palestine. The drama of "giving Adam and Eve another chance" is about to begin! We have a new Adam whose desire and intent is to rescue and reclaim Eve!

6

Seeking Eve:
I Will Always Find You

"No matter where you go I will find you, if it takes a long, long, time. No matter where you go I will find you, if it takes a thousand years."

(Ciaran Marion Brennan/Clannad)

In one of the most dramatic moments portrayed on film is a scene from the 1992 version of the "Last of the Mohicans" wherein Nathaniel Hawkeye, played by Daniel Day-Lewis, cries out to the young English woman, Cora Munro, played by Madeleine Stowe, in a cavernous indentation behind a waterfall who is about to be overtaken and made prisoner by French allied American Indians during the North American French and Indian War. "You stay alive, no matter what occurs! I will find you. No matter how long it takes, no matter how far, I will find you!" Nathaniel Hawkeye promises and proclaims that he will spare nothing to locate, rescue, and liberate her. In this moment, he is, to me, a Christ-like figure, for is not this what Jesus has done for us? In my theory of the "Relationship of One", is not this what Jesus, the last Adam, has done for Eve? "I Will Find You" is also a popular Celtic song whose lyrics state, "No matter where you go, I will find you, if it takes a thousand years!" Certainly, the outworking of God's Plan has taken many thousands of years, particularly if you affirm as likely, as I do, the research perspective of the "Reasons to Believe" group based in Los Angeles, California. Their dating of human/Biblical events greatly extends the time frame, particularly of the Genesis accounts, over that which has been popularly believed and advanced in Christian cultural thought.

One of the better and most heart-felt stories of my 30-year ministry at Natrona Heights Presbyterian Church (now an Evangelical Presbyterian Church congregation) concerns a woman named Helen Dougherty. Now with the Lord, Helen was one of those many special ladies I had the privilege to get to know and serve during my career at NHPC. At a time in her latter years, she was recuperating physically at a rehabilitation facility in Pittsburgh. One day I went to this residence to visit with her and she was not there. I was told that she had been moved. The residence helped me locate her new temporary home. When I got there, I was told that she was not there either. "Where is she?" I inquired. "She has been taken to Shadyside Hospital," I was told. So, I went to Shadyside Hospital, and at the hospital I was told, "She hasn't been admitted here!" I then asked the person at the desk, "Well, if she hasn't been admitted to the hospital, could she be in the ER?" After engaging a search, I was told, "Yes, she is in the emergency room!" So off to the emergency room went I. Asking permission to enter, I pulled back the curtain of an identified cubicle and here was Helen! With a surprised look on her face, she asked, "How did you know I was here? How did you find me?" Never was Helen more surprised! Under the circumstances she was never happier to see a friendly face who could comfort her and help her understand her medical situation. I remember well my reply: "Helen, I will always find you!"

Finding is very much a God thing. While much ink in the Bible is devoted to our search and discovery of God such as Proverbs 8:17 wherein God says, "I love those who love me, and those who seek me find me!" The fact of the matter is, as Luke 19:10 records Jesus saying, "For the Son of man came to seek and to save what was lost." What was lost includes us! Jesus' entry on the human scene is, in reality, a seek and save operation. He has come to seek us! He has come to rescue us! His finding of us is his assignment on planet earth never more put into story than the teaching stories (parables) of the Lost found in Luke 15. Let us look at the first story of the three (really four) parables, the Lost Sheep.

According to the late Dr. Kenneth Bailey, whose statements and writings to which I make reference here, the religious establishment at the time of Jesus views Jesus as a religious innovator and feels threatened by him. He shares table fellowship with and ministers to all forms of "bad company"[111] (the categories of which number more than a dozen according to my count and listing). These include "the unclean", the breakers of Jewish law, and imperialist (Roman) collaborators. They murmur against Jesus as he receives or engages in fellowship with those whom they (the religious elite) would never be found in their presence. Jesus knows their complaint and so addresses it in story form. He tells a simple story out of the life of those in the village. He does not talk the language of the law. He lumps the listeners in with the shepherds. He includes the religious elite (John 10) in with the hired under-shepherds. In the Middle Eastern culture, according to Dr. Bailey, one never places the blame on oneself for anything. Here Jesus squarely places the responsibility for the missing sheep on the shepherd. It must be noted that the willingness to go after the lost one is only after the 99 are cared for and properly secured, according to Dr. Bailey. Jesus describes the search as a wilderness one. He employs the wilderness here reminding the audience of the discontent that Moses and Aaron also faced. This is a discontent that historically would eventually reach its crescendo in

---

111   Adolf Holl, *Jesus in Bad Company*, trans. Simon King (Austin, Texas: Holt, Rinehart, and Winston, Inc., 1973), 26-34.

the shout, "Crucify him!" In this story, Jesus is actually insulting the scribes and Pharisees. They who were to be the shepherds of the people would never discomfort themselves to go out after the one which is lost. They would never accept responsibility for the lost. The cost of the search would discourage them. The shepherd's task of finding the lost sheep is daunting. Lost and frightened sheep make no noise and "get small". They lie down trying to hide themselves. It is not an easy find! The shepherd, however, continues the search until he discovers the location of the missing sheep. When he finds him or her, he revels in joy! He is not celebrating the fact that the task is completed. According to Ken Bailey, the shepherd is rejoicing in the one who is found through this burdensome effort of restoration. Do not miss this point! The Good Shepherd searches diligently for the one lost and will sacrifice himself completely in order to accomplish this task. Is not this what the second Adam has engaged to find the lost, particularly the one, Eve? I would like to advance another observation here. Notice that the rescue operation becomes a "hands on" event. The shepherd embraces the one who is lost and holds that one tight. The rescued one is comforted and assured of liberation from all the evil that "lostness" entertains. The frightened sheep cannot be led back. Sheep in this condition, so I am told, will not walk. The good shepherd must secure its hooves with his hands, wrap the sheep around his shoulders and carry it back. The shepherd then announces to the community the success of the restoration and calls everyone in the community to rejoice with him. Jesus says that there will be more rejoicing in heaven over one sinner who repents than over 99 righteous person who do not need to repent. Here, according to Ken, Jesus employs a subtle humor. The righteous who do not need to repent DO NOT EXIST! There will be no heaven's joy for the religious elite because they will not be there. They have missed the injunction, "we all, like sheep, have gone astray" (Isaiah 53:6 & 1 Peter 2:25), refusing to be found and carried. They have refused to embrace Jesus. They have refused Jesus' offered embrace! The Christ, as the Good Shepherd, has left the security of heaven and has proceeded at great risk, placing himself in "harm's way", so that we will not be left behind subject to the consequences of sin. Finding is very much a God thing. We might search for God, but it is God who always does the finding.[112]

Have you ever noticed, when it comes to the Resurrection narratives of Jesus in the Gospels and some of the divine interactions in the rest of the New Testament (ie. Paul on the Damascus Road), that which ties all these stories of the risen Christ together? One of the common themes of Easter and the 40 days of Resurrection is that Jesus is always the one who does the finding! It all starts, of course, with Mary Magdalene. She thinks Jesus is lost. His body, after all, is missing from the tomb. It is she, however, who is the lost one. Jesus finds her. The one whom she hoped to find finds her!

Look at all the resurrection stories. Jesus finds his own. He comes to them and stands right in their presence. Again, and again, Jesus walks right into their presence. We have here the fulfillment of the promise of Psalm 23. The "with me" God is right there by our side to take us through the gloomy valleys where death's shadows stretch over us and threaten to envelop us. Our Jesus, however, has other plans. He remains by our side and takes us all the way to the place of provision and rejoicing. His finding of us never ends until we are in the safe fold of his permanent security.

When Jesus found Mary Magdalene, as we will examine, the two embrace. That embrace is absolutely huge and communicates much! In terms of this chapter, Jesus' message is clear – "I will always find you".

---

112   Kenneth E. Bailey, *Poet and Peasant and Through Peasant Eyes: A Literary-Cultural Approach to the Parables in Luke* (Grand Rapids, Michigan: William B, Eerdmans Publishing Co., 1976), 142-156.

7

A Kite or A Windjammer

"There's a man who leads a life of danger.... With every move he makes, another chance he takes. Odds are he won't live to see tomorrow. Secret agent man, secret agent man, they've given you a number and taken away your name."

(Steve Barri, and P. F. Sloan/Johnny Rivers)

"I will always find you!", has taken us another step toward the drama of the second Adam finding, rescuing, redeeming, and restoring Eve. To fully grasp the extent of the drama being played out here, we must review some aspects of Holy Week, particularly Thursday night, the Crucifixion, the entombment of Jesus, and the immediate circumstances and setting of Christ's Resurrection.

Over my career, much to my disdain, Biblical and theological acumen seem to have receded among not only the general population of the United States but critically among those who claim Christ and have some sort of church affiliation. In the culture today, people do not seem to have a good handle on the late Paul E. Little's book titles, "Know What You Believe", "Know Why You Believe", and "Know Who You Believe".[113] In today's culture it seems to me that people pick and choose, in much a cafeteria style, what they will believe from Scripture, what they will follow from Scripture, what they will reject from the Bible, and what they will decline to practice from the Bible. My experience has been that very few people really understand what is going on in the Bible cover to cover, and, sadly, their ignorance does not bother them. Our narcissistic culture has produced a catering in many Christian communities toward what God can do for you and your life, rather than how you can know and serve God. Toward the end of my ministry when ordered by the Session to preach on Reformed theology, and particularly the "Five Solas",[114] I heard murmurings among the congregation concerning the "boring" nature of the material and how they "get nothing" out of my sermons. Has the Christian faith so deteriorated in North America that the main church theme expression is "all about your life" and not God's? Has church become less of an academy of learning and more of an entertainment venue? I think it has! In fact, I am sure of it!

While I have not made an extensive study on this, I certainly have noticed as I have written above, that the Bible is a book of themes, many of which are quick to be set out in its pages. Like a steel rake, whose metal tongs make their mark on the ground moving straight and true covering a wide swath, the themes revealed in the Bible travel from one end of the book to the other. To me, this thematic reality of the compilation of 66 books helps to verify what I believe is the divine imprint of the text, as well as being a valuable tool in the defense of its validity! What I have also noticed is that the Bible is really one big circle. Its starting point and ending point are both linear and circular. The Bible repeats itself again and again. It is a circle, like a cyclone, that moves!

---

113   For bibliographic information on the book titles of Paul E. Little listed here, please see the Bibliography.
114   The Five Solas ("Sola" is Latin meaning "alone" or "only") of Reformed theology are: "Sola Scriptura" (Scripture Alone); "Sola Fide" (Faith Alone); "Sola Gratia" (Grace Alone); "Solus Christus" (Christ Alone); and "Soli Deo Gloria" (Glory to God Alone).

The Bible goes around and around, in my estimation, but advances at the same time. The Bible also spins out smaller circles that go around and around, yet advance as well! The big question in the Bible for people like me is where does the book, on the circle, really begin and end. I think I have discovered that, and it is not what or where people think! Of course, I will be sharing that in an upcoming chapter.

When the latest edition (2015) of the James Bond movie series, "Spectre" was released, I found myself viewing it for a second time. In the movie one of the characters makes a reference to Bond, a British MI6 (Military Intelligence Department 6) agent, as "a kite dancing in a hurricane." Immediately I said to myself, "that's a good expression for Jesus during his hours of opposition and persecution Thursday night (Maundy Thursday) and through the daylight hours on Friday (Good Friday)." I fancied, at that moment, Jesus as God's "Secret Agent Man", and as Johnny Rivers recorded, "They've given you a number and taken away your name." Bond was given the number 007 by the late Ian Fleming from the digits on a hotel room he once resided or noticed in passing. Jesus has a number, though most do not know it. Christ's number is 888, playing off of God's 777, and the Satanic trinity of 666,[115] of which the derivation and identification of the last number is highly debated by scholars and others (although I appreciate Dr. Ken Bailey's assertions on the subject).[116] Upon further reflection, I thought to myself, "No, Jesus was not a kite dancing helplessly in a hurricane. Jesus was in his Passion a mighty 'windjammer'

---

115   In Christian Numerology "666" is either the number of humankind (created on the 6th day), but signifying our fallenness, or the Luciferian (Antichrist) trinity. It generally is understood to refer to humanity or Lucifer as coming up short of God's perfection. See Revelation 13:15-18 as the mark of the beast being the sign of the Antichrist. "777" is generally understood to represent the Christian Trinitarian God. The number 7 represents perfection in Hebrew numerology. It refers to God's perfection and completeness. "888" is understood to be the number of the new creation, of victory, and Jesus as Christ the Redeemer. Christian and Biblical numerology is a study in which one must proceed with caution, particularly to assigning numbers, symbolic and literal, to personages, events, ideas, and time periods. Plenty of information on the subject can be found in the internet.

116   Dr. Kenneth Bailey made a very good case for the Beast of Revelation 13 to be the Roman Emperor, Nero. He, among others, have presented this argument or advocated this position. There are many scholars who disagree. This debate is most complicated with a great deal of speculative writing on the subject.

who steered into the wind, challenged it, and rode through it coming out the other side. As he did with other storms in the Gospels, he also calmed it". Here is yet another mini-Biblical theme no one has apparently equated between the life events of Jesus and his Passion. What is a windjammer? Windjammers were the large sailing ships of the 19th and early 20th centuries which hauled much cargo a long distance. They were merchant ships of four to five masts with square sails. The term, "windjammer" comes from the German word meaning "to wail". It is the typical sound that strong winds bring as they blow through the rigging. In England, the term referred to sails so large that they seemed to "jam the wind." Jesus, in the upper room, at Gethsemane, during his six interviews and trials, and on the cross was certainly not a kite caught helplessly in a gale. Jesus defied the elements and rode them out to complete victory. He was, as he commented to Pilate, always in charge and always in control of the things that happened to him. In my opinion, everything was scripted. He followed the script to the end of his self-sacrifice. He chose the moment of his earthly, physical, human death. In reality, no one killed Jesus. His death, and his moment of dying, were always in his power to control. To continue onward with this imagery, by the end of his self-sacrifice, Jesus, one might say, was wind-tossed, battered, and bruised. After harboring for re-fitting for several hours in Sheol, however, he put out to sea again no worse for wear and mightier than before!

As a reader of the commentary of the late John Marsh on the Gospel of John, I observed how superb he was in detecting Biblical symbolism and possible multiple meanings in the text. John, he advanced, was written with such a high degree of intelligence behind it that much of its verbiage has two or three meanings. Marsh writes about the phrase, "and it was night" (John 13:30), referring to both the time on the clock with daylight having waned, and a reference to the dark night of Judas' soul as he is cut off from the light of the world, going from the presence of Christ into complete darkness.[117] I do not remember Marsh writing

---

117   John Marsh, *Saint John*, ed. D. E. Nineham, *The Pelican New Testament Commentaries* (Harmondsworth, Middlesex, England: Penguin Books., Inc., 1968), 493-495.

about a third possibility or meaning here, though if he had I most certainly would have jotted it down in my Bible. What is a possible triple meaning here to add to the previously two noted? What if, "and it was night", is also a reference to the beginning of Jesus' time of darkness and distress? What if this is the beginning note of Jesus' night-time experience culminating in both the wrenching of the Trinity and his physical death? What if this is also to denote that with Judas' departure and movement to "turn him in", that darkness has now come to Jesus? Is this statement the proverbial "and so it begins!"? To quote the title of an old book on the Korean War, "Hold Back the Night",[118] Jesus, thus far, had done just that during his wilderness temptation, the counter-productive statements by Peter, the escape through the crowd on the cliff edge of Nazareth, and all the possible and notable schemes of men to "do him in." Jesus had held back the night to the moment the night, as planned, was to envelop him! And so, with Judas' departure, the "night of his soul's anguish, passion, and resolution began!"

What did the dark night of his soul include? It included the horrors and terrors of Gethsemane. The Garden of Gethsemane was an intensified repeat of his wilderness temptation experience. In this olive grove Jesus wrestled with dark inclinations and the fiercest spiritual warfare ever known to man. It included his arrest. It included the brutality and injustice of six trials and vicious interviews (Annas, Caiaphas, the minimalist Sanhedrin, Pilate, Herod, and Pilate again). It included all the physical beatings and tearing of his body to sink his person and soul, yet Jesus jammed through it not giving into an SOS. It included the via Dolorosa, the agony of being placed on the cross, and the ghastly horrors of the crucifixion itself. It included the "Great Darkness". It included the fractured Godhead becoming totally sin and taking on all evil in the human past, present, and future. It included the aftershocks of the great earthquake, the opening of the tombs, and the rising of the blood moon as his physical countenance is placed in a "stone cold tomb". "And it was night" signals that the time of the dousing of the light of the world is now upon Jesus and all humanity. Of course, John

---

118   Pat Frank, *Hold Back the Night* (Philadelphia: Lippincott, 1952).

19:41-42,[119] is not the end of the story as Andrew Lloyd Webber and Tim Rice's "Jesus Christ Superstar", would have you believe.[120] Jesus is no frail kite in hurricane-force winds. He is that windjammer who took on the storm challenging the chaos. Just when we think he is sunk in a deep trough going down and underneath the waves; just when we think that it is over and that he is finished; we find to our surprise and amazement that, although he is initially hidden by a tumultuous wave, he rises up on its crest, calming the seas on the other side.

I like looking for themes of Jesus in culture as we were instructed to discover at Pittsburgh Theological Seminary. The American Western and Anti-Western genre provides much in terms of the classic engagement between good and evil. One of my favorite all-time movies is the 1952 film "High Noon" from a story entitled, "The Tin Star", by John W. Cunningham (screen play by Carl Foreman), starring Gary Cooper as Will Kane and Grace Kelly as Amy Kane. Will Kane is a long-time sheriff who is retiring from his office and seeking to relocate. On his final day on the job, he marries a young woman who wants him to put aside his guns forever. The villainous Frank Miller has just been released from the territorial penitentiary, and, with his gang, is coming to gun down the sheriff who put him behind bars. Will and Amy Kane begin their flight out of town, charging away on a buckboard wagon when the former sheriff suddenly stops, thinks for a moment, and, much to the dismay of his new bride, turns around to pick up his star again, don his 6-shooters, and face his adversaries. He knows he cannot run away. He knows he must face evil up close and personal. He knows he must gun it down. And, he discovers that he must do it alone.

The portrayal of the sheriff in "High Noon" reminds me much of Jesus, who probably would have liked to have run away. He would have liked to have dismissed the whole thing (Gethsemane tells us that much). He knew, however, that he could not run away. He knew that

---

119   John 19:41-42 (NIV), "At the place where Jesus was crucified, there was a garden, and in the garden a new tomb, in which no one had ever been laid. Because it was the Jewish Day of Preparation and since the tomb was nearby, they laid Jesus there."

120   Andrew Lloyd Webber and Tim Rice, *Jesus Christ Superstar* (London, England: Leeds Music Ltd., 1970), 26.

the evil, for the sake of those whom he loved in this world (particularly personified in the women at Golgotha and at the tomb) and for all of humanity beginning with Eve, had to be forever decapitated, defeated, and destroyed. The question many have entertained is, "What if Jesus had not gone to the cross? What then?" Paul understood that we would be left in our sins and be a people without hope.[121] To me, such a question is implausible and impossible. Jesus is God in human flesh. God is always true to God's Word. God never loses. In the cross, both love and eternity intersected!

I also find it interesting in the movie "High Noon" that the character Grace Kelly plays, though dismayed as the events play out, never runs away or hides like all the others. She stays. She does not leave. She is present. She is there to provide assistance and help. She triumphs first hand in the victory. Her reward is bountiful! She reminds me of a woman who becomes a stalwart in Jesus' life, and one whom he must save.

Jesus emerges from his "night", as Gustaf Aulen so proudly declares, as "Christus Victor".[122] We too need to proclaim Jesus as such, triumphantly and boldly, as we face the continued maelstrom that storms about us. Jesus journeyed through the deepest and darkest night so that we might embrace him as Savior and Lord, expelling all darkness and gracing us with his light and love and presence for all of eternity!

---

121   1 Corinthians 15:12-20. Note: If there is no crucifixion there is no resurrection. Without the cross there is no empty tomb. Without the empty tomb there is no eternality.

122   Gustaf Aulen, *Christus Victor: An Historical Study of the Three Main Types of the Idea of the Atonement*, trans. A. G. Hebert (New York, NY: Macmillan Publishing Co., Inc., 1977), 4, 158-159.

8

Crossing That Deadly Forbidden Zone

"When the woes of life o'ertake me, hopes deceive, and fears annoy, never shall the cross forsake me: Lo! It glows with peace and joy. Bane and blessing, pain and pleasure, by the cross are sanctified; Peace is there that knows no measure, joys that thro'all time abide."

(John Bowring)

It happened 106 years ago. The line stretched for 700 kilometers (435 miles) across northeastern France and northwestern Belgium separating the armies of France, Britain, Belgium, Portugal, Germany, and a token Austro-Hungarian contingent, among others.[123] The space between them was a deadly killing zone known in infamy as "No Man's Land." This desolate expanse represented the ultimate in godless chaos

---

123   This line of battle in World War I is known as "the Western Front". The "Eastern Front", in the same war, pitted Russia and Romania on one side and the Austro-Hungarian Empire, Bulgaria, the Ottoman Empire and Germany on the other.

and vacancy. It was a void where millions died not only of bullets, artillery bursts and mustard gas, but also of illness, plague, vermin, and exposure. It stands as one of the most significant symbols in human history of the totality of evil, the baseness of humanity, and the human need for the deadly forbidden zone to be eradicated.

Into that void in 1914, the thought of one person shrunk the abyss into nothingness and brought those at enmity with each other together in mirth, joy, and brotherhood. The spontaneous cease-fire and celebration of December 25th in 1914 came about as it could only be brought about, with the memory of, and in honor of the Prince of Peace who could transcend the evils of this world and eradicate that which ails us. It lasted not more than a day, but just the thought of Jesus caused a revolutionary action in the hearts of many Christian based men of several tongues.

The deadly forbidden zone, and the crossing of such, is another one of those themes interwoven through the Bible that I would like to suggest to you is evident in this divinely inspired book. This deadly forsaken space begins with the expulsion of Adam and Eve from Eden guarded by the presence of a fierce angelic warrior.[124] The relational void between God and humanity, filled with demonic influence and evil machinations of all kinds, is what the incarnate God came to bridge, eradicating all of that which keeps us a part. Over and over we see in the Old Testament how this expanse is bridged by God. It occurred in two ways at the Reed Sea. It occurred at the Jordan River and at Jericho. It was part of the story of Samson, David, Ruth, Esther, Jehoshaphat, Daniel, and many others in the Bible. All these stories and circumstances are predictive of God's great power to be our "bridge over troubled waters"[125] and to accomplish that which eliminates the deadly forbidden zone forever.

With Jesus it all comes down to the feet. Let us consider the feet. During the time of Christ in Palestine, human waste of all kinds was

---

124   Genesis 3:24.
125   Paul Simon, *Bridge over Troubled Waters*, performed by Paul Simon and Arthur Garfunkel, Columbia Hall of Fame recording, 1970.

often dumped into the streets. Animal waste and other debris was also frequently trampled underfoot. The towel and the bowl became a significant part of Hebrew custom. Upon entering a building, these implements were often provided to clean the feet. This was often accomplished by the person who was invited to enter the dwelling, by a servant of the host, or by the host himself. It is no accident that in the stories of the Gospel we have people falling and prostrating themselves at the feet of Jesus. It is no accident that in the stories of the Gospel, as we shall see, we have people washing and anointing Jesus' feet. It is no accident that in the Gospel accounts we have Jesus himself, the great host of us all, washing disciples' feet at the beginning of the inauguration of his death remembrance ritualistic event.

In a sense, salvation is gained by the action of the feet. Someone needs to walk into the deadly forbidden zone and do the work needed to reclaim "no man's land", transform it, and eliminate its deadliness forever. Jesus did just that! He walked the walk we could not walk. His whole incarnation was designed to walk in our shoes. Jesus came to walk as we walk. Being God, he came to walk into the place we could not walk. He went to the place deadly for us. He went to a place we could not go or hope to redeem. He walked the Via Dolorosa[126] and was lifted up on a tree[127] in the middle of that deadly forbidden zone. On the one side were perpetrators of great evil. On the other side were those sinful and evil but sympathetic to the man. John and many women were present at the edge of the deadly forbidden zone, where one was always close but held at a distance. Jesus' mother, Mary, was there. So was Mary Magdalene; John's mother, Salome; the Mary of James and Joses; Mary, the wife of Cleopas; Mary's sister; and others whose identity we do not currently know.[128] All of them, with tear-soaked eyes and bowed countenance, were staring at the feet of Jesus dripping streams of blood. While it is believed that those crucified were not lifted way above the

---

126   The "Via Dolorosa" is Latin for "way of grief (or sorrow, suffering, pain)". It is approximately a 2000-foot (600 meter) pathway believed to be the route the Romans employed taking Jesus to the execution site.

127   Deuteronomy 21:22-23; Acts 5:30; Galatians 3:13; 1 Peter 2:24.

128   Matthew 27:55-5; Mark 14:40; Luke 23:49; John 19:25.

viewers,[129] Jesus' feet were right there in front of them. The whole thing was a bloody mess, but one which beckons a strange call to come. In Jesus' crucifixion there is a beckoning call to come to the foot of the tree. At his feet a cleansing was occurring. It was a reminder of what Jesus stated concerning the feet: that if the feet are clean the whole body is clean.[130]

Perhaps the women at the cross would have desired to cross that deadly forbidden zone and clasp the soiled feet of Jesus in their hands, bowing cheek pressed against his precious feet.[131] The execution space, however, was forbidden to all but the victims (including, in this case, "the sacrifice"), and those discharging the gruesome task. The deadly forbidden zone was a place unchallenged which no one could alter. Jesus came to challenge the place and eradicate it forever. With his death, the deadly forbidden zone ceases to exist. Nicodemus and Joseph of Arimathea physically remove his body from the cross and take possession of his corpse.[132] We know that many of the women were present when they took charge of the lifeless Jesus.[133] The garden tomb of Joseph of Arimathea is very close to the execution site.[134] Mary Magdalene walks the short distance and observes the attempt to initiate the embalming requirements and the entombment.[135] She lingers until the Sabbath is inaugurated by the setting sun. Little does she know that she will soon become the one, symbolically, which will forever testify to humankind the eternal termination of that deadly forbidden zone. In just a few hours, with her own feet, she will walk across ground no longer forbidden into the intimate presence of the twin tasked (securing the work of perfection the first Adam was charged to perform and satisfying the death sentence upon our sin) victorious second Adam. At that moment comes the realization that everything has changed,

---

129   Bart D. Ehrman, *How Jesus Became God: The Exaltation of a Jewish Preacher from Galilee* (New York, NY: Harper Collins, 2014), 135-165.
130   John 13:10
131   Matthew 27:55; Mark 15:40; Luke 23:49; John 19:25-26.
132   Matthew 27:57-60; Mark 15:42-46; Luke 23:50-54; John 19:38-39.
133   Matthew 27:61; Mark 15:47; Luke 23:55.
134   John 19:41.
135   Matthew 27:61; Mark 15:47; Luke 23:55.

and that everything is new. She walks across space that is no longer deadly. Once across, she discovers both love and eternity. After some very significant moments, her feet become employed in a new task. As with Mary Magdalene, so it is with us. We can follow in her footsteps!

9

"Romancing the Stone"

"All I need is a miracle, all I need is you!"

(Mike Rutherford and Christopher Neil/Mike + The Mechanics)

"Romancing the Stone" is a title I borrowed from a 1984 Michael Douglas movie of the same name. This book is much about the Resurrection of Jesus Christ, and, in particular, one of the 13 to 15 (depending on how you reference them) Resurrection appearance stories in the Bible. To accomplish the purpose of this writer, we must examine the circumstances and literary evidence available to us in order to detail the story and the chronology of events. Many scholars and authors have attempted to fit all the Resurrection narratives into a seamless flow of events.[136] They have done a commendable job. The chronological appearance theories I am employing in this chapter comes from the work

---

136   Johnston M. Cheney, *The Life of Christ in Stereo: The Four Gospels Combined as One* (Portland, Oregon: Western Baptist Seminary Press, 1969), 204-214.

of a number of people who have shared their thoughts in writing about Resurrection Day and beyond over many decades.

The work of the Second Adam has culminated on the cross. Jesus, as the second and last Adam, has accomplished the work of obedience that Adam failed to perform. As the perfect sacrifice to take away the sins of the world, Jesus' death on the cross fulfills what was necessary to liberate sinful humanity in terms of all the legitimate Atonement theories advanced by scholars.[137] The work intended by the incarnation/virgin birth has now been accomplished. The work of saving Eve, and all of humanity chosen by God, is complete. What has not been finished is the drama of the Resurrection itself, and the declaration of its multi-faceted meaning for humankind, including the ultimate intersection of love and eternity!

To help digest the circumstances and events of the Resurrection, I will turn to a critique of the movie "Risen." Please note that my knowledge of the resurrection has been shaped by many authors including, but not exhaustive of, Hank Hanegraaff, C. S. Lewis, Walter Martin, Paul E. Little, Dr. D. James Kennedy, Paul L. Maier, Gary Habermas, John

---

137   It has been suggested that "atonement" mean "at-one-ment". The idea advanced here is the bringing together of those who are alienated, separated and estranged. The word actually means "to cover." In the Old Testament the animal sacrificial system foreshadowed a covering for sin that Christ's death on the cross secured. Of the eleven theories of atonement known to this author there are several which it is believed here have significant or at least some validity: a Covering (the viewpoint that our sin is covered over and taken out of the view of God by Christ); Reconciliation (the viewpoint that the opposition between contending parties is over with the alienation of sinners removed and the former opponents of God newly embraces); Propitiation (the viewpoint that advocates that God's wrath and anger concerning our sin has been removed by the offering of the gift of the sacrifice of the Christ on the cross); Ransom (this theory advances the idea that Christ paid the price to meet the holy requirement of God's law and redeem us from its curse. There has been debate over whether this price was paid to God or to Satan as some advocate); Substitution (the concept that Christ suffered and died in our place); Recapitulation (the idea that Christ repeats all stages of human life in his incarnation and work. This theory is not totally accurate as only Christ's death is vicarious [to act or to do for another] and not his life as some might advance); Satisfaction (this theory has been known in the past as the "Commercial Theory." This viewpoint advances the idea that God's righteousness is appeased and the Father is honored by the punishment of Jesus whose work on the cross satisfied God's justice. This theory has some merit but fails to include the idea that Christ died in penalty for our sins). The theories rejected here are the "Moral Influence" theory, the "Example" theory, the "Accidental" theory, and the "Martyrdom" theory.

Ankerberg, R. C. Sproul, John Warwick Montgomery, Josh McDowell, and Sean McDowell.

Directed by Kevin Reynolds and written by Reynolds and Paul Aiello, the 2016 movie stars Joseph Fiennes, Tom Felton, Peter Firth, Cliff Curtis, and Maria Botto, and is a hypothetical depiction of the Resurrection by the Roman military Tribune, Clavius, and his subordinate, Lucius. The movie attempts to look at certain aspects of Jesus' resurrection from the perspective of this fictitious Roman officer. Upon its release, the drama sparked conversation concerning the Biblical accuracy of the presentation. While this author found the movie to possess a quality worth viewing and examining, as certain scenes were depicted accurately Biblically, historically, and culturally, several scenes were poorly rendered and downright inaccurate. Much of the attention of this writer centered around the tomb of Jesus and the large stone rolled into place blocking the entrance.

When it comes to the portrayal of the tomb of Jesus Christ, the writers of the film borrow some information from the pseudepigraphical work known as the Gospel of Peter. Pseudepigraphical is a designation by scholars for a work that bears the name of an historical figure, in this case the Peter of New Testament fame, but was not written by the person to whom it is attributed. In fact, the book dates from 150 to 200 AD. It was first mentioned by other historical documents and circulated between 190 and 203 AD. The earliest surviving manuscripts we have of this book are from the 8th and 9th centuries. The book is considered by critics to have Gnostic leanings and sympathies.[138] Gnosticism was, and still is in its continuing influence, a rival religion to Christianity. When comparing Gnosticism to Christianity, one must understand two things as it pertains to our current discussion. Christianity is, in the first place, a faith-based religion indicating that salvation is by grace alone. Gnosticism advocates salvation through the attainment of special knowledge and rejects both sola fide and sola gratia. Secondly, and this is of major importance, all the books of the

---

138   Ryan Turner, "Does the Gospel of Peter Belong in the New Testament?" *Christian Apologetics Research Ministry.* https://www.carm.org. (accessed April 4, 2019).

New Testament were written in the 33 to 37 years after the death of Jesus, including, in my estimation, Revelation! This is my educated opinion of which I am absolutely convinced! The latest evidence points to a crucifixion date for Jesus of April 3rd, 33 AD. Jesus would be just a little more than two months shy of 35 years old (if a June 17, 2 BC birthdate is accurate). Of course, this date places the Resurrection of Jesus on April 5th, 33 AD. In Matthew, Mark, and Luke (Matthew 24, Mark 13:1-37, and Luke 21:5-36) Jesus makes a significant prediction (prophecy) which gets much ink. Sadly, most Christians mistake the time frame reference for this prophecy and believe that Jesus is talking about his second physical coming to planet earth and what most people mistakenly reference as "the end of the world." R. C. Sproul, who is a leading proponent of what I am referencing here, indicates that this prophecy, known as the "Olivet Discourse", is not about the "end of the world" but the end of the "Jewish age", wherein God comes in judgment of the Jewish religious elite.[139] Known as the "First Jewish War" (there were three Jewish Wars, as known from the Roman perspective, the other two being The Kitos War of 115-117 AD, and the Bar Kokhba's Revolt of 132-136 AD)[140], according to Josephus who chronicles the events,[141] the rebellious Jews who attempt to cast off Roman Imperial rule are finally beaten back, after some stunning early success. After a lengthy siege of Jerusalem, the Romans finally breech the walls, take the city, destroy the Temple, and kill, according to some estimates, up to 1.2 million people in the process.[142] The results of the Jewish defeat are among some of the most savage circumstances ever faced by a people in history. This war occurred, roughly, between 66 and 70 AD (with final "clean-up" operations lasting into 73 and 74 AD, including the fall

---

139   R. C. Sproul, *The Last Days According to Jesus: When Did Jesus Say He Would Return?* (Grand Rapids, Michigan: Baker Books, 1998), 14-48.
140   "Jewish-Roman Wars," *Wikipedia*, https: //en.wikipedia.org/wiki/jewish-roman wars. (accessed April 4, 2019).
141   See Flavius Josephus, *The Works of Flavius Josephus: A History of the Jewish Wars,* trans. William Whiston (Philadelphia, David McKay, Publisher, 1910) for a complete recording of the events.
142   "First Jewish-Roman War," *Wikipedia*, military.wikia.com/wiki/First Jewish-Roman War (accessed April 4, 2019).

of Masada on April 16, 73 AD). The interesting fact about the Olivet Discourse is that Jesus predicts everything down to the smallest detail.[143] Jesus told his followers, when the end of the current age or era is upon them, to flee the city for the mountains and the wilderness. For the most part, Christ's followers at that time, did just that. Most of the remainder of the Jewish people flooded into the city, which was then besieged by the Romans. This is an absolutely shattering occurrence and yet not one word of it taking place, and the prophecy being fulfilled, is described in the New Testament. Certainly, had any of the books of the New Testament been written after the event, there is no way one would not include this holocaust and fulfillment of Jesus' prediction verifying him as a true prophet! It is the conclusion of this writer, as it is of others beforehand, that all the books in the New Testament had to be early writings. All of the 27 books had to have been written in about 33 years after Jesus' death, and in the lifetimes of those who witnessed the words and events of Jesus' life.[144] This is huge! It means, as many others have labored to point out, that if there were inaccuracies in the New Testament, especially the four Gospels,[145] many people who witnessed Jesus would still be alive acting as a corrective![146] All of this becomes important because many of the circumstances surrounding the tomb are only reported by Matthew, and many are the scholars of the 19th century who speculated that Matthew invented parts of the story.

Another critique of the Resurrection stories in the four Gospels were made, particularly during the 19th century, surrounding what appears to many readers to be the absolute confusion of the four Gospel writers as to what actually happened at the tomb when Jesus arose. Yes, confusion seems apparent, but many apologists have written that this actually strengthens the case for the historicity of the Resurrection.[147] It

---

143   Mathew 24:1-44; Mark 13:1-37; Luke 21:5-36.

144   John A. T. Robinson, "The New Testament Dating Game," *Time*, Vol. 109, March 21, 1977, 95.

145   Josh McDowell, *The Resurrection Factor*, (San Bernardino, CA: Here's Life Publishers, Inc., 1981), 26-35.

146   Josh McDowell, "The Case of the Empty Tomb," *Campus Crusade for Christ International*, 1973, 13.

147   *Compelling Truth*. "Do the Gospel Resurrection Accounts Contradict Each Other?" God

is worth, for the serious reader, the time to examine the arguments others have made about these apparent inconsistencies in the texts. It is the opinion of this writer that the work of others, over time to sort out the difficulties in the stories and suggest a chronological narrative moving forward, is quite helpful to potentially overcome these inconsistencies and give us a clear picture of a momentous day in Jesus' resurrected life and in the new life he came to gift humanity.[148]

We all need to read the Gospel resurrection accounts very carefully, particularly of the first day, and do diligent study. I am suggesting below one way to understand the flow of events. This is not my own formulation, but what I have understood from the suggested order of events others have proposed. The order of events is critical, especially at the outset of the day, to my main premise in this book, and so, in the opinion of this author, we should pay some attention to the proposed chronology others have suggested. The following is a suggested account of the flow of events on the day of Jesus' resurrection.

According to the Jewish way of counting days, the Resurrection had to occur at least by the crack of dawn, with the sighting of the top of the sun appearing on Sunday, April 5, AD 33, in order for Jesus to be, by the Jewish count, in the tomb for three days. (Any part of one day was counted as a full day, including his entombing just prior to the vanishing of the setting sun on Friday, and his rising just after the sun top makes its appearance over the Jerusalem horizon. Please remember also that one day in this culture was considered from sundown to sunup). Prior to dawn on this day, there are two things we need to note. First, there is a Roman military guard detachment at the tomb site.[149] Secondly, now that the Sabbath (Saturday) is waning a number of women are preparing and traveling to the tomb site to complete what they had perceived as an incomplete burial (external embalming) on Friday before dusk by

Questions Ministries (2011-2019), https://www.compellingtruth.org/resurrection-account.html (accessed May 3, 2019).

148   Tim Chaffey, "Christ's Resurrection – Four Accounts, One Reality: Biblical Authority," *Answers Magazine*, (April 5, 2015), https://answersingenesis.org/jesus-christ/resurrection/christs... (accessed April 5, 2019).

149   Matthew 27:62 – 28:4,11-15.

Joseph of Arimathea and Nicodemus; or to perform what they could do in their cultural tradition to further honor his body by the placement of additional spices and ointments.[150]

As the sun cracks the horizon, some sort of display of energy, light, might, and power takes place in and around the sepulcher. The visualization of what we would call angelic entities appears to have also played a role. As recorded in John, the round and large 1 ½ - ton to 2-½ ton stone that blocks the entrance is blown off and at some distance away from the rock encasement. Josh McDowell, in particular, has provided much in his writings about the removal of the large stone which was a barrier to the entrance. All four Gospels mention the stone. The key root word in Koine Greek for the action concerning the stone is the word "kulio", which means "to roll something". As McDowell points out, Matthew 27:60 and 28:2 employs this root word. A large stone, on a slight tracked incline, was released from the position that held it in place, to travel down the slope and block the entrance of the tomb. The key in all four Gospels is the use of a preposition explaining the position of the stone. Mark adds the preposition "ana" meaning "up" or "upward" (Mark 16:4). "Anakulio" refers to rolling the stone back up the slope or track. Luke employs the preposition "apo" (Luke 24:2) which refers to the stone being rolled so far away from the entrance that there is separation of the stone from the sepulcher. In other words, the stone was removed at "a distance from" the tomb. It is John's account which employs the preposition "airo" (John 20:1), meaning "lift up, take up, pick up". This not only confirms what Luke has written, it also informs us that the stone was a great distance from the entrance as if someone picked up the stone and physically carried it across the garden. Of course, why would someone, or a group of people, do that if they only sought entrance to the cave to quietly evacuate the body? How could the Roman guard, as well, permit such a removal? Even if one might presume they all fell asleep, as McDowell points out, "they are not deaf."[151] The combination of the visual display and the action at

---

150   Mark 16:1; Luke 24:1.
151   McDowell, *The Resurrection Factor*, 53-54, 66-68.

the entrance terrifies the Roman military detachment, freezing them in fear, and then causing them to flee this otherworldly happening.[152] The situation, for them, becomes chaotic, but whatever they saw, heard, and felt, I am convinced that the resurrected Jesus, in the way he appeared to his followers, was not seen by them. I am convinced that they did not encounter the resurrected human Jesus.[153] His initial sighting, following his Resurrection, is uniquely scripted and reserved for another. The Roman legionnaires, in some way at least, are the first ones to learn about, or assume, an empty tomb. Next, those faithful female followers of Jesus, some of whom had watched Joseph of Arimathea and Nicodemus place his body in Joseph's new and never-before-used garden tomb, are truly the first to learn that the tomb was empty. The women, and there were several of them, perhaps as many as eight to just beyond a dozen, do not represent some tiny little group. They knew nothing of the Roman guard and pondered, prior to and on their dawn journey, just how they would roll back the stone up the small incline into the open position.[154] Something that is rarely noted by those who have researched the Resurrection is the fact that since this was the Passover pilgrimage season,[155] tens of thousands (or more) of people would be camping out on the hillsides all around Jerusalem. It would be a tent city of enormous proportions.[156] The sheer numbers of people in the area might have influenced the authorities to post a rather generous Roman guard. Perhaps, the woman believed that it would not be too hard to find help and strength to perform the opening of Joseph's tomb in their time of need. Many of the women, finding the stone at some distance from the sepulcher and the tomb completely open, venture into the tomb and find no corpse. Mary may not have entered the tomb. Seeing the tomb open and the stone resting at some puzzling distance away from the entrance, she assumes that either foul play or the remov-

---

152 Matthew 27:4, 11.
153 Matthew 27:2-4.
154 Mark 16:3
155 John 11:55.
156 *Scripture Backdrops: Relevant Historical Insights into Scripture.* "Jerusalem at Passover" Bible History On-Line, http://www/bible-history.com (accessed April 5, 2019).

al of Jesus' body by his enemies had occurred. She might have reasoned that, perhaps, his opponents in the Jewish religious elite thought it was unfitting for Jesus to be buried in a garden tomb recently hewn and prepared by a member of their own ruling council, the Sanhedrin. Perhaps she might have reasoned that Jesus' opponents did not want his grave site to become some sort of memorial to the man and a rallying point for any possible evolution of his movement. Mary runs back to inform Peter and John, who were apparently at John's lodging (perhaps this was John's Jerusalem home).[157] This would probably be the location John has taken Jesus' mother, Mary, to give her care, comfort, and security in the light of the events of the crucifixion two days earlier. Meanwhile, the women who enter the tomb to inspect it find the body of Jesus missing, encounter two personages (angels who had assumed some sort of human form, we presume) who tell them the marvelous, absolutely incredible news, that Jesus has risen from the dead as he stated previously that he would![158] Mary Magdalene is not present at this time to hear this announcement and declaration for she has already rushed back to inform John and Peter that someone, or some persons, have taken the body out of the tomb. She probably says this with the hope that they can go and discover the what, who, and why of it all and retrieve Jesus' physical remains. The other women, by the time John and Peter end their foot race to the tomb, had already left the site. These other women are going to inform the disciples of the news of the Resurrection as the angels had informed them.[159] Apparently, it takes the women longer to reach the disciples than it took Mary Magdalene to find John and Peter and get back to the tomb.[160] The run is much of a sprint with John arriving first, looking in, and Peter arriving and bypassing the stationary John going into the tomb.[161] Mary Magdalene also runs and hurries, following them, as she can. John and Peter inspect the con-

---

157   Mark 16:5; John 20:1-2, 10.
158   Mark 16:5.
159   This author understands the Lukan account (Luke 24:1-2) to be a generalized report or summary of which the other Gospels provide more specific information.
160   Chaffey, *Christ's Resurrection: Four Accounts and One Reality.*
161   John 20:3-9.

tents of the tomb. The body is missing, which is quite obvious. What is mysterious is the grave clothes. How spice and ointment laden they might, or might not have been, is unknown. They are, however, lying there in exactly the position where Jesus' body had been, but the body was not in them. The head cloth which had been wound around his head was collapsed inward in proper position as well. It was clear to Peter and John that someone had not simply come and removed the wrappings from the body and taken the body away. The appearance of the grave clothes seemed to testify to John that, in some miraculous unexplained way, the body had simply passed through the wrappings, leaving them there in place and collapsed inwardly as if undisturbed. Peter, at first, fails to understand the significance of the grave clothes. John, at this point, testifies that he came to realize more than just what Mary Magdalene had told him about the disturbed tomb: that Jesus, in all probability was alive again, his resurrection body having passed through the linen wrappings. When the women first saw this sight, the positioning of the grave clothes confused them as to the circumstances that had transpired.[162]

Mary Magdalene cannot run nearly as fast as the youthful and athletic cousins. She arrives back at Joseph's garden just after Peter and John had departed the scene. Perhaps she followed them, arrived before they departed, and stays behind lingering outside the tomb.[163] It appears they did not pass each other on the way, as one party or the other had taken a different route. It is here, at this moment, weeping deeply, that Mary enters over the threshold and under the head of the tomb entrance and, inside the opening of the sepulcher, looks in.[164] Two angels, who were not present moments before when John and Peter were there, are spied sitting at the head and feet of where the corpse would have laid. Their appearance, to this writer, is symbolically important, as we shall see! They address the grieving Mary as to her tearful countenance. Whether Mary is surprised or fearful of their presence is unrecorded.

---

162   John 20:5-9.
163   Chaffey, *Christ's Resurrection: Four Accounts and One Reality.*
164   John 20:11.

Mary proceeds to explain her weeping which is caused by her anxiety over the missing body.[165] At this, Mary hears a disturbance behind her and turns to see a clothed figure at a speaking distance from the tomb. The figure speaks to her, inquiring as to her crying. Mary now thinks that she might be in the presence of a gardener of this private tomb area, and as such, he might know the circumstances surrounding the removal of the body and its present location. Her motivation is to retrieve the body and give Jesus a decent burial.[166] It only takes Jesus one word to grant her the true identification of the man. Christ speaks her name, "Mary"![167] Remember, Jesus taught that the sheep know the voice of the shepherd and respond. This is a significant teaching in the Gospel of John (John 10:27). This writer presumes that something in the way Jesus states her name causes Mary to note the familiar. Her response is an immediate identification of the person of Jesus. She proclaims, "Rabboni", highly significant for a number of reasons, "Rabboni" is defined in the text as "teacher", but it means more than "rabbi".[168] It is frequently a term that is reserved only for God.[169] This statement by Mary is a one-word confession of the nature of Jesus.[170] It is one of the three great professions of faith (John 11:27 and John 20:28) recorded in the Gospel of John and ranks right up there with Peter's great confession found in the Synoptics. The word carries great significance in terms of our story here.[171] Instantly, Mary Magdalene exits the open inside en-

---

165   John 20:12-13.

166   John 20:14-15.

167   John 20:16.

168   Rabboni is a Jewish title of respect and honor for their teachers. While the word "rabbi" (meaning "master" or "teacher") is employed on 15 occasions in the New Testament, "Rabboni" (rhabboni, rhabbouni, rhabbounei) is used just twice: here in John 20:16 and in Mark 10:51. The word can be translated "great master" or "my great master". It appears to represent a deeper or higher respect from a student toward a master or teacher. Commentator, Leon Morris understands it to be a "mode of address...confined to addressing God in prayer."

169   Leon Morris, *The Gospel According to John*. The New International Commentary on the New Testament (Grand Rapids, Michigan: Wm. B. Eerdmans Publishing Co., 1971) 839-840.

170   John Marsh, *Saint John*. The Pelican New Testament Commentaries (Hammondsworth, Middlesex, England: Penguin Books Inc.), 633.

171   This term is interpreted by John to mean "Teacher". Leon Morris says, "This last point is probably decisive. We should hold that Mary's understanding of Jesus' person is not complete" (see footnote #34). However, Mary's surprised reaction to Jesus' presence seems to indicate an elevated awareness of Jesus' person which will be refined shortly in Christ's days of resurrection.

trance covering of the tomb and rushes forward.[172] She fully and firmly embraces Jesus.[173] Jesus reciprocates.[174] After a time of this clenching reunion, Jesus instructs her to go and share the encounter with his followers, giving the first indication that much of his weeks of resurrection will be spent in his home territory of Galilee.[175] This meeting, which is the purpose of this book, is actually the most extraordinary encounter in the entire Bible according to this author. Far more is happening and being communicated here than Dr. Leon Morris writes, "Her unique love had been rewarded with this very special privilege." We will pick up the precise details and explanation of this in upcoming chapters.

Immediately after his appearance to Mary Magdalene, he appears to the throng of women just before they reach the remainder of the eleven,[176] which would have been, we presume, eight of them together. The eight react with skepticism, culturally colored, in all reality, not to receive the testimony of the excited women.[177] The women, however, tell them that the tomb is empty. They report on the angelic message.[178] And they share Jesus' appearance to them, and that he spoke to them on their return trip. At this point in the story, Paul records that Jesus appeared one on one with Peter, but we have no content.[179] Jesus spends most of the rest of the day walking with two of his followers, including Cleopas (who might have been his uncle), cloaking his presence, but sharing in apologetics from the Old Testament (explaining the prophecies concerning the Christ). He reveals himself at mealtime to the two on the road to Emmaus. They then "high tail" it, even at that late hour, back the miles to Jerusalem. Locating and meeting with the disciples and assembled followers of Jesus, they make their report. While they

---

172   Marsh, 637.

173   Morris, 841.

174   It is the opinion of this writer, based on the language and words employed describing the action presented here, that this is not a similar action as described in Matthew 28:9. The precise action of Mary, whether bowed and grasping his feet or clinging to a full body-hugging action is the subject of debate.

175   John 20:17.

176   Matthew 28:8-9.

177   Luke 24:9-11.

178   Luke 24:22-24.

179   1 Corinthians 15:5.

are confirming the news of the Resurrection, Jesus suddenly material-
izes and appears in their midst. He demonstrates the truth of his personhood and physicality. And then he does something almost everyone
misses. He takes the Old Testament and proves through it his person,
nature, and historicity. Do you understand what Jesus was doing here?
He proves the whole Christ event through an exposition of the Word![180]
"And there was morning and evening of the first day" of the new creation, and God and God's people saw that is was "very good!"

Before we advance taking a microscopic look at the encounter of
Jesus with Mary Magdalene, let us make sure that we have examined
much of the background information concerning the tomb and the setting just prior to Mary Magdalene's revelatory moment, which is much
the purpose of this chapter.

Many of the events of salvation history occur either in a garden or
a house. That is the summation of this author concerning the setting
for much of the core essence of the Biblical drama. Concerning the garden imagery of the Bible, consider the following: Humanity is placed
in a garden paradise where relationship with God can be considered
quite intimate. It is also the setting where sin enters the picture, and the
garden paradise is forfeited and lost. The word in Greek for "garden"
is "kepos", which refers to any plot of land where trees, flowers, spices,
fruit, and vegetables are grown for consumption and/or beauty. The
word can also be understood and translated as orchard. The Garden
of Gethsemane, for example, was an olive tree orchard. John 19:41
indicates that the tomb of Jesus was near the place where Jesus was
crucified. John 19:41 also states that the crucifixion took place in or by a
garden. Most crucifixions were accomplished along well traveled roads,
highways, and byways for political shock value and a warning against
imperial transgressions.[181] Evidently, the crucifixion of Jesus occurred
in or by an area of private burial gardens of the more well-heeled of
Jerusalem society. It seems that the private garden tomb of Joseph of
Arimathea was right at hand or nearby. Of course, the Resurrection

---

180   Luke 24:13-46.
181   Crucifixion was always intended to be a gruesome public event.

takes place in a garden. The final disposition of humankind, the eschaton, is portrayed as a massive garden city.[182]

The tomb, according to Matthew, Mark, and Luke, belonged to Joseph of Arimathea. This tomb, which was for Joseph's burial, was "hewn out in the rock"[183] indicating the wealth of this man, only the wealthy could afford to have their tombs carved out of a stone formation.[184] The word, "hewn" means to both "cut" and "polish". The stone enclosure was, in other words, a very special and splendid tomb. In a rich man's tomb, according to Isaiah's prophecy, they placed (set or deposited) Jesus.[185] Carefully, the body of the deceased crucified one was laid in its place in the tomb. These types of tombs included a space or spaces for the deceased to be place down full extended, and then shelving or compartments for ossuaries (boxes)[186] wherein the bones of the deceased were eventually deposited.[187] The spices and ointments were to render a good odor, rather than that of the decaying body, if and when the tomb had to be accessed for the laying of additional deceased persons.

As Joseph and Nicodemus wrapped the body and presumably (depending on the time of day remaining for them) placed spices and ointments between the layers of this long winding strip of cloth, Mary Magdalene and Mary the mother of Joses "beheld where he was laid".[188] The imperfect tense in Mark's reporting of the event indicates that they took their time, being very observant of the action taking place. This would include, among other things, noting the location of the burial garden and the extent of the embalming that was (or was not) accomplished by Joseph and Nicodemus. They lingered around the tomb and

---

182   Revelation 21 & 22.
183   Luke 23:53; Mark 15:46; Matthew 27:60.
184   Josh McDowell and Sean McDowell, *Evidence for the Resurrection* (Ventura, California: Regal, 2009), 172.
185   Isaiah 53:9.
186   An ossuary was generally a stone rectangular box (also made of alabaster or ceramic) employed as a final depository for the skeletal remains of the deceased. It made the use of a solitary stone tomb for multiple burials possible.
187   Ralph F. Wilson, "Burial in Joseph's Tomb," *Jesus Walk Bible Study Series* 107 (2019), http://www.jesuswalk.com (accessed April 5, 2019).
188   Mark 15:47.

were very observant. The Greek word, *theaomai*, indicates that they "gazed upon" and "fully visualized" the identity of the body and the action occurring. Due to the fact that the burial site was near the execution site, that this was probably a significant garden tomb location, that this site had particularities relating to Joseph of Arimathea, and the significant time they spent there, no possible misidentification of the precise garden tomb would be possible in the upcoming days. It is apparent that the setting of the sun inaugurating the Sabbath, in which no one could work according to the law, put pressure on Nicodemus and Joseph to conclude or cut short their work. During that time, additional spices and ointments would be added to the embalming for one to be entombed who was held in very high esteem by others. For significant individuals, anything above 100 pounds would be likely.[189] It could be that the women were convinced that more was needed to honor Jesus but not in that twilight hour. As the sun fell below the horizon, Joseph of Arimathea released, or had others release, the stone secured on a small incline, and it rolled down and blocked the entrance to the tomb. While many Jewish tombs in those days had doors with hinges, a large stone rolled before the tomb was a rarity.[190] It made, however, the burial site more secure due to the difficulty of placing the stone back up the incline once again.[191]

The ruling elite, who had convicted Jesus of blasphemy and sought the death penalty, were not so sure that the site was secure. Knowing that Jesus had made statements about coming back from the dead in three days when he talked about the destruction and re-building of the Temple, members of the Sanhedrin feared that Jesus' followers would come and steal the body, claiming that he had been raised from the dead or had risen himself from the dead. So, the Jewish leadership that had led the opposition against Jesus went to the Roman procurator, Pilate, and asked him to command the sepulcher be made sure.[192] The

---

189   McDowell, *The Resurrection Factor*, 52.
190   Kenneth E. Bailey, "Burial Customs," *Oxford Biblical Studies Online*, www.oxfordbiblicalstudies.com (accessed April 5, 2019).
191   McDowell and McDowell, 176.
192   Matthew 27:62-66.

Greek word, *sphragidzo*, is found here. This word refers to a legal seal that was placed on government letters, documents, and other items to provide a warning if they are breeched. In this case, the item is a tomb. The purpose of "sealing the tomb" legally was to indicate that any violation of the site was unlawful and punishable by the full weight of the Roman Empire. Authentication of the sealed item was important. Prior to the seal being placed, the contents should have been inspected to determine that that which they were sealing was present and proper. The seal was a string that would have been stretched across the entrance of the tomb and stamped on both sides by the order and authority of the Roman Empire. While Matthew does not mention this, it is worthy to note that the authorities were first required to inspect the inside of the tomb to see that the body of Jesus was actually there. His body would have to be identified as that of the beaten and crucified Jesus. The authorities would have to guarantee that what they were sealing and guarding was actually present. Their lives depended on it! After a proper and thorough inspection, the stone was returned to its resting position covering the opening and the seal was attached. While this action is rarely explained by apologists of the Resurrection, it is the reason so many of them indicate in their writings that the last people to possess the body were the authorities, chief among them the Romans.[193] Once this action was completed, an imperial guard detachment that Pilate had authorized took up their position. What this all means is that the tomb, which was unguarded on Friday night, was undisturbed on Friday night. The body of Jesus spent Friday night in the tomb.

Concerning the guard stationed at the tomb, the movie "Risen" certainly took some liberties with the text. It is inaccurate according to Roman military manuals, as Josh McDowell and others have researched and point out, that only two soldiers were placed at the tomb, but also, according to Roman discipline, that they would have become inebriated.[194] Skeptics also charge, at this juncture, that since only Matthew records the placing and happenings of the guard, that the story has been

---

193   McDowell and McDowell, 184-185.
194   Ibid, 176-181.

fabricated. Other than Matthew, only the second century writing, the Gospel of Peter (which was not authored by Peter and is a Gnostic work) speaks of the guard. The movie, however, takes the sealing of the tomb from the Gospel of Peter as it portrays seven strings and seven sealings. What then about the placing of the guard and the guard itself? Once more, as indicated above, the tomb was left unguarded on Friday night. The decision and action to seal the tomb and place a guard to enforce it occurred on Saturday.[195] The circumstance rarely noted by writers on the subject of the Resurrection deals with the Passover. The potential for trouble at the tomb concerning the body of Jesus was intensified because of the Passover. There were tens, perhaps, hundreds of thousands of visitors to Jerusalem who had made pilgrimage for this event. The area outside of Jerusalem in the surrounding hills were crawling with people. Tents were everywhere as they were camping out around the city. Many of them were Galileans. Many of the Galileans would be fans, if not outright supporters, of Jesus. The Romans knew this and so did the Jewish religious elite. They both knew that the potential for mischief was present. It would not be difficult to believe that there might be an attempt to steal away the body, either to create a story of resurrection or to get the corpse out of the hands of one of the Sanhedrin for a number of other possibilities. So how many guards does one send to guard the stone? As pointed out by a number of people I have read over the years, the Greek word, "some" in Matthew pertains to a guard of at least four soldiers. There is some debate as to whether the guard was Roman or the Jewish Temple soldiers. Most writers understand that when Pilate states, "take a guard", it is in reference to the dispatching of imperial troops. Let us be clear, why would the chief priests come to Pilate in the first place? They had their own soldiers. The word "guard" refers to a "squad". The authorities know, that at a minimum, there are at least 11 core disciples. They also know that Jesus has several other circles of disciples and radically loyal followers. They feared an attempt on the tomb, and to thwart such action, the guard must be robust.[196] As pointed out

---

195   Matthew 27:62.
196   Anthony Horvath, "How Many Guards at Jesus' Tomb?", *SntJohnny.com* (April 6, 2009),

by Josh McDowell and others, Roman military manuals of the time in-dicate that a guard of between 11, with its officer, and 16 is probable.[197] If you want to discourage any attempt to violate the tomb and retrieve the body, and also defend the position properly, a detachment of approx-imately 20 to 40 personnel, as some have suggested, would not be out of the question. Penalty for failure was, of course, death.[198] The method of death was usually being burned at the stake.[199] The guard, whatever its numerical disposition, would be rotationally dispatched and placed. Several soldiers, perhaps up to four, would stand at attention in front of the tomb. The remainder of the contingent, save for any keeping watch on an outer perimeter, would be at rest, even sleeping, in front of the tomb with their heads toward the tomb facing outward. The total guard would not be asleep at one time. Even if they were, any attempt to open the tomb, carry the rock some distance away from the entrance, take the time to unwrap the body leaving the cloths with the appearance of being undisturbed, and escape with the naked body of Jesus would be impossible to carry out without awakening them. I find it highly likely, as have others who have thought about and written on this matter, that when the guard detachment was sent to the tomb, some Jewish Temple guards or representatives of the Sanhedrin, including perhaps some of the chief priests themselves, would have accompanied the Romans to the tomb, even on the Sabbath. Remember, this matter was deemed critical from the perspective of the ruling elite. It is also highly plausible that representatives of the chief priest and Pharisees participated in the inspection of the tomb alongside the Romans prior to the sealing. It has also been suggested that at least a couple Jewish guards would remain in the vicinity to keep an eye, not only on the tomb, but the Roman guard

---

https://www.scribd.com/book/194951629/How-Many-Guards-at-the-Tomb (accessed February 5, 2018). Please note that in the spring of 2013 a series of essays were added including "Were They Roman Guards or Jewish Guards?"; "The Disciple of her Roman Soldier."; "The Romans and Jesus: So (un)Happy Together."; "Pilate Puts Jesus On Trial, The Jews Put Pilate on Trial."; "Evidence of Jewish Guards at Jesus' Tomb". These were also accessed as this subject was pursued.

197   McDowell and McDowell, 181.

198   Roman execution for derelictions of duty, including cowardice, included the summary execution of the offender being beaten to death (stoning or clubbing) by fellow soldiers, the practice of "decimation" (random execution fo every 10th man in an offending unit).

199   McDowell and McDowell, 193-194.

as well.[200] The key thing to note, at this point, once again, is that it is Christ's opponents who are in possession of the body Saturday morning through sunrise Sunday morning. They are the last people to have Jesus, and they are responsible for the lifeless body of Christ.

The guard, however, is most unprepared for what is to happen at the crack of dawn. No military or combat training, activity or experience would have prepared them, or anyone, for what they were about to witness. From the Gospel accounts, we can surmise that some sort of unfathomable display of light, energy, power, and incomprehensible beings stunned the guard and psychologically froze them in place. While not a hostile display of might meant to harm them, the drama displayed at the point of initial resurrection, including the displacement of the stone through their midst, would be absolutely "alien" to them. When God's light and power show was quickly over, the soldiers recovered themselves and flee the site rightly deciding that these alien sights, sounds, and beings are more to be feared than the priests, their commanders, or even the governor. But what do they do next? They realize that the events, including their flight, will soon become known. They realize that they very well could be tried and sentenced to death for deserting their post. That some of them go and seek an audience with the chief priests does not necessarily mean that it was a Jewish guard. Perhaps they thought that explaining these things to this religious assemblage of leaders was their best bet! Perhaps, if a Jewish presence was there with them, it would collaborate their story. Since the Jewish religious elite and the Romans participated and cooperated together in the money bonanza of the Temple (concerning which others have written),[201] they were not opponents of one another as many people might think. Through this means, it was probably thought, some sort of influence by the Jewish religious officials might be rendered with Pilate and their commanders. Very soon after the soldier's report to the priests, the news must have reached Roman authorities, including Pilate. It is

---

200   Bill O'Reilly and Martin Dugard, *Killing Jesus* (New York: NY: Henry Holt and Company, LLC, 2013), 228-229, 238, 240.
201   McDowell, 80.

highly possible that the "hush money" the Jewish religious elite gave the Roman soldiers and the ridiculous lie they told would not have set well with Pilate. As has been pointed out by many, if they were asleep, how would they know it was the disciples who came and stole the body? Sleeping at their post is one thing, but lying about it and running away in the face of danger, even if it appeared to be otherworldly, would be quite difficult for him to tolerate. Surely, he, if not their commanders, would have forced the truth out of them. Regardless, one can be certain that both Jewish and Roman authorities would have gone and inspected the tomb and the immediate area (the rock at a distance from the entrance and the positioning of the grave clothes), finding that it would be impossible for any group to come and steal away the body in the manner the lie described. While not wanting to admit it, something very strange, indeed, happened in Joseph's garden which may, or may not, for we do not know, got the guard off the hook and perpetuated the ridiculous lie.

In any case, the tomb was empty and both Jewish and Roman authorities did not have and could not find the body that, in the words of Josh McDowell, would have forever killed any notion or story of resurrection. Displaying the dead body would have stamped out any movement by Jesus' followers forever! The tomb was, in fact, empty. It was then reported that the previously deceased body was experienced and witnessed alive and moving about again. Hundreds of people saw Jesus,[202] talked with him, and spent much time with him during the five or six weeks of Resurrection.[203] In fact, all of Jerusalem knew that the tomb was empty, and those who had not seen or heard Jesus alive knew people who claimed both.[204] This is why, on Pentecost, about 50 days later, all Peter had to do was give a credible explanation for the situation which led to thousands upon thousands that day, and in the days and weeks to follow, embrace Jesus as Christ, Savior, and Lord![205]

---

202   1 Corinthians 15:6.
203   *BibleStudy.org.* "Meaning of Numbers in the Bible: The Number 40." www.biblestudy.org/bibleref/meaning-of-numbers-in-bible/1.html (accessed April 5, 2019).
204   Acts 2:14-47.
205   McDowell, 91.

To summarize, even though Matthew is the only Gospel writer to inform us of the guard and the sealing of the tomb, its historicity is most plausible and ultimately cannot be urged as legendary as some polemic in the debate of the missing body and empty tomb. Matthew is written within the 33 years following Christ's death. Certainly, if the story and text were false, witnesses would have provided the corrective. To fabricate such a story was unnecessary and far outside the character of this highly ethical follower of Jesus. Matthew mentions this story almost as an afterthought, according to others I have read, which lends credence to its authenticity. Matthew does not give us all the details. We would like to know more. He tells us only the main points of the story because the story he tells is really the story. The story Matthew tells really happened, and so he chooses to record it even if the other three Gospel writers find no reason to do so as well.

Jesus, upon the third day, is no longer in bondage and neither are the people he came to save, particularly Eve. The time has now come for the announcement of the liberation, of Eve and all of her children so chosen by God. The liberation has been completed. At the time of Jesus' resurrection no one knew that yet, but they are about to in a very startling way!

10

"It Ain't Over Yet!"

"We've only just begun to live...."

(Roger Nichols & Paul Williams/The Carpenters)

"General Burgoyne, it ain't over yet!"

As a student and instructor on the subject of the American Revolution, my favorite quote of America's effort to achieve independence from Great Britain originates from an unknown American soldier during the Wilderness Campaign of 1777. In 1776 and 1777 the British attempted to divide the American states by an assault on Washington's Northern Department of War. The plan was to move southward from Quebec, Canada up the Richelieu River into Lake Champlain and Lake George, and then down into the Hudson River Valley. There they would join up with British forces sweeping eastward from Oswego on Lake Ontario down the Mohawk Valley to Albany, and those moving northward from New York City. The British General

135

Carlton initiated the effort in 1776 but was held off by Benedict Arnold and his Lake Champlain naval flotilla, culminating late in the year by the American naval defeat at Valcour Island. The effort was renewed in 1777 by "Gentleman Johnny" Burgoyne with an army of more than 8,000 troops. Things did not go well for the American effort to halt the British advance. Not only was the American naval presence on Lake Champlain significantly diminished at Valcour Island, but the British juggernaut took the American fortress at Fort Ticonderoga, captured Fort Independence, destroyed the remaining American fleet at Skenesborough, defeated an American land force at the battle of Hubbardton and, moving south, took Fort Anne. The Americans had been soundly defeated, and it appeared to the British that it would be a cakewalk the few remaining miles separating Fort Anne and the Hudson River Valley. It looked like the British strategic effort to separate the Middle and Southern states from New England was going to succeed. The Americans, however, were not finished or ready to give up the fight. On a tree just outside of Fort Anne, an American soldier had posted a message for the British. That message read, "General Burgoyne – It ain't over yet!" History records that when General Burgoyne received the message, he shuddered and viewed it as something quite ominous. Apparently, he believed that its words forecast a prophecy of doom. The retreating Americans were giving him a message that they were not beaten or defeated and would fight on with great resolve.[206] From the reception of that message on, British fortunes rapidly deteriorated as approximately 40,000 to 45,000 American troops engaged the British in that theatre of war surrounding, defeating, and capturing Burgoyne's entire British army helping to change the entire outlook of the war for George Washington.[207]

"It ain't over yet"! To this writer, these words can also be understood in terms of Christ's crucifixion and resurrection. While Jesus did say on the cross, "It is finished!",[208] what he meant by that was the termination

---

206   Michael O. Logusz, *With Musket and Tomahawk: The Saratoga Campaign and the Wilderness War of 1777* (Havertown, PA: Casemate Publishers, 2010), 114-115.
207   Logusz, 306.
208   John 19:30.

of the work of the second Adam. While the work of obedience and the sacrificial offering were now completed, the fact of the matter is that "we have only just begun!" When everyone thought that Jesus was dead and done and gone forever, they were in for the greatest shock and most tumultuous reversal in history. Truly, the resurrection cries out words similar to that solitary, unknown American soldier at Fort Anne, "It ain't over yet!"

The followers of Jesus were pretty slow on the uptake when it came to understanding what Jesus had told them about his death and return. Jesus had discussed the "sign of Jonah" (three days imprisoned in the internals of the great fish)[209] and had made both surprising and shocking comments about taking down and rebuilding the Temple in three days.[210] He had indicated to his disciples that he would be going away but returning to them. He had stated that a time of significant sorrow would be replaced by overwhelming joy.[211] Christians have often wondered how the disciples and followers of Jesus could have, seemingly, totally missed the meaning of Jesus' words. Certainly, the opposition to Jesus seemed to have more clarity when it came to predictions of his death and resurrection, in that they did not want the body stolen and a claim that he had risen advanced![212] So how did they miss, what to us seems clear in the aftermath, his assertion of resurrection? It appears to this writer that there were three things that clouded their understanding. First of all, it appears that Jewish prophecy of the Messiah, which has both a "suffering servant" component and a "kingly" component, was not held in tension as we discover in the Bible. During Jesus' lifetime, the emphasis appears to be, almost exclusively, on the "kingly" aspects of messianic prophecy. It appears that the suffering servant passages in Isaiah[213] were greatly ignored as the Jews of Galilee and Judea desired national and political independence from the Romans. Taking the role of a great national political and military leader seeking earthly

---

209   Matthew 12:39-41; Luke 11:29-32.
210   Matthew 26:61; John 2:19; Matthew 27:40; Mark 14:58; Mark 15:29, Acts 6:14.
211   Matthew 16:21; John 13:33-14:6; 14:18-31; 16:5-20, 28; 17:11, 13.
212   Matthew 27:63-64.
213   Isaiah 42:1-4; 49:1-6; 50:4-9; 52:13-53:12.

independence and the re-establishment of a greater Davidic Kingdom and Empire was one of the three great temptations Jesus had to deal with in the Wilderness following his self-identification with humanity in his baptism by John.[214] It was not yet understood that the suffering servant passages related to Jesus, personally (see Dr. Walter Ralston Martin's exegesis on this subject),[215] and were, by necessity, a pre-requisite for the fulfillment of the kingly prophecies. The people, including the followers of Jesus, did not have full clarity on the specifics of his mission.[216] Martha comes close in her confession of the person of Jesus in John 11:27 through the employment by John of the continuous tense in terms of Christ's coming. John, of course, seems to gets it immediately upon the visualization of the empty tomb and the positioning of the grave clothes.[217]

Secondly, the followers of Jesus, like the Pharisees, did affirm the miraculous and a coming resurrection. When it came to the word resurrection, religiously and culturally their mind set was fixed on the doctrine and concept of a resurrection of the dead in the last days. A reanimation of the body to a tangible, corporeal, and physical life was their great expectation. Please note that this was not the expectation of every Jew in Palestine at that time. So, when Jesus spoke of coming back from the dead, their response would be, "of course, Jesus will rise again just as we all will in that great day of resurrection"!

Thirdly, I also think that they did not think deeply enough when it came time to reflect on Jesus' statements about three days! Jesus was, perhaps, just cryptic enough in his messaging that they did not quite connect things. Maybe that is the way it was supposed to be. With the way things play out, I am convinced that this was God's plan all along.

Whatever the reasoning, and perhaps others have thought and written about this in greater depth than what is represented here, the expectation of a Sunday or Monday reanimation and departure from the

---

214   Matthew 4:8,9; Luke 4:5-7.
215   Dr. Walter R. Martin did an exegetical expose on Isaiah 52:13-53:12, this author does not know if the video presentation is still available.
216   Luke 24:8; 25-27; 44-46.
217   John 20:8-9.

tomb was totally foreign to them. Had it been otherwise, there would have been a vigil at the tomb with Jesus' followers excitedly anticipating his exit. The loudest and clearest statement that they anticipated no immediate resurrection was the fact that the women came on the day following the Sabbath to perform, finish or add to the embalming that had been initiated on Friday.[218] We need to note also that the initial understanding of the empty tomb by the women and Mary Magdalene was not one of resurrection.[219] The women and Mary had to be told what had, indeed, happened!

Our conclusion has to be that there was present among the followers of Jesus no expectation of an immediate resurrection. This lack of expectation sets up, of course, what I have referred to above as the greatest exhibition of "shock and awe" in human history.

---

218   Mark 16:1; Luke 24:1
219   John 20:2, 13-15; Mark 15:4-6; Luke 24:1-8.

11

Scripted

"Try? There is no try!"

"If you think you've found someone you'll love forevermore, then its worth the price you'll have to pay. To have, to hold's important when forever is the phrase that means the love you've found is going to stay."

(Jack Sigler, Jr./Mercy)

Back in 1994 when I was 40 years old, a group of us from Western Pennsylvania had hired guides to help us scale the Grand Teton (roughly 13,777 feet) of the Grand Teton mountain range in Wyoming. Three of us in the group, after a day of training and practice climbs, were cleared to engage a two-day mountaineering venture and technical climb up the sheer western face of the mountain. Starting out at 3 am on the second day, we reached the jump off point for the main technical climb to the peak. Dawn had broken, and we from the East were exhausted by the altitude as we reached the site known as the start of the Pownall/Gilkey Route up the summit. Our guides, Wes and Pete, pointed out to us the traverse we would have to make along a narrow (but easily passable) ledge. Next was a technical climb vertically up the mountain's sheer and smooth western rock face to a point we could go off belay, and scramble up the last remaining boulders and elevation to the summit. All three of us were wondering, at that moment, if we had the energy to complete the ascent. When I stated to Wes and Pete that I had come too far not to try, I was met with the reply, "Try? There is no try!" We were informed that once we began the long technical phase, we would have to finish it by making the top. For a number of reasons, once we engaged in the motion, there was no turning back. We actually succeeded in making the summit quicker and easier than we ever imagined. The ending was super fun, and the 40 minutes we spent on the summit were most joyful. Those words, however, "Try? There is no try!" have always stuck with me. There are times in life where the cliché is true, "failure is not an option!" Historically, I am reminded of Joshua Lawrence Chamberlain and the 20th Maine Regiment on Little Round Top during the 2nd day at Gettysburg, of which many have written. Certain circumstances and actions by Biblical characters such as Moses, Joshua, Elijah, and Esther also come to mind. Perhaps, the greatest example of "Try? There is no try!" echoes in regards to the person of Jesus Christ.

With Jesus, there is no try, and failure was, absolutely, not an option. There is no individual in history of whom this is truer. In the wilderness temptation of Jesus, the tempter presents Jesus with three options in terms of the conduct of the ministry he is about to initiate.[220] Would Jesus feature the social welfare concerns of the people to ride a wave of popularity? Would he gain a following by entertaining the crowds like a magician putting on a mysterious and dazzling performance with great feats of the supernatural? Or would he delve into politics, particularly from a military perspective, force the issue and take over? Jesus would have none of it! The only way open to him if he were to satisfy the purposes of his incarnation, and the meaning of his human life as the last

---

220   Matthew 4:1-11; Luke 4:1-13.

Adam, was to go the way of the cross, living life sacrificially. Though the tempter and others sought to deter him, Jesus was steadfast in his terrible resolve! Try to make it? Try to get to the finish line? Do your best and try to complete your mission? For Jesus, there was no try. He had to stick to the game plan, execute it completely, and go all the way to the prescribed finish! In so doing, as shared previously, the great theologian Gustaf Aulen assigns to Jesus the thunderous proclamation, "Christus Victor!"[221] Jesus, though tempted to pursue other paths, conquers his human temptations, unlike the first Adam, and fulfills the meaning of his human life becoming the victorious Christ!

Christ's destiny was prescribed from the outset of Creation. The life of Jesus and his mission, in the belief of this author, was completely "scripted". What do I mean by scripted? I am a Penn State football fan and was a season ticket holder for 33 years starting in 1978. While I do not know if this is entirely true, I have been told that one of the innovations that former Penn State offensive coordinator, Fran Ganter, made to college football many years ago was to plan out the first 16 or so offensive plays. These plays were drawn up and practiced by the offensive squad. It was noted that Penn State's offensive unit seemed to perform well early in the game, only to be frequently less successful after the second or third offensive series. This innovation was known as "scripting". The initial play-calling was "scripted". In similar fashion, the events of Jesus' coming, the major outline of his ministry, and particularly the details of his Passion and Resurrection were planned out beforehand in great detail. Jesus was just following the plan! This "script" was a difficult one, particularly considering his trials and execution. Yet as we have seen, he was obedient to it, embraced it, and followed through with it. This includes his Resurrection and particularly in the thesis of this author, everything that surrounds his first appearance to the person of Mary Magdalene. It was scripted that she would be the first to encounter the Christ. It was essential that she be the first person to see, touch, and converse with Jesus. Before Jesus began appearing to and inaugurating his resurrection apologetics concerning his identity

---

221   Gustaf Aulen, *Christus Victor* (New York, NY: MacMillan Publishing Co., Inc., 1969), 4.

and mission, he had critical business to engage with Mary Magdalene. It was absolutely crucial that he appear to her and engage her person, alone! To this author, the encounter between Jesus and Mary Magdalene is the greatest part of the greatest story ever told, and yet, it appears to have been missed and its great meaning never fleshed out!

The questions now before us are who, what, and why! Who is Mary Magdalene? What is Mary Magdalene? And why is Mary Magdalene, to this author, an absolutely critical figure in the life of Jesus and in story of salvation history?

12

New Testament Eve

"But I'd like to get to know you (yes I would). But I'd like to get to know you (if I could). But I'd like to get to know you, know you, know!"

(Stuart Scharf/Spanky & Our Gang)

Who is the person of Mary Magdalene? In relationship to salvation history, what is Mary Magdalene? And, why is Mary Magdalene a crucial figure in the drama that is portrayed in the Bible?

Mary Magdalene represents the fallen and restored Eve in the New Testament account of the garden and Jesus' Resurrection. She is symbolically and figuratively, Eve. She is, in this perspective, the New Testament Eve! There are many parallels between the Garden of Eden and the Garden of Joseph of Arimathea. As we noted previously, these gardens, the people present in them, and the action that occurs in them is characterized by the number 2. In terms of these gardens, there are four people (four divided by two), a man and a woman in each; two Adams', Adam and Jesus; two Eves', Eve and Mary Magdalene; two

lights; two messages; two stories of relationship; two callings; two waiting periods; two dispositions of the tempter; two circumstances dealing
with sin; two occurrences of sleeping; two placements of people; the
donning of clothing; two moments of excitement; a flight from God and
a flight toward God; splitting and a re-unification; a paradise lost and
a paradise restored. Each seem to echo aspects of Ecclesiastes 3, in its
own time. The parallels between the two stories separated by thousands
of years are uncanny and, in the estimation of this writer, scripted. Eve
was the "perfect woman" who discarded and fell from her lofty status
with God. Mary Magdalene is the "perfected woman". She represents
Eve's perfection before God restored. Mary Magdalene is the "perfected
Eve." Mary Magdalene is the "redeemed Eve."

To understand the who, what, and why of Mary Magdalene as the
New Testament Eve, we need to delve into what we know and what we
do not know about Mary of Magdala. Who was Mary Magdalene? The
name Mary was very common in Palestine during her lifetime, with
23 to 28 percent of all women apparently sharing that moniker.[222] The
name Mary is found in the New Testament about 61 times in about 53
verses. At least seven Marys are mentioned in the New Testament including Mary of Magdala (Luke 8:1-3); Jesus' mother Mary (Luke 1:38);
Mary of Bethany, the sister of Martha and Lazarus (Luke 10:38-42);
Mary, the mother of James the younger and of Joses (Mark 15:40, possibly the James, son of Alphaeus, but also possibly referred to as Mary
the mother of James in Mark 16:1 & Luke 24:10, and Mary, the mother
of James and Joseph in Matthew 27:55-61); Mary the wife (or daughter)
of Clopas or Cleophas or Cleopas (John 19:25); Mary the mother of
John Mark (Acts 12:12-14); and Mary, a Roman disciple (Romans 16:6).
Mary Magdalene is named 12 times in the Gospels. In five of six listings
of women in the Gospels (all but the Gospel of John, chapter 19:25) she
appears first on the list (Luke 24:10 at the Resurrection; Mark 15:40 at

---

222   Derek Leman, "Yeshua In Context: The Life and Times of Yeshua (Jesus) the Messiah,
Jewish Names in Galilee and Judea," *Yeshua in Context* (March 29, 2011): YeshuaInContexct.com.
(accessed April 8, 2019).

the crucifixion; Matthew 27:56 at the crucifixion; Matthew 27:61 at the burial; and Matthew 28:1 at the Resurrection).

People usually have three opinions concerning Mary. There is the widely held view of her as a repentant prostitute or a repentant business woman of a house of prostitution. The town from which she apparently resided, Magdala (a Galilean town located on the western side of the Sea of Tiberius), was "renowned for its wealth and immorality" at the time of Jesus.[223] There are those who believe that she was the bride of Jesus. If they were not officially married, she was what we would say today, his girlfriend. Perhaps, some might call it a friendship "with benefits." That she was a friend of Jesus is true. There is no evidence that she and Jesus were "more than friends" in the current common understanding of the phrase. It is possible that Mary Magdalene became Jesus' best female friend. Perhaps she was Jesus' best friend -- period! Regardless of all this speculation, she was a follower and supporter of Jesus. It is likely that she possessed wealth, leading to speculation that her wherewithal came from her lucrative business in prostitution. While there does not appear to be any evidence to support this, she may have inherited her wealth, or been involved in some other sort of trade like the woman of valor described in Proverbs 31. There is also speculation that her name, Magdalene, may come from the Hebrew "Migdal", which refers to a "tall fortified position" or a "tower". In Aramaic, the word "magdala" can imply the words "tower", "magnificent", "great", or "elevated".[224] Some have suggested that she might have been tall in stature, or this is a reference to the height of her faith. Others have suggested that she had a "tower-

---

223   Madeleine Sweeney Miller and John Lane Miller, *Harper's Bible Dictionary* (New York: NY: Harper & Row Publishers, Inc., 1952), 423. It is known that the Romans destroyed this town due, in part, to its moral depravity. It is often repeated that Magdala, a fishing village, had a reputation for illicit immoral practices and depravity. Throughout my career I read material commenting that it was a "center of prostitution." In writing this book such language was not uncovered.

224   Abarim Publication, "The Name Magdalene in the Bible: Etymology and Meaning of the Name Magdalene," *Abarim Publication.com.* (November 21, 2017), www.abarim-publications.com/Meaning/Magdalene.html (accessed April 8, 2019).
Wikipedia, "Mary Magdalene," *Wikipedia, The Free Encyclopedia,* https://en.wikipedia.org/wiki/Mary_Magdalene. (accessed 4/8/19).

ing hairdo", and worked as a hairdresser.[225] There does not appear to be any evidence that she had a husband, was previously married, or had children. As a follower of Jesus, she appears to have fulfilled three roles: a female disciple (one of the supposed 120), a witness to the words and events of the Christ (as she appeared to be a frequent traveling companion of the 12), and, presumably, being a person of means, a financial supporter of Jesus' ministry and the 12. Mary Magdalene might also be referred to as an apostle ("Apostle to the Apostles" in some traditions), in that she is sent by Jesus to announce his Resurrection to others.[226] Of the three opinions above, in the view of this author, all three could be true, at least according to one point of reference.

Mary Magdalene's life was changed drastically after meeting Jesus who delivered her from seven demons[227] (Luke 8:1-3 and Mark 16:9, and yes, I am aware of the scholarship concerning Mark 16:9-20, which does not have to invalidate the truth or historicity of this statement about her). This is significant and indicates that she was captive to sin and its ill-circumstances. Opinions on demon possession vary from outright "entity" oppression (known as "possession" to many) to having succumbed to numerous diseases thought to be the work of, and indicating the presence of, Satan and his minions. If, as this author asserts, Mary Magdalene is the New Testament Eve, she is a perfect candidate of a fallen one captured in the clutches of sin and evil and in need of deliverance, just like the Old Testament Eve. In a sermon (Homily 33) delivered on Easter Sunday in 591 AD, Pope Gregory I (Gregory the Great) appears to have confused the woman of Luke 7 and Mary Magdalene in Luke 8. It appears that this is where the idea that she was a prostitute originated, although Ephrem the Syrian in the fourth century advanced

---

225   Christianity Stack Exchange, "Why is Mary Magdalene the Patron Saint of Hairdressers: Theory 2: Actual Hairdresser," *Christianity Stack Exchange, Inc.* (2017), Christianity.stackexchange. com/questions/33729 (accessed April 8, 2019).
Wikipedia, "Mary Magdalene," *Wikipedia, The Free Encyclopedia,* https//en.wikipedia.org/wiki/ Mary_Magdalene. (accessed April 8, 2019).
226   Wikipedia, "Mary Magdalene," *Wikipedia, The Free Encyclopedia,* https//en.wikipedia.org/ wiki/Mary_Magdalene, (accessed April 8, 2019).
227   Since the number seven represents the idea of completion in Jewish thought, perhaps this number is symbolic representing the totality of Evil's domination over her.

the notion of Mary Magdalene as a repentant sinner.[228] Biblically, there is no indication that she was a prostitute, which was made nearly universal by the rock opera "Jesus Christ Superstar", and through many other films and songs (among them Martin Scorsese's adaptation of Nikos Kazantzakis's novel in the film "The Last Temptation of Christ"; Jose' Saramago's "The Gospel According to Jesus Christ"; Mel Gibson's "The Passion of the Christ"; and even in two of Lady Gaga's songs). Though Magdala may have experienced a great deal of prostitution traffic, as noted above, the Bible never states the identity of or names the demons which possessed her.[229] The Vatican officially corrected Pope Gregory's error during the 20th century.[230] The Bible also does not know, or comments, on any romantic relationship between the two. As evidence, I advance the "Rabboni" statement in the John 20 passage, the lack of a care statement (or recording of a care statement) from the cross during the crucifixion as Jesus spoke to John about his mother, Mary, and the imagery Jesus employs in the Gospels, of which we will address as we proceed.[231]

---

228   Ephraim or Ephrem "the Syrian" was apparently the first person to identify Mary Magdalene with the unnamed sinful woman depicted in Luke 7:36-50. St. Gregory the Great accepted this association and declared it publicly late in the sixth century as well.

229   The identity of the demonic suffering she experienced could have been regarded as mental illness, psychological and/or emotional distress, physical maladies, spiritual anguish, or afflictions causing immoral behavior. It is possible that it was a combination of some or all of the above. It must, however, be noted that immoral conduct may not have been part of her package of deviant behavior.

230   There have been in recent decades and years three papal declarations on the person of Mary Magdalene. All of these can be easily referenced online. The first was on April 3, 1969. In an edition of the Roman Missal published under Pope Paul VI, the link that Pope Gregory I identified between Mary Magdalene and the Lucan Passage of the sinful woman (Luke 7:36-50) was severed. Mary of Bethany was now identified as the sinful woman. This official declaration occurred quietly without any fanfare. The second papal declaration occurred on August 15, 1988 in Pope John Paul II's *Mulieris Dignitatem* concerning the Dignity and Vocation of Woman. Here Mary Magdalene's courage, loyalty, faith, and fidelity during Christ's passion was noted as well as her role in sharing the news of the Resurrection with the Apostles. The third Papal declaration was Pope Francis' July 22, 2016 decree elevating the liturgical celebration honoring Mary Magdalene from the status of a memorial to the position of a feast. Mary Magdalene was now granted equal footing with the Apostles.

231   Philip Neal in his article "Was Jesus Really Married to Mary Magdalene?" advances more criteria for the lack of a romantic relationship between the two in his article's section entitled, "Why Jesus Could Never Have Married", which is insightful and worth serious consideration. It can be found at truthofgod.org., from Hollister, California, 2018.

Mary Magdalene is not mentioned in the New Testament beyond the Gospels. It does appear that she was among the followers of Jesus at Pentecost and a member of the early New Testament church. Following the ascension of Jesus, there are a number of ideas concerning the remainder of her life. Eastern Orthodoxy has her living with Jesus' mother, Mary, having accompanied the apostle John to Ephesus, where she is believed to have died.[232] There is the legend that she went into a life of contemplation for several decades, living in a cave and communicating with angels.[233] The idea that Mary travelled to southern France with Joseph of Arimathea and had a daughter named Sarah to Jesus apparently appeared in the 9th century and has become known as the Magdalene Heresy.[234] This notion garnered more inventive ideas to it in the 12th century. Gregory of Tours in the 6th century places her in Ephesus,[235] but medieval Roman Catholic speculation believes she ended up in the south of France, dying at Saint-Maximin-la-Sainte-Baume.[236] The Magdalene Heresy also links Mary Magdalene to the goddess Isis.[237] While I greatly enjoyed Dan Brown's novel, "The Da Vinci Code", having read it twice and watched the Tom Hanks' movie multiple times, the theory the novel presents, appears not to have any real basis in history as far as the examination of this author goes. This writer has taken the time to review several books on the subject and has advanced, in the past, a number of presentations on this matter. The John 20 text of Mary Magdalene and Jesus at the tomb seems to have aided to the spark in people's imagination of the relationship between the couple. While the relationship between the two was most serious, it is the opinion of this author that the normal variant track that alternative views take is just off the mark. Much has been written about Brown's "Da Vinci Code" and all the thoughts and theories of Rosslyn

---

232 Wikipedia, "Mary Magdalene," *Wikipedia, The Free Encyclopedia*, https://en.wikipedia.org/wiki/Mary_Magdalene (accessed April 8, 2019).
233 Ibid.
234 Ibid.
235 Ibid.
236 Ibid.
237 A plethora of esoteric articles concerning a connection between the goddess Isis and Mary Magdalene exist on-line.

Chapel and the Knights Templar that surrounds it. I leave it to those who have written numerous articles, pamphlets, and books on the subject to guide your investigation of this matter. It is not the purpose of this author to debunk these theories, though this author finds nothing to substantiate them.

It is worth mentioning that some scholars have suggested that Mary Magdalene represents a "composite individual" made up of the lives of two or three personages. Mary of Bethany has been suggested as one such possibility.[238] The idea of a "composite Mary Magdalene", or that she has been merged with Mary of Bethany or even the unnamed adulterous woman in Luke 7 or John 8, seems to be far-fetched to this author. It appears that the Cisterian monk, Peter of Vaux de Cernay, in the 13th century, suggested that Mary Magdalene was the woman caught in adultery as recorded in John 8.[239]

Of all the Resurrection scenes in the Bible, John 20:1-18 is, by far, the most significant and meaningful. It is important for a number of reasons: It's historicity is crucial to the legitimacy of the text; Mary Magdalene with Jesus carries a great amount of symbolism in terms of the themes of the Bible, the story of the Bible, and the completion of salvation history; Mary Magdalene with Jesus is the keynote event of eternity; Mary Magdalene's story speaks to the liberation of women and their proper place within God's plan of living for humanity; and the interaction between Jesus and Mary Magdalene informs us about the conduct of our present and future relationship with God. All of these things we will examine in this chapter or in the chapters to come. While people have been intrigued with the person of Mary Magdalene for two millennia now, and this has been particularly true in the last couple decades with Dan Brown's novel, reliable historical sources (note that I used the term "reliable", which is of course ultimately, a subjective opinion) indicate that Jesus' initial encounter with Mary Magdalene occurs during his ministry, not during his pre-ministerial years. Mary, as

---

238   Wikipedia, "Mary Magdalene," *Wikipedia, The Free Encyclopedia*, http://en.wikipedia.org/wiki/Mary_Magdalene (accessed April 8, 2019).
239   Ibid.

we know, was a very troubled person afflicted by seven demons which could reference mental and physical illness but also demonic oppression which this author affirms, in terms of spiritual warfare, as a legitimate phenomenon. The Bible, as we have noted, never indicates that she was a prostitute. After her deliverance, Mary Magdalene becomes one of the female disciples of Jesus, who appears to be the first (or among the first) Rabbi to include female disciples. While the women were not a part of his inner core, the 12, they were absolutely invaluable to his ministry. They were more than just "camp followers" in the sense of this terminology throughout history, but integral to his ministry and received instruction as well.

It is the staunch opinion of this writer that there is a major difference between 1st century writings (the New Testament) and the writings of the subsequent centuries, particularly the 2nd, 3rd, and 4th. As previously stated, it is the position of his writer that the entire New Testament, including Revelation, represents early, and not latter 1st century production. The position here is that the entire New Testament is written prior to AD 66, which would be in the lifetime of those who witnessed the life, the statements, and the events of Jesus. There is no historic recording in the Bible that states that Jesus celebrated a traditional Jewish marriage or that anyone produced his offspring. Jesus was here on a grave mission which dominated his psyche and total life outlook. As the Wilderness experience, certain responses during his ministry,[240] and Gethsemane reveal, in the studied opinion of this author, there appears to be a certain haunting of his mind as he approached Calvary, particularly by being made sin and cut off from the love of the Father. For the last three years or so of his life, he set his face squarely on Jerusalem. In that he was God incarnate and his whole young life was wrapped up in his mission, which was humanly terminal, there was no reason for engaging in certain other aspects of human normality. It is also interesting to note that, while on the cross, Jesus calls out to the disciple John to oversee the care of his mother (at this time, his four brothers and two sisters do not appear to be available or affirm his

---

240   Matthew 16:21-23.

unique personhood). As the eldest in his nuclear family, he is responsible for her in light of the demise of his father and he performs this last duty out of both a cultural requirement and a heart of love. Nowhere is there a mention that he turned over the responsibility or care of an alleged wife or children to a disciple or another. Mary Magdalene was at the execution site, and her presence is highly significant. We have, however, no wordage that passed between them at this time (seven last words or statements were all that was recorded). It is the opinion here that while Mary Magdalene and Jesus were best friends and interlocked in the story of salvation history, there was no cultural regard or responsibility due her by him. This is something that should be noted.

Since much has been alleged about the person of Mary Magdalene and her relationship with Jesus, we need to look at the passages that some have linked to her, and then begin to delve into her real meaning and the invaluable role her person plays in salvation history.

Some people have surmised that John 7:53 – 8:11 is a story related to Mary Magdalene. While, it is true, the earliest texts we have of John's Gospel do not record this pericope, that does not mean that the story is fictitious and improperly placed. I have reviewed commentary on this story from many different sources during my career, but Dr. Robert Kelley, Dr. John Marsh, and Dr. Ken Bailey, have been particularly helpful in informing my views about Jesus and the woman taken in adultery. The placing of the story here may help to amplify John 8:15's comment by Jesus on the subject of "judging". According to Ken Bailey (whose teaching and views are represented below), this story is taking place on the Sabbath when papyrus cannot be inscribed with ink due to the observance of the day. The location of this incident is in the temple with the guards watching from above. This has no characteristics of a riot or demonstration. Through this incident we learn from Jesus that no one should judge another from inappropriate motives. The whole incident is a trap. The story is one of entrapment of the woman, in order to spring a trap on Jesus. The men who bring the woman to Jesus are doing so to see if Jesus, through his own words and actions in this case, might incriminate himself by violating the Law. A woman is brought to

Jesus at dawn and she stands, surrounded by a gathering crowd and her accusers, in front of Jesus. Please note her position. She is not groveling on the ground as in Mel Gibson's movie. The woman is also unidentified. Her accusers say to Jesus, "Teacher, this woman was caught in the act of adultery. In the Law, Moses commanded us to stone (execute) such women. Now what do you say?" Jesus is no dummy. He knows immediately what is going on here and he, being astute, knows how to deal with it. True justice, in the first place, would require them to apprehend and bring the man to stand before Jesus as well. The act of physical adultery takes two! Jesus knows that his accusers set a trap for the woman with a male accomplice and allowed him to escape. They employed a man to catch the woman, possibly to rid themselves of her, besides testing Jesus. Also, there is a Jewish maxim that there can be "no penalty without a warning." Witnesses of events like this are required to warn the perpetrators before they apprehend them or bring charges against them. Likewise, the woman's accusers show a special kind of vindictiveness against her because there is no reason to publicly bring her along with them. They could have just held her in custody, referring the case to Jesus. He knows what is going on here and must deal with the dilemma they have set up for him. Among the issues he has to circumnavigate is to deal with her sin while upholding the validity of the Law in regards to stoning. If he does uphold its validity and charge her with the death penalty he runs afoul the Romans who reserve for themselves, only, the right to inflict capital punishment. Jesus is smart! After all, this situation is not unlike Eden: How do you charge sin and punish it while rescuing those from sin's deadly clutches? Jesus knows!

Slowly Jesus bends down and begins to inscribe letters in the dust. Why does he write in the dusty soil and what does he write? As he does so, he may have a couple historical episodes in mind. Besides the circumstances of Eve's sin and the departure from the fertile Eden to the harsh ground outside of Paradise, he may also have in mind the compassion his father, Joseph, demonstrated with his mother, Mary, not so long ago. According to Roman criminal law, a sentence for an offense is written down and then read aloud. In so doing, is Jesus pronouncing the sentence on the woman in the best imperial style, but in a way in which it could not be carried out? Was he writing an aspect of the law in the dust? Was he writing the sins of the accusers in the dust? Was inscribing the dirty loose unfertile soil when considering the wind (maybe symbolic of the work of the Spirit), a way in which Jesus declares and demonstrates that sin can be wiped away containing no lasting or permanent record? Was he indicating that even this sin can be forgiven, removed, and erased? When Jesus is finished, he stands erect once more, bravely and boldly challenging the accusers, "If any one of you is without sin, let him be the first to throw a stone at her." He utters the challenge, then stoops down and writes some more. Slowly, one by one, the crowd of accusers, the wisest ones first, slowly back off, depart, and fade away. To me this is one of the most haunting scenes in the Bible. When all have departed, it is just the woman and Jesus standing alone. Perhaps, a breeze is already beginning to brush away the inscribed ground. Jesus stands erect once more and looks her square in the face. "Woman," he says, "where are they? Has no one condemned you?" Speaking respectfully to her advocate, she replies, "No one, sir." "Then neither do I condemn you. Go now and leave your life of sin." Many people miss what Jesus is really saying and doing here. He has declared that her sin is sin! He has judged her sin as sin! And he declares that she has no license to sin again! She must change her life and sin no more. In essence he is declaring to her, "Would you please stop it, your sin is sin, and you must engage it no more!" The woman is not off the hook with Jesus![241]

What Jesus has done here in this encounter is exactly what he came to do with Eve. As the second Adam, he accomplishes this and then demonstrates its results to the second Eve, Mary Magdalene. In some ways, it might have been neat to have the woman actually be Mary Magdalene, as some historically have envisioned. The fact of the matter is that this woman is not and, in any way in which this writer has looked at it, could not be Mary Magdalene.

---

241   Kenneth E. Bailey, *Jesus Through Middle Eastern Eyes* (Downers Grove, Illinois: InterVarsity Press, 2008), 227-238.

Another passage that is often associated with Mary Magdalene is Luke 7:36-50. Once again, I find the work of the late Dr. Robert Kelley and the late Kenneth Bailey helpful in wrestling with this text. According to Dr. Kelley, Luke 7:36-50 is the second meal scene in Luke. Dr. Kelley believed that the meal scenes in Luke's Gospel, of which he numbers as 10 (Luke 5:27-32; Luke 7:36-50; Luke 9:10-17; Luke 10:38-42; Luke 11:37-54; Luke 14:15-24; Luke 19:1-10; Luke 22:7-38; Luke 24:13-35; Luke 22:36-49), are critical thematically to the book. [242] They are also critical thematically in terms of God being a relational God (Revelation 3:20). This meal scene deals with an outcast woman. The action in the story has Jesus flanked by two sinners, the woman and Simon the Pharisee. According to the theology of Jesus as described and outlined by Ken Bailey (whose thoughts and teaching on the subject are represented below), the woman, who is "bad company" (according to the book, "Jesus in Bad Company" and my own compilation, the bad company designated by the religious elite included the following: the ceremonially impure or "sinners"; tax collectors known as "publicans"; the immoral, adulterers and others of low moral character; the mentally and/or spiritually deranged; women; Samaritans; the diseased and physically afflicted; those who rejected their Jewish heritage; Gentiles; fisherman, and other uncouth lowlifes such as shepherds; and criminals) according to the religious elite, is a law-breaking sinner.[243] Simon, of the religious elite (according to the theology of Jesus as outlined by Dr. Ken Bailey), is a law-keeping sinner. Both categories are in need of repentance and salvation. This is the first time Jesus, in Luke, eats with a Pharisee. This scene is a foreshadowing of Calvary. Like the cross, Jesus ends up being flanked by two sinners. According to Ken Bailey, the drama is portrayed in seven scenes.

Scene one is the introduction (verses 36 and 37). Simon the Pharisee invites Jesus to share table fellowship with him. Eating dinner with someone at that time was a major social event encrusted with much

---

242   Robert E. Kelley, "Greek Reading: Luke" (Lecture, Pittsburgh Theological Seminary, Pittsburgh, PA, 1979).
243   Kenneth E. Bailey, "The Theology of Jesus" (Lecture, Pittsburgh Theological Seminary, Pittsburgh, PA, July 8-12, 1998).

custom and was significant in meaning. Jesus, as well as Simon and other principal guests, are reclining at table on couches Roman style (as he was to do in the Upper Room at the Last Supper) with their feet in the air away from the table and the food, usually resting on the left arm. Guests, who are lower on the social scale, would be seated on chairs along the walls of the courtyard or enclosure and served last. It is possible, as Ken Bailey points out, that Jesus is dining with a group of very pious Jews whose intent, since Jesus is in their village, is to talk with him to form some sort of opinion about him or in opposition to him. A woman, a resident of that town who had practiced a very sinful life, learns of the meal and Jesus' upcoming presence there and decides to go and attempt to witness the proceedings, bringing along with her an alabaster jar of perfume. Alabaster jars of ointments and perfumes were items typical in the plying of the prostitution trade. In all likelihood, this woman had lived a life exercising and promoting this business. The fact that she brings along with her the jar of perfume speaks to the performance of some sort of planned action on her part. Often meals like this were set in courtyards, with people who were uninvited to the dinner attempting to peer around walls or over the top of the wall to view the activity and listen to the conversation. This woman appears to be one of such a crowd. Apparently, she arrives at the location prior to Jesus and observes his entry.

It is at this moment, in scene two (verse 38), that the woman makes observation and is aghast at what she sees or, in this case, does not see. Here is Jesus, a man whom she has heard teach and preach on the subject of forgiveness and it has changed her life. According to the Jewish understanding of repentance as outlined by Dr. Bailey, she cannot possibly make up for her sin and is a lost soul forever. In hearing Jesus, she understands that God, in terms of forgiveness, operates in a way wherein she can receive God's acceptance and the opportunity to embrace a new way of life. She embraces the grace that has been offered, and its internalization has made her new. In feeling the love and compassion of God firsthand through Jesus, she now wants to offer Jesus an expression of her gratitude and a demonstration of her intent to live a new life. Nervously, perhaps, she awaits her opportunity to express herself, and finds that such an opportunity is afforded to her early in the meal. She advances upon and approaches Jesus from behind in the vicinity of his feet. She is upset and immediately succumbs to a profuse weeping, her tears so large and numerous they fall upon and wet Jesus' feet. She then proceeds to let down her hair, which is a disgraceful act in public, and to touch Jesus. Without a towel she employs her hair in the wiping of the soil off of his feet, kisses his feet with her lips, opens the jar and pours her perfume, anointing his feet. This alabaster jar of perfume is not only a probable tool of her trade but very expensive as well. We are to understand here that it is Jesus who has convinced her to give up her profession, and so she surrenders the tools of her trade in thankfulness for the grace, forgiveness, mercy, and salvation she has received. To be touched by a woman, particularly in this way, is, once again, a most disgraceful act both to perform and receive. The actions of both, however, are full of grace. The woman is communicating to Jesus that she has terminated her life employment of sin, but is also expressing her thankfulness for the liberation he has offered to her and to which she has received. Jesus can do nothing else but sit quietly and receive the gift of the woman. If he halted her action, what detrimental impact might this have on her? He knows that her expression is vital to complete the spiritual healing that she needs in her new relationship with God.

The third scene (verses 39 and 40) deals with the reaction of the woman's bold anointing and Jesus' reception of it. The witnesses had to be aghast! This action has sexual overtones to it. Simon the Pharisee was certainly annoyed and openly challenges Jesus' prophethood. Contact equals contamination in this instance, and Jesus, who claims to be of God, has permitted it! Simon speaks to himself, probably in a low voice that those near him can hear, "If this man were a prophet, he would know who is touching him and what kind of woman she is – that she is a sinner." Notice Simon's use of the present tense! In all actuality, everything about the woman and her sin should now be described by the employment of the past tense. Jesus, upon hearing Simon mumble, or knowing what Simon is thinking, prepares to respond. Jesus' intent here is to challenge and to get Simon to think about his own self-righteousness, and the fact that he will soon be leaving the village and wants to help the woman by dealing with people's opinion of her.

Jesus responds by sharing a teaching story (parable) in scene four (verses 41 and 43). The story concerns two debtors who could not repay a money lender or banker. The money lender graces both of them by forgiving (cancelling) their debt. One debtor owes a denomination of 500, the other 50. Jesus then asks Simon which of the two individuals will love the money lender more?

Scene five is Simon's reply (verse 43). Simon answers, "I suppose the one who had the bigger debt canceled." Jesus then informs him that he has answered or "judged" rightly.

After this dialogue with the sinner Simon, Jesus proceeds in scene six (verses 44-47) to explain the actions of the woman. Here Jesus, according to Ken Bailey, goes on the attack! Jesus knows that Simon has no respect for him due to the fact that he broke all the rules of hospitality. Simon, and his servants, did not provide the customary bowl and towel for the washing of the feet upon entering the house from the polluted streets. This would be particularly poignant while eating on couches Roman style. Simon did not greet Jesus with the customary kiss due one Rabbi to another, nor did he provide ointment (olive oil) for the hair and hands to freshen up before partaking of the meal. The woman, seeing the violation of all these acts of hospitality is crushed by Simon's disregard and disrespect to someone she holds in high esteem. She cannot stand that Jesus is being treated so poorly. Hence, she moves to make up, on her own, for these intentional, gross omissions. In reality, the woman has compensated for all of Simon's callous attitude and actions toward Jesus. If there is a sinner to avoid here, according to Bailey, it is Simon. In so doing, Jesus has completely turned things around on Simon and placed him under scrutiny for sin, including his self-righteousness, willful neglect in the performance of the responsibilities of hospitality, and failure to see what God is doing by offering forgiveness, granting grace and mercy, and accepting the penitent. Jesus makes it clear that Simon is the greater sinner here, and not her. Jesus then says, "I tell you, her many sins have been forgiven, therefore she loved much". According to Ken Bailey, the Greek here should not be translated "for she loved much" as if she is forgiven and rewarded for her work or good deed performed upon and for the Christ. "Therefore" is preferred, according to Bailey, as a response of her love for the gift Jesus has already, prior to the dinner, given to her. Her expression of love is simply her gift of gratitude.

Verses 48 through 50 represent the story's conclusion. Jesus turns to the woman, a daughter of Eve, and pronounces forgiveness. "Your sins are forgiven!" What a marvelous declaration this truly is! Jesus finally says to her, "Your faith has saved you; go in peace." Her faith expression in embracing God's love and mercy, and accepting her new gifted status as righteous, has placed her in the company of those the incarnate God came to save. Her salvation has nothing to do with her tears or perfume and the performance of serving Jesus to which she did not hesitate to accomplish. God granted the grace, and the woman responded with thankfulness! Salvation, after all, is something that cannot be earned. Salvation is a gift of God's grace freely received. The woman received it and her actions testify that, indeed, she is saved for all time and eternity![244]

There is nothing in this passage which ties the woman with Mary Magdalene. This is the story of a woman not afflicted with and delivered from seven demons, but one who has come to realize that repentance and forgiveness for her sins is not completely out of the question as she once thought. Her sins, which are many, have already been forgiven and so she embraces her new status with God. She will remain in the village. She will not be joining, as did Mary Magdalene, the travelling company of his disciples. As with the woman caught in adultery, this encounter also fits what Jesus came to do with Eve. Once more, as the second Adam, he comes seeking the sinful Eve, and demonstrates the fulfillment of his purpose by appearing to and receiving the second Eve, Mary Magdalene as the perfected woman.

---

244   Kenneth E. Bailey, *Jesus Through Middle Eastern Eyes*, 239-260.

A further passage associated with Mary Magdalene, in the opinion of some, is Mark 14:3-9. It is what we now refer to as "Holy Week". It appears to be a Tuesday or possibly a Wednesday evening, depending upon whether one celebrates the Galilean or the Judean Passover which were on different days. Jesus is residing in Bethany, a suburb of Jerusalem about two miles away, probably at the home of Lazarus, with his sisters Martha and Mary. In this story, he is once again reclining, Roman style, at the home of another Simon, known as "the leper". The man is apparently afflicted with the dreaded disease, or, more likely, has been healed by Jesus of the malady. Simon is apparently a wealthy individual and is hosting Jesus in one of the final moments of respite he has prior to the tumultuous events that would soon encompass him. It has always appeared to this author that the women surrounding and ministering to Jesus understood more about his mission and coming Passion than did his male disciples. At least it appears that way! An unnamed woman carrying an alabaster jar arrives at the feast, breaks the jar in this story, and, in this case, pours the perfume on Jesus' head. The circumstances in this setting are much different than in the previous story examined above. Here the concern of the onlookers is not about the woman's character, profession, and disgraceful conduct in public with sexual overtones. The complaint of those sharing in this meal concerns the waste of a valuable resource which could have been employed to lessen the pains of the poor and needy. Perhaps Judas, the treasurer of Jesus' ministry band who may have embezzled ministry funds, was the lead antagonist in the murmuring and harsh rebuking of her action. Jesus rapidly comes to her defense. Here Jesus utters one of the most marvelous statements in the Bible, "She has done a beautiful thing to me!" This statement by Jesus is full of grace and blessed appreciation for the fact that she knows what is about to happen to him. She may not know all the details and the theology behind it, including the time frame reference to the Resurrection, but she does know that he is going to his death to do something about the breach existing between God and humanity. Jesus rebukes those who rebuked her. At this, Judas decides to make his move against Jesus. The woman in this story could be Mary Magdalene. It is entirely possible that it could be her due to the presence at this meal of many of Jesus' disciples and followers. This anointing appears to be an "inside job" by a follower close to him, rather than the situation of the lady in Luke 7. Mary Magdalene is, however, unnamed. The opinion of this writer is, due to her prominence with and among the disciples, and with the backward gaze of John Mark, that if this woman in the story would have been Mary Magdalene, she would be accredited with this action. The woman, however, remains unnamed, and so it is believed here that she was not one of the more prominent women assisting Jesus and his ministry band.

The Synoptic parallel to the Marcan account is found in Matthew 26:6-13. The story is exactly the same one detailed by Mark. There is nothing new that we can discover here and so we will proceed to examine the anointing described in John.

The Johannine account of Jesus' anointing at Bethany is found in the 12th chapter of the Gospel, verses 1 through 8. Once again, we are at the close of Jesus' public ministry just prior to Jesus' "Triumphal Entry" into Jerusalem if John's chronology, which is more theological than actual, is to be affirmed as it appears. Here the time frame reference is prior to the anointing Jesus receives by the unnamed woman in the home of Simon the Leper. It is entirely possible that Jesus received this type of anointing multiple times during his ministry. This meal is at the estate of Lazarus and his sisters, Martha and Mary. The perpetrator of the anointing in this report, is Mary of Bethany. The Mary spoken of here is not Mary Magdalene. The setting and the identification of the individual who anoints Jesus is clearly Lazarus' sister, Mary. Mary Magdalene and Mary of Bethany are two different individuals. While Mary of Bethany appears to be in the circle of Jesus' best friends, it does not appear that she traveled with and accompanied the 12. She was greatly interested in Jesus' teachings, to be sure, but she appears to be very attached to the family dwelling and location. Any attempt to merge them into a "composite Mary" is bogus from the study of this author. The remainder of the circumstances of the meal and the reaction of the participants, including Judas, appears to be similar to that of Simon the Leper, which appears to follow on a subsequent night. There are six divergent points between the story in Mark 14 and John's account here in chapter 12. John's account places the action prior to Holy Week, while Mark's is during Holy Week. In John, Jesus' feet are anointed and not his head as in Mark. In John, the perpetrator is named. She is unnamed in Mark. In the two versions, there are some differences in wordage and the order of the account. In Mark, the vial is broken. This is not the case in John. In John, Judas is more prominent in his indignation. It is a group of individuals who are named as indignant in Mark. It is interesting to note that the disciples are named as indignant in the Matthean chapter 26 account. Mary of Bethany, unlike the woman at the home of Simon the Leper, anoints Jesus' feet and wipes them with her hair as did the woman in Luke 7. Wiping the feet with her hair is curious in this household setting with Mary living there. The act, however, of anointing the feet, while cultural, may be, at the same time, symbolic for anointing the whole body. This is an act of utter humility and interpreted by Jesus as foreshadowing his death and burial. Unlike many commentators, this author thinks that the dual anointing of Jesus are two separate incidents and may be "copy-cat" occurrences. This is only conjecture, of course, on my part. The point is, that in both cases, it is greatly in doubt that the performance of the anointing was by Mary Magdalene.

It is my contention that one of the themes of the Bible is that of the perfect woman. Eve was originally the "perfect woman". As a result of her sin, there is no longer a woman in the Bible who holds the title of "the perfect woman". Mary, the mother of Jesus, as we briefly discussed above, although marvelous, was also in need of the shed blood of her Son. After Eve, there is no "perfect woman". Hints of perfection do exist throughout the Bible outside of the creation stories. Proverbs 31:10-31 is the honoring of a "woman of valor" who is near perfect and, in the estimation of this author, picks up the theme of God's goodly creation of woman. This writer also asserts, as we will see, that John 14:1-6 is a part of the theme of the "perfect woman" as well. Revelation 21:1-7, with the declaration of "making everything new", is the culmination of this theme in the Bible according to my point of view. God is intent on redeeming and restoring Eve. As there is a second Adam who recapitulates the first Adam and succeeds in the Adamic enterprise, so there is a second Eve who is the representative recipient of perfection restored. Mary Magdalene represents the redeemed, restored, and perfected Eve.

Once again, there is no woman in the Old Testament who is more identified with sin than Eve, although Jezebel is a great candidate for this title. There is no woman in the New Testament more identified with sin than Mary Magdalene. She has been imagined, as we have seen, and perhaps wrongly so, as the worst of the worst. Eve is informed in Genesis 3 that a remedy for sin is coming. Mary Magdalene is informed that the remedy for sin has taken place and she receives it. In truth, she receives it prior to Christ's Passion in her personal deliverance. And she also receives it again in the good news of human restoration as the second Eve following Christ's Passion. In Eden, Eve is cast out of the garden and removed from the immediate presence of God. In Joseph's garden, Mary Magdalene is welcomed and embraced. The story comes full circle on Easter morning. Jesus stands for Adam. Mary stands for Eve. Eve and her children are, on Easter, represented by Mary Magdalene. That is why I call her the New Testament Eve. The one disgraced and cast out has now been retrieved and restored. The original garden circumstances have been dealt with and reversed. What is now set up are the circumstances of the new sinless future and all of it involves Mary Magdalene, as the perfected Eve, and all the forthcoming children who will share in the new birth from above!

It is now time to gaze through a magnifying glass at the wondrous story granting Mary Magdalene New Testament Eve-like status, and along with it all the implications for Mary, and for us, that it bears. Before we do so, however, let us take a brief look at Gethsemane and one important aspect of the cross!

13

A Very Sad Song

"Abide with me! Fast falls the eventide. The darkness deepens; Lord with me abide! When other helpers fail and comforts flee, Help of the helpless, oh, abide with me! Swift to its close ebbs out life's little day. Earth's joys grow dim; its glories pass away. Change and decay in all around I see; O Thou who changest not, abide with me!"

(Henry F. Lyte)

Consider the importance and value of a song sung sad, or as Neal Diamond sings, "Song sung blue, everybody knows one." Sad songs have been much a part of the American experience. Many sad songs were written about the circumstances of war in this country. This is particularly true during the War Between the States, the music and lyrics of which have almost completely vanished from American consciousness. Many of the songs of World War II were sad as well, but they were also very hopeful of a coming time with a bright future. Sad songs have been written in this country about growing up and growing old, about times of separation, about re-location, and, of course, about death. The song, "Shenandoah", still pulls the heart strings of those who reminisce. Eric Clapton's "Tears in Heaven", I have associated with the untimely and unfortunate demise of a number of people in my life, and to this day still causes me to well up in tears. I have heard Christians comment that there is no place in the church for a sad song. They say that sad songs should not be a part of the Christian experience. It has been stated that the only songs Christians should sing are songs of triumph, victory, glory, and joy. I disagree. Israel's hymnbook, The Psalms, contain many laments or sad songs. Some of the hymns that a few churches still continue to sing today, such as "Abide with Me" tend to be sorrowful and sad. I have always agreed with Sir Elton John, "Sad Songs" do "Say so Much!" Sad songs are much of the human experience, because we need to be able to express sorrow, loss, and disappointment in our lives. Sadness and sorrow is part of the reality in which we live. We cannot escape that, at least not yet! My favorite Beatles' song is the sad and sorrowing "Long and Winding Road". "Yesterday" is another sad song of theirs. Early in my life "Green Leaves of Summer" and "Greenfields" by the Brothers Four, I found particularly sorrowful. My all time favorite sad song is by Jimmy Webb and sung by the late Richard Harris, "MacArthur Park". "Lara's Song", the theme to the movie Dr. Zhivago is a particularly sad song. "Traces of Love" by the Classic 4 is hauntingly sad. And how about Mary Fahl's "Going Home" (she also does a beautiful rendition of "Both Sides Now"), the theme song of the movie "Gods and Generals"? Frank Lloyd Wright said, "The longer I live the more beautiful life becomes!"[245] There is a lot of truth in that, particularly if a person is centered upon and has their eyes fixed on Jesus. A Spanish Proverb says, "I wept when I was born and every day shows why!"[246] George Herbert is correct as well, especially when viewing the circumstances of this world. The first book I endeavored to write was a history of individuals, couples, and families in the church I had served

---

245   John Rattenbury, "A Living Architecture: Frank Lloyd Wright and Taliesin Architects," *AZ Quotes: Frank Lloyd Wright Quotes* (October 31, 2000), https://www.azquotes.com/author/15963-Frank_Llyod_Wright (accessed April 9, 2019).
246   Thinkexist.com. Quotations, www.thinkexist.com (accessed April 9, 2019).

for 30 years. One of the things I noticed in writing this most unique and lengthy history was the large number of things in the area that are not here anymore! More sobering was the large number of people who are no longer present as well. My history ended up being much a "Who's Who" in terms of a funeral record. It was very depressing and quite melancholy emotionally. One of the cultural aspects of America, particularly in the 1860's was the symbolism of the "empty chair". Portrayed both in song and in the Jimmy Stewart movie "Shenandoah", the chair or chairs of the deceased were left unoccupied at family table. This became a stark reminder of what once was and those who were once joyfully present. A number of years ago a significant elderly sports figure was honored and all he could initially vocalize were the words, "all the people", meaning, in part, all the people who were once here and valued in his life and were now gone from the stage of life and his presence. The experience of this life now is much a sad one. That is reality. That is the way things are. Sadness, sorrow, and disappointment need a release. Do not take the sad song, and its expression, away. Sad songs really do help us cope with life, and they also provide the backdrop for the new coming reality, made ever so much more magnificent for us because of the earthly sorrows we have had to endure. Reason communicates to me that we cannot possibly know the heights of joy, unless we know the depths of sorrow.

To date, I have officiated more than 500 funerals in my career, including many family members. I do them well, both in sadness and in joy. Each one is unique for each person and circumstance is unique. I have never gotten used to doing them. With the performance of each one, a little slice of self and person seems to die as well; but with each death, I also find THE GOOD HOPE rising and burning brighter and brighter. One of things that my family is experiencing is the aging and physical devolution of our 14-year-old beloved pet, an American beagle named Scupper (Scupper died on September 1, 2019 at the age of 15 years, 4 months, and 2 weeks). Scup Pup is very much my dog and really tuned into me. During one period of time in his 11th year of life, his legs failed him and he couldn't stand up, or once placed up, remain standing, due to a spinal issue not uncommon for beagles. On the first night wherein his inability became grave, I rolled out my sleeping bag and determined to sleep on the living room floor with him. I placed him about a yard away on cloths specially designed to catch and hold bodily elimination. We settled down. Then I noticed that the poor dog was struggling in his attempt to crawl over to me. He accomplished this, curling himself into me, and stayed against me all that night. He had to make contact with me. The contact was necessary, soothing, and re-affirming to him. The situation reminded me of the time we purchased him from a pet store when he was 7 months old. He shook violently as I placed him down on the front seat of the car, completely terrified about being taken out of his environment by these strange people. All I had to do, I learned, as I drove carefully home was place my hand on him, and keep it on him. As long as there was contact, he shook no more. The loving and caring presence of another is vital for us as we live our lives and confront the terrors of this world.

I have always been interested in what one might term "the psychological Jesus". Over the past few years, this writer has spent a good bit of time reflecting on Jesus' mental and emotional state during his ministry, but particularly in his Wilderness experience, at Gethsemane, during his Passion, and in the moments immediately following his Resurrection. Nothing too terribly profound has been discovered, but some interesting thoughts, ideas, and notions have played over and over again in my mind. The big question I have entertained is, "How could Jesus possibly get through all of his personal "demolition" without humanly experiencing a complete mental, psychological, and emotional collapse? I have entertained some possibilities which may, or may not, provide the answer.

Dr. Stanley Ott, formerly of Pittsburgh Presbytery, PCUSA, and the Pleasant Hills Community Presbyterian Church in the South Hills of the greater Pittsburgh area, always made reference to something called, "People Eyes". In ministry, Dr. Ott maintained that pastors and churches "needed to be properly double focused" with "one eye fixed on Christ, and the other eye fixed on people."[247] I think there is a clue here to how Jesus psychologically managed to survive his Passion.

In the movie, "The Lion, The Witch, and The Wardrobe" the embattled and outnumbered heroes and heroines go into battle crying "For Narnia and for Aslan!"[248] Aslan is C. S. Lewis' Christ-like figure in the tale. Narnia is the land which represents the hoped-for restoration of all goodness, peace, and righteousness. In a similar vein, Jesus' battle cry approaching the cross could actually be imagined to be "For the Father and for those the Father has given me!" Jesus primarily addresses the Father in Gethsemane.[249] He primarily addresses those whom the Father has given him in the Upper Room.[250] His concern for both the Father and those the Father has given him are quite evident while he is on the cross.[251]

The Upper Room experience is just absolutely dripping with emotion. There is no more emotionally charged section of the Bible than this one. Called the "Farewell Discourse", it covers a whopping five chapters in the Gospel of John, nearly 25% of the book. There is more written about this moment in the life of Jesus than any other moment in his life including the passion and following Resurrection.

What is the subject of Jesus' sharing with them? It is all about his goings, and comings, and goings, and comings, and goings, and comings again and how, through it all, they are to be, act, and react. Much of the same can apply to us today as well! There are three specific departures and four specific divine comings that this author finds in the text: Jesus' departure that night culminating in his death; his unanticipated (by

---

247   Dr. Stanley Ott is founder and president of the Vital Churches Institute (VCI). He discussed "people eyes" in his Book, *The Vibrant Church: A People Building Plan for Congregational Health.* One can access this book from Regal Books of Ventura, California published in 1989. Also note his sermon series on-line entitled *Journey of Transformation.* Here he specifically mentions "People Eyes" in his message series from Vienna Presbyterian Church, Vienna, Virginia, March 28, 2010. This author learned of his teaching concerning "People Eyes" from numerous conversations and presentations by the Rev. Dr. Ott over his years as a member of Pittsburgh Presbytery pastoring the Pleasant Hills Community Presbyterian Church (PCUSA).

248   *The Chronicles of Narnia – The Lion, The Witch, and The Wardrobe,* directed by Andrew Adamson, Walt Disney Pictures and Walden Media, 2005, final battle scene.

249   Matthew 26:36-46; Mark 14:32-42; Luke 22:39-46.

250   John 13:1 – 17:26.

251   Luke 23:26-46; John 19:25-27.

them) early bodily Resurrection; his departure again, known to us as the Ascension; his still future expectation, of which we term the Second (physical or bodily) Coming (in the meantime, the coming and the abiding of the Holy Spirit is a prime focus as well); the departure known as our earthly demise or death; and his coming to us to translate us and appropriate us to the "intermediate heaven."[252] The whole experience is not all going to be parades, parties, and fireworks in a celebratory sense. It is going to have its gut-wrenching, anxiety-producing, life-shattering, and person-obliterating moments. What they all are going to need is a continuing invisible touch of love, care, and confidence by their friend and Lord through the blessed three persons of the Trinity. Jesus, in the Upper Room at the Last Supper, amidst all the angst and stress and sorrow, is giving them a touch of his hand and heart and assuring them of God's presence to calm, comfort, and console them in his passion and absence. He is communicating that that which appears to be his end, is not an ending at all. Human relationships with the divine go on. Someday they will be together again, and again, and again. Permanently separated love is not Jesus' destiny, nor is it theirs. A great truth is spoken here. With and in Jesus' love, permanent separation is anathema!

Gethsemane is the Wilderness Experience (Matthew 4:1-11; Mark 1:12,13; and Luke 4:1-13) recapitulated. In the desert, as Jesus fortified himself for his grueling three-year ministry, he faced three major temptations concerning the means, methodology, and precise ends of his divinely ordained assignment. The great temptation of his incarnation had nothing to do with Mary Magdalene or sexual activity. His great temptation was all about cross avoidance. He knew that his trials and crucifixion were going to be absolutely brutal, not only physically, but spiritually as well. The thing that seems to have terrorized him was being cut off from the love of the Father – a splitting or shredding of the Trinity, perhaps. We cannot fully understand or comprehend what being cut off from the love of the Father would be like (at least at this point in our lives, and it is my hope for the reader that they never will),

---

252   Randy Alcorn, *Heaven* (Carol Stream, Illinois: Tyndale House Publishers, Inc., 2004), 41-42, 44-45.

but for Jesus it appears to have been the focal point of his concern and anxiety as he approaches the cross. Avoidance of being made sin, and the removal of the love and presence of the Father, was something not too far from his awareness (Matthew 16:23) through the exercise of his ministry. It may be too strong to say that it haunted him, but the contemplation of what was to come may have been a constant in his life. The temptations in the wilderness dealt with whether he would cater to the social welfare needs of the people in order to gain a following; practice showmanship to dazzle the crowds; or become a political/military leader vanquishing the Romans and re-establishing a greater Davidic empire. What he chooses, as scripted, is the way of the cross. He chooses the path of humiliation and self-sacrifice as found in the prophecies of the suffering servant. Temptation aside, he knows that he can do no other. Nothing else will produce what the second Adam needs to do to rescue Eve and her children. And this rescue operation means everything!

Jesus, the person, and his life experience, is all about the relational! In fact, Jesus was (and is) super relational. This should be no surprise to us as an Augustinian and Edwardsian (the puritan, Jonathan Edwards) understanding of the Trinity screams the relational.[253] Our God is all of a relational God. Jesus, being God incarnate, is much about establishing and living relationally. Jesus developed the deepest and most personal relationships of anyone who ever lived, presumably during his pre-ministerial life in the building trades industry, and in the three years or so leading up to his passion. His relationships of which we read in the Gospels appear to be very close and very intense, so much so that these become a significant part of him. My guess is that he could not conceive of life and living without them. And so, for them and their eternal salvation, which translates into relationships that are exercised eternally, becomes that prize his work as the second Adam and the suffering servant must secure. Neither "hell or high water", as the old

---

253   John H. Gerstner, *Jonathan Edwards and God* (Philadelphia, PA: Tenth, a quarterly publication of the Philadelphia Conference on Reformed Theology and Tenth Presbyterian Church, January 1980), 53-66.

expression goes, was going to keep him from their rescue. Jesus sets his face completely toward Jerusalem and the cross as the late Bob Kelley liked to reference in seminary.[254] Regardless of what it will cost him and the horrors of it personally, physically, and spiritually, he must engage the struggle to secure the prize.

Having made a presentation on the 70th anniversary of Bastogne a few years ago, one impression that I carried away from my study was the complete determination of General George Patton, and in partic-ular, the commander of the 4th Armored Division, General Creighton Abrams. Abrams and the men of the 4th Armored Division were the spearhead of Patton's Third Army winter march and fight to relieve the surrounded 101st Airborne Division in the Battle of the Bulge. Abrams and his tank crews had to make their way through the hellish fire of the German 88s, tank destroyers, and Tigers to rescue those who refused to surrender. They took terrible casualties, but to a man were determined, regardless of the loss of life and limb, and throwing caution to the wind, to relieve the town. They succeeded, and it was the best Christmas gift the men of the beleaguered 101st ever received![255] This, and more, is the stern determination of our Christ. The rescue, by all means, and no matter the cost, had to be secured! He had to succeed!

In the Upper Room, Jesus carefully prepares the 11 for the trauma he, and they, are about to endure. The discourse reveals the depth of his love for them, and because of the intense human connection he has made with them, the rescue operation must proceed. In his self-sac-rifice, he has them very much in mind. In Gethsemane, he confronts, for a final time, the temptation to refrain from the plan that will bring the totality of hell upon him. His concern here is for the Father. In Trinitarian terms, his love for the Father is immense. This time of great spiritual angst and struggle reveals something of the depth of divine

---

254   Dr. Robert E. Kelley commented in class lectures at Pittsburgh Theological Seminary that the goal of Luke's Gospel was to get Jesus to Jerusalem. Luke's goal in Acts, according to Kelley, was to get Paul to Rome.
255   Stanley Weintraub, *11 Days in December: Christmas at the Bulge, 1944* (New York, NY: NAL Caliber, published by New American Library, a division of Penguin Group, 2006), 91, 103, 105, 108-109, 175.

love. This rescue operation of God's most precious creation must proceed for the Father is unwilling to let humanity totally flounder and sink into the abyss. In his self-sacrifice he has the Father and the Father's love for humanity very much in mind. I think that Mel Gibson portrays Gethsemane remarkably well in the "Passion", catching much of the turmoil and determination of the Christ, and the spiritual battle that swirls around and inside him. I have always remarked to people that in Gethsemane Jesus "puts his game face on". I understand that this is a rather crude expression, but I think it is true. He comes out of his time of prayer with a steely resolve, ready to face and endure the challenge, and to get it over with! To me, there almost appears to be a "step count" mentality[256] to Jesus during his passion. He faces 12 or so hours of the worst that a being can experience. With each horror that he endures and passes during his trials and crucifixion, he is one step closer to the end of this personal reign of terror which has besieged him. With each passing minute and hour, he can mentally cross off, one by one, the precise and specific horrors he will never have to experience again. Keeping his eyes, "properly double focused", on the Father and those he came to rescue from the eternal terrors he is now experiencing, he proceeds knowing he will never have to pass this way again. In so doing, he knows that neither will those whom the Father calls his own.

In the reflections of this author, there is one more aspect to which Jesus might have fixed his gaze. Perhaps he was properly triple focused! In terms of the "step count" concept of his passion, it is the opinion here that Jesus is also focused on what immediately follows the terminal moment when "it is finished!"[257] He knows that just beyond his death on the cross is the release of Paradise.[258] With the end of his self-sacrifice his human bodily anguish is over. His spiritual anguish ends as well as the breech between the Father and Son is healed instantaneously.

---

256   The author understands the concept of "step count" to mean a pre-planned organization of intended happenings that must take place in a prescribed order to render or reach the desired end. With the passage of each happening, event, or activity one gets closer to the termination of the specific action that must take place.
257   John 19:30.
258   Luke 23:43.

If as Tony Campolo has written that "heaven is a party",[259] he awaits a whole series of celebratory experiences besides whatever congratulatory circumstances exist within the Trinity. His appearance to the Old Testament saints in Sheol is the first human reactions of the triumph of his enduring work. This is followed by the shock, awe, surprise, joy, and embrace of those he ministered to and with for three years. Aside from all the emotion of love reconnecting face to face again, it had to be fun for him to see their surprised countenance and the "now I get it" understanding that followed. It must have also been a relief for him to now engage these relationships, knowing that the terrors of the coming sacrifice were no longer part of the mix. Then, following all this, is his homecoming to heaven. There is no way to truly understand this cosmic celebration, but it must far exceed those celebratory moments portrayed in the Star Wars series and in the Tales of Narnia as displayed on the silver screen. These times and expectations must have motivated him to get it over and get it done.

At the foot of the cross there is something else that helps him keep his focus. Before him is a six-hour presence that provides support, undergirding and strengthening his will and determination. Right before his eyes is very much the reason for the action he has taken. Present among those who love him are the big three: the disciple whom Jesus loved, John; Mary, his earthly mother who has borne and bears much sorrow; and the one who has become the representative of the beloved for whom the whole thing was initiated, Mary Magdalene, as the second Eve. He will not fail them now. His love transcends the fires of hell he is experiencing. Truly, his motto is "For the Father and for those whom the Father has given me!" Let us now turn and examine the text that reveals Mary Magdalene as the New Testament Eve.

---

259   Anthony Campolo, *The Kingdom of God is a Party* (Dallas, Texas: Word Publishing, 1980), 9.

14

"Could We Start Again Please!"

"Could we start again please!"

***(Andrew Lloyd Webber & Tim Rice/ Yvonne Elliman,
Jesus Christ Super Star)***

The song sung by Yvonne Elliman, "Could We Start Again Please!"
is found in the film version (not the vinyl recording) of the rock opera Jesus Christ Superstar. While the plea made in the song by Mary
Magdalene and Peter is set prior to Jesus' crucifixion, pleading with him
not to go through with it, in reality starting again is the foundation of
the action in Chapter 20:1-18 in John's Gospel. Let us take a closer look
at this text and begin to flesh out what is actually happening here. In
this chapter, and in the chapters that follow, this author will indicate
both the actions that have been missed in this poignant encounter and
why Mary Magdalene is a worthy candidate for the title *New Testament
Eve*. According to R. V. G. Tasker, chapter 20 is the eighth section of the

Gospel.[260] It is also the 20th movement found within the book.[261] Verses 1 through 29 detail the Resurrection. Verses 1 through 10, deal with the empty tomb. Verses 11-29 are known as, "The Appearances." The "Appearance to Mary Magdalene" is found in verses 11 through 18.[262]

Early on Sunday morning, following both the Sabbath and the Passover, while the sun was dawning and yet still dark, Mary Magdalene ventures to the tomb of Jesus. John's purpose in writing is to anchor the circumstances surrounding the empty tomb, the resurrected Lord, and Mary. He does not mention the other women. His purpose is to center on the importance of the Jesus' coming encounter with Mary. John communicates a great deal within 18 verses. He leaves it to the reader, however, to draw out both the import of the action and the symbolism it represents. Mary goes to the entrance of Joseph's tomb and notices the curious positioning of the large stone covering. According to the Greek word here, it is found at some distance from the rock face of this carved cavity.[263] There is no mention of the guard because they have already fled the scene. The site is vacant. Mary's statement upon her rapid flight to Peter and John is that the tomb is empty. We can assume here that she had to have entered the burial cavity and examined it (though this might be in conflict with the Matthean account) or she relied on the comments of the ladies with whom she travelled that the tomb was violated. Either way she is quick to speed away and make report! Notice the pronouns in verse 2. "They have taken the Lord out of the tomb, and we don't know where they have put him!" Mary does not presume a resurrection here despite the curious location of the stone. "They", probably means Christ's enemies – most likely the religious elite, as the Romans had surrendered the body and she knows nothing of the Saturday circumstances of attaining a Roman guard

260   R. V. G. Tasker, *The Gospel According to St. John: An Introduction and Commentary*, Tyndale New Testament Commentaries (Grand Rapids, Michigan: Wm. B. Eerdmans Publishing Co., 1980), 39-40.

261   Joseph Hopkins, "John" (lecture, Westminster College, New Wilmington, PA, January 1974).

262   Leon Morris, *The Gospel According to John*, *The New International Commentary on the New Testament* (Grand Rapids, Michigan: Wm. B. Eerdmans Publishing Co., 1979), 69.

263   Josh McDowell, *The Resurrection Factor* (San Bernardino, CA: Here's Life Publishers, Inc., 1981), 68.

and the examination of the tomb. It is doubtful that she is referring to Joseph of Arimathea for why would he remove Christ's body? The tomb is big enough to hold many bodies over time with decay and placement in ossuaries. Notice that she also employs the first-person plural, "we"! I take this as a reference to the unmentioned women that accompanied her.

Ever in competition with each other as John's writing shares in a number of personal glimpses,[264] Simon Peter and John conduct a foot race to the sepulcher. John, the writer of the gospel, makes sure that he informs his readers that he was first to arrive on the scene. At the threshold, he bends over and looks in and sees the grave clothes just lying there. He goes no further. Peter catches up with him and, typical of the personality of this disciple,[265] rushes straight forward and past John. Peter sees the strange positioning of the grave cloths and the head piece. They are arranged in a neat and orderly fashion, not haphazardly as if stripped off by grave robbers or those in a hurry to exit with the body. Peter comes to no particular conclusion from what he sees. Finally, John goes further inside the tomb to examine the contents, and he records that he reaches a conclusion, he "believes." What is his belief? At this point does he believe in the resurrection of Jesus, or is this statement indicating to us that he believed Mary's story? Verse 9 may tip us off that the three of them still did not come to the correct conclusion. Or does the pronoun "they" speak only of Peter and Mary Magdalene?

Peter and John return to their lodging. Does Mary catch up with them at the end of their brief examination of the contents lingering alone at the site following their departure, or does she come after they have departed, whether or not they passed each other on the way? The text does not provide us with the answer! Notice her position. At first, she stands outside the entrance to the tomb weeping. Then she bends over and looks inside. Such an action suggests that she has her head and part of her body inside the rock cavity, just like John. She is not

---

264   Most notably, John 21:20-23.

265   Peter has often been characterized by the word, "impetuous." "Impetuous" refers to rapid or quick action or statements without reflection, thought, or consideration of the consequences.

fully inside the crypt, but she has partially entered the interior space. This would have been necessary for Mary to adjust her eyes to see into the darkness of the cavity as daylight grew in the outside environment. Only this time, the tomb contains more than just the wrappings. John reports that Mary is greeted by two angels, one at the head of where Jesus has previously been placed and the other at his feet. The presence of the angels is interesting, if only for symbolic reasons as we will see! It should be noted that the angels were not present when Peter and John were in the crypt. The divine purpose is for Jesus to appear to Mary first, not to the disciples. The angelic appearance, however, begins to answer the question as to what happened to Jesus' body. The conversation never reaches that point, and Mary Magdalene still assumes some sort of relocation happenstance. The angels ask her, "Woman, why are you crying?" Little does Mary Magdalene know that her tears of grief, sorrow, and travail should be those of joy and ecstasy! "They have taken my Lord away, and I don't know where they have put him!" she replies. It is not the purpose and the place of the angels to answer her. God has scripted this encounter in another way so that the divine answer is delivered directly and personally. While the sepulcher has no real threshold, jam, or door frame, she is within the area wherein today we would apply these terms. Her head and at least part of her body, if not her whole body, is bent down and within the entrance. We do not know if she took a step or two forward and stood erect (if that was possible). What we do know is precisely at this moment, there is some sort of sound or disturbance outside and behind her. She leaves the entrance-way, turns around, and sees a figure standing there. A man is near her, but still at some sort of a distance away. She does not recognize that the figure she sees standing there is Jesus. Why the lack of recognition? This has been much debated. In the first place she has no anticipation of the near (three-day) Resurrection of Jesus. Her intent is all about finding a corpse. She is not looking for a living person! It may also be factual that there was something different about Jesus' resurrection body so that he was not always easily recognizable. We have strong evidence of this in Luke 24:13-35 with the encounter on the road to Emmaus. Further evidence for this might be Luke 24:37, John 21:4, Matthew 28:17. We can logically assume that Jesus is clothed, perhaps, hooded. We also know that his wounds have been healed, revealing only scar tissue of which at this moment they are mostly covered. Maybe the position of the sun coming into the garden area presented difficulty for Mary. Perhaps she cannot make identification due to the shadows of dawn in the garden. Maybe her blurry eyes have something to do with it. Whatever is the case, she thinks the personage within her eyesight is the gardener. This is the conclusion to which she instantaneously arrives, as he may be the very one who has taken the body away. He may be the one who is in possession of the corpse at this very moment! If he knows the present location of the body, and if he is in personal possession of it now, she asserts her initiative to secure it, unto her person, immediately. She wants to make sure that Jesus gets a proper burial, which has been the purpose of that day all along. Her desire to secure and take possession of the body of Jesus I find interesting. In moments she will do just that, only not of a corpse, but of a living, moving, breathing individual.

The mysterious unidentified figure then speaks to her, "Woman, why are you crying? Whom is it you are looking for?" The word for crying in Greek is best translated "weeping", referring to a heavy and tearful lament.[266] The words "looking for" are best translated by the theologically significant word "seeking".[267] As Mary responds to the mysterious stranger, she apparently turns her body back to the tomb as her point of reference. It is at this point that Jesus speaks the one revelatory word upon which the story turns. He speaks her name! The mysterious stranger knows her name! The way in which Jesus speaks her name strikes a chord of instantaneous recognition deep within her being. She does not have to play a guessing game any more concerning the identity of the man standing near her. She knows by something in the man's vocal tone and inflection that it is Jesus. Only Jesus speaks her name in such a manner! With her back turned toward him, Jesus

---

266   Klaieis comes from the Koine Greek word klaiw meaning "to weep or cry". It is employed in the New Testament to refer to a bitter lament or a vehement cry of mourning among its uses.

267   Zeteis, comes from the Koine Greek word zetew which means "seek or look for". The seeking is in order to discover or find what may be lost and secure it.

speaks her name in the most loving, caring, and revealing way. In this case "hearing is believing"!

Astonished, she whips her body around and replies. Her reply to the man is as instantaneous as her recognition of the man. "Rabboni!", she excitedly exclaims. John, at this point in the drama, provides definition of the Aramaic term, meaning "teacher". Rabboni, however, is a title which was almost exclusively employed to address God. Mary's expression and employment of the word indicates a rapid ascent in her coming to terms with Jesus' personhood. It is not that previously she denied Jesus as the incarnate God, but now Jesus' identity is fully exploding upon her heart and mind. Her response of "Rabboni" is much more than an OMG ("Oh My God") expression of shock and awe today (whether in today's culture this highly overused expression is employed correctly or illegitimately). It seems to be weighty with the idea, at least to me, that the Jesus of the Resurrection might be worshipful. Amid all the myriad of emotions and thoughts swirling within her head is the idea that Jesus might be worshipped as God is worshipped, for the one resurrected may be none other than God himself. It is believed by some that John's short and incomplete definition of "Rabboni" is meant to carry the meaning that Mary's understanding of Jesus is still incomplete. I disagree. While some fog of unknowing might be evident here, I think that Mary gets it, at least on an elementary or beginning level. What she needs is some time to digest and reflect upon the sudden circumstances she has abruptly encountered in order to advance and make concrete her understanding of this happening in real life. Jesus has now, in his Resurrection, fully demonstrated his personage. Mary is now processing what rapidly becomes a full assurance that Jesus is, in fact, the Christ, meaning God in human flesh. All of this happens with great speed in her mind (though the full implications of it may require the balance of the day). Her response, to this writer, is just as much a profession of faith as Martha at the resurrection of her brother, and Thomas in Jesus' appearance to him. She gets it! And more so, her next movement communicates that "she's got it!"

Verse 17 is a controversial verse which few have properly under-stood. Many people in my generation were steeped in the Authorized Version (KJV) of the Bible. My first Bible, given by the "Sabbath School" of the former First United Presbyterian Church of Tarentum, UPNA, (which became known as "Hillside" Presbyterian, and later, "Highview" Presbyterian, before merging with First Presbyterian of Tarentum, PCUSA) was a King James Bible. The KJV reads here, "Touch me not, for I am not yet ascended to my Father." This statement of Jesus never made sense to me. It is as if Jesus stops Mary in her tracks holding out his arm with hand raised to prohibit her approach and embrace of him. Why would not Jesus want Mary to embrace him, particularly in this highly emotionally charged moment in both of their lives? Is Jesus' new resurrected body radioactive or toxic to her? Why would Jesus prohibit Mary from touching him when he encourages demonstrations of his physicality (John 1:1) in all his subsequent appearances? In particular, he encourages Thomas to touch him, to which Thomas touches him not! While the Greek Interlinear translates the initial three-word clause, "Not me touch", the fact of the matter is that the Greek construction im-plies, according to Ken Bailey, to "stop doing something than do not do something." Ken Bailey translates the phrase as, "Stop clinging to me!"[268] The NIV translates the phrase as "Do not hold on to me." The Concise Bible Commentary translates it as "Cease touching me!"[269] The Wycliffe Bible Commentary is in agreement with Bailey that "the Greek calls for a different rendering: 'Stop clinging to me.'"[270] John Marsh writes, "The Greek here uses a present imperative with a particular form of the neg-ative, and the use indicates that an action is already in progress is to be stopped. The best way to render the imperative in English therefore is to say, 'Cease from clinging to me'".[271] Tasker also understands the verb "touch" as a present imperative "and when used as a prohibition this

268   Kenneth E. Bailey, "Leadership in the New Testament" (lecture, Pittsburgh Theological Seminary, Pittsburgh, PA, June 8-12, 1998).

269   W. K. Lowther Clarke, ed., *Concise Bible Commentary* (Aylesbury and London SPCK: Hazell, Watson, and Viney LTD, 1952), 795.

270   Everett F. Harrison, *The Wycliffe Bible Commentary* (Chicago, IL: Moody Press, 1962), 1119.

271   John Marsh, *Saint John, The Pelican New Testament Commentaries* (Hammondsworth, Middlesex, England: Penguin Books Ltd, 1968), 637.

should normally give the meaning 'stop touching me' or 'Do not touch me any more'. The right translation would therefore seem to be, 'do not cling to me' (RSV 'Do not hold me')."[272] Leon Morris writes, "This verse presents us with some problems. The first is in the words 'Touch me not'. There seems no reason why Mary should not touch Him, and indeed Matthew tells us that when the women first saw the risen Lord 'they came and took hold of his feet, and worshipped him'. Probably we should understand the Greek tense here in the strict sense. The present imperative with a negative means 'stop doing something' rather than 'do not start something'. Here it means 'stop clinging to me', and not 'Do not begin to touch me'. Evidently Mary in her joy at seeing the Lord has laid hold of him...."[273] Mary apparently has proceeded to do what many of us in an intense, intimate relationship with someone would do, she immediately lunges at Jesus, recovering the space denied her by the deadly forbidden zone, which, due to Christ's Resurrection, has evaporated. She is now holding Jesus in a full embrace. Those who have translated this passage correctly have taken two options here. Some, like Rev. W. K. Lowther Clarke of the Concise Bible Commentary, affirm that Mary has bowed herself before Jesus and is embracing his feet as the women recorded in Matthew 28:9 perform when Jesus appears to them.[274] Morris writes "Evidently Mary in her joy at seeing the Lord laid hold on Him, possibly in the same way and for the same purpose as the ladies of whom Matthew writes."[275] Marsh writes, "The calling of her name as she went away brought her swiftly round, and back to her Lord to embrace him in a clinging embrace, with the word Rabboni. This was a moment highly charged with feeling, but the word she used indicates the nature of it, for it is a word used characteristically for the deity. Imagination can picture her clasping the feet of Christ in humble adoration."[276] We cannot assume that what took place in the subsequent appearance before the women on their return trip from the sepulcher

---

272   Tasker, 225.
273   Morris, 840.
274   Clarke, 795.
275   Morris, 840.
276   Marsh, 637.

is the same here for Mary Magdalene.[277] I never asked Ken Bailey about this because I always took him to mean a full bodily embrace rather than hands touching Jesus' feet. What is interesting here is William Barclay's take on the moment. Barclay calls this story "the greatest recognition scene in all literature.... The whole story is scattered with indications of Mary's love."[278] Concerning Jesus' statement "Touch me not", Barclay writes:

(i)   The whole matter has been given a spiritual significance. It has been argued that the only real contact with Jesus does in fact come after His Ascension; that it is not the physical touch of hand to hand that is important, but the contact which comes through faith with the Risen and Ever-living Lord; that the importance is not that a body can be touched, but that spirit with spirit can meet. That is certainly true, and certainly precious, but it does not seem to be the meaning of the passage here.

(ii)   It is suggested that the Greek is really a mistranslation of an Aramaic original. Jesus of course would speak in Aramaic, and not in Greek; and what John gives us is a translation into Greek of what Jesus said. It is suggested that what Jesus really said was: "Touch me not; but before I ascend to my Father go to my brethren and say to them..." It would be as if Jesus said: "Do not spend so long in worshipping me in the joy of your new discovery. Go and tell the good news to the rest of the disciples." It may well be that here we have the explanation. The imperative in the Greek is a present imperative, and strictly speaking it ought to mean: "Stop touching me." It may be that Jesus was saying to Mary: "Don't go on clutching me selfishly to yourself. In a short time I am going back to my Father. I want you to meet my disciples as often as possible before then. Go and tell them the good news that none of the time that we and they should have together may be wasted." This may be a commandment to Mary to leave go of Jesus, not to clutch Him to herself, but to

---

277   Note the story of Martha and Mary with Jesus in John 11:20-32. Martha remains standing before Jesus, while Mary bows. The actions of the two are different. While it is clear Mary bows before Jesus, one cannot assume the same of Martha. If Martha had bowed, it would have been recorded!

278   William Barclay, *The Gospel of John, Volume 2, The Daily Study Bible Series* (Edinburgh, Scotland: The Saint Andrew Press, 1955), 312.

go and tell the blessed news to others. That would make excellent sense, and that in fact is what Mary did.

(iii)   There is one further possibility. In the other three gospels, the fear of those who suddenly recognized Jesus is always stressed. In Matthew 28:10 Jesus' words are: "Be not afraid." In Mark 16:8 the story finishes: "For they were afraid." In Luke 24:5 it is said that they were "sore afraid." In John's story as it stands there is no mention of this awe-stricken fear. Now, sometimes the eyes of the scribes who copied the manuscripts made mistakes, for the manuscripts are not easy to read. Some scholars think that what John originally wrote was not ME APTOU, Do not touch me, but, ME PTOOU, Do not be afraid. The verb PTOEIN means to flutter with fear. In that case Jesus would have said to Mary: "Don't be afraid; I haven't gone to my Father yet; I am still here with you."

Barclay thinks that the second option is the superior one![279]

The Interpreters' Bible rejects the notion that Mary Magdalene, as it was with the other women was "badly frightened." According to Interpreter's, "…Mary Magdalene has no fear at all. She is distracted and miserable, but markedly it is emphasized that she has not a trace of terror. The vision of angels in no way disturbs her. She seems not greatly interested in it. What she is seeking, what she must find, is the body of her Lord. And nothing else is of much consequence to her. If this report is accepted as authentic, then the suggestion falls. Christ does not throw words about for nothing. He does not say 'Do not be frightened' to one who was not in the least bit afraid."[280] Interpreter's also debunks the claim of Bernard that "cease clinging to me" should be translated "be not affrighted." Interpreter's claims "this has no MS support."[281]

Tasker does not directly comment on whether Mary's clinging to Jesus is one of hands clasp to feet or an embrace. He does write,

---

279   Barclay, 314-315.

280   Arthur John Gossip, *The Interpreter's Bible in Twelve Volumes: The Gospel According to St. John*, vol. 8, ed. George Arthur Buttrick (Nashville: Abingdon, 1982), 794.

281   Wilbert F. Howard, *The interpreter's Bible in Twelve Volumes: The Gospel According to St. John*, vol.8, ed. George Arthur Buttrick (Nashville: Abingdon, 1982), 794.

"When she tries to cling to her Master and keep him at her side, she is accordingly told that she must cease touching him..."[282] While no firm conclusion can be reached, it is the perspective of this writer that the scenario, setting, and circumstances between Mary in John 20:17 and the women in Matthew 28:9 is entirely different. Jesus suddenly appears in front of the women in Matthew's account. His mysterious sudden appearance and their startling recognition of one dead now alive produces anxiety and fear. It causes them to bow before him. Mary, on the other hand, is already engaged in conversation with an unidentified individual. There is no sudden appearance here or startling recognition. According to Tasker Jesus' "one-word utterance" is "charged with emotion...."[283] Mary's response to Jesus' emotional declaration of her name may be one full of mystery, but the leading reaction is one of joy. The one she seeks is right before her! Her response is a quick closing of the distance between them and enveloping him, in the same motion, in her arms. Since no statement of bowing, clasping of the feet, and prostrated worship is recorded here, the verbiage speaks to a full embrace. Those who think the revelation leads immediately to a worshipful display miss the pure human emotion and love reaction of the Magdalene for Jesus, and, I would think, of Jesus for his Mary! That which appeared to be lost is found. True, it was Jesus seeking Mary. In that regard also, in the thesis of this writing, Eve has been re-embraced. The whole scene does not portray a pure act of worship and solely an act of worship, but the excitement, delight, and awakening to reunion, reconciliation, and a vital re-connection of separated love.

Another curious thing here is the reference to the Ascension. The Greek Interlinear states the second phrase of Jesus' assertion to Mary as "for not yet have I ascended to the Father." Ken Bailey takes Jesus' words in verses 17 and 18, as this author has understood him to mean, that Jesus is not yet at the "point of permanent departure". His ascension from planet earth is certainly coming, but not yet! Implied here is the certainty of presence, visitation, and the allowance of time spent

---

282   Tasker, 221.
283   Ibid, 221.

with Mary, the disciples, and his followers before his physical change in location. It is possible that also implied in Jesus' statement is a message that the Ascension will follow his Resurrection appearances. Unlike the raising of Lazarus, Jesus will not be returning to the way of his previous life. Bailey's transliteration of verses 17 and 18 are as follows, "Stop clinging to me. There is no need for this, as I am not yet at the point of permanent departure. You will have the opportunity of seeing me.."; and/or "Stop clinging to me. I have not yet ascended to my Father, it is true. But I shall certainly do so. Tell this to my brothers!" Leon Morris recites the same exact words as I recorded from Bailey uttered in lecture, "Stop clinging to me. There is no need for this, as I am not yet at the point of permanent ascension. You will have opportunity of seeing me." The one, perhaps, quotes the other.[284] The words I heard Bailey pronounce are found in Morris' commentary. This writer does not remember and/or did not record Bailey's attribution of the transliteration, but these words appear to come directly from Morris. Morris writes, "In the message to the 'brothers' the verb 'I ascend' is in the present tense. This tense may denote further action, but if so it is with the thought either of imminence or certainty. It is the latter which is required here. We should probably accept Lagrange's suggestion that the adversative conjunction appended to 'go' applies also to 'ascend.' The words will then mean, 'Stop clinging to me. I have not yet ascended to my Father, it is true. But I shall certainly do so. Tell this to my brothers.'" [285]

I think that the action being described in verses 17 and 18 is the ending of Jesus' self-revelation to Mary Magdalene, and the initiation of his resurrection event to the rest of his followers. Verses 17 and 18 are transitional. In verses 15 and 16 Jesus reveals himself to Mary Magdalene. Recognizing Jesus, Mary rushes to embrace him. This embrace, in the opinion of this author, is a long one. It is so long that Jesus has to break it off, due to the time schedule he must keep in order to appear to many others, particularly the other women and Peter.

---

284 While note-taking captured the main tenet and even the exact words of Dr. Bailey, the memory of documentation here and proper ascription is not remembered.
285 Morris, 841.

Jesus affirms his coming ascension, but remarks to Mary that it is not imminent. He will be around for a while. He tasks Mary with the assignment to announce his bodily resurrection to his prime followers, helping to pave the way and prepare them for his visitation before the end of the day. In this Mary takes on a missional and even apostolic role. Somewhat like Paul Revere, William Dawes, Samuel Prescott, Israel Bissell, and Sybil Ludington in April of 1775, and Pheidippides of Marathon fame, Mary Magdalene is charged with the task of making a stupendous announcement. Revelation, providentially, always leads to mission! Mary, as the New Testament Eve, is the proper one to first make announcement of the divine reversal. What is divine reversal? The banishment from Eden has now been terminated. Paradise is open for business and occupation again!

We must, however, take a closer look at the ascension verbiage of John 20:17b. The NIV (New International Version) records Jesus saying, "Go instead to my brothers and tell them, 'I am returning to my Father and your Father, to my God and your God.'" Marsh emphasizes the translation "gone up" for ascending and returning.[286] Marsh comments that "the word ascend is the same one used earlier in the gospel to speak of Jesus being 'lifted up'" (John 6:62).[287] Marsh further comments about Jesus "going up" to Jerusalem to die, being "lifted up" upon the cross, and "going up" in terms of his ascension:

> The Johannine answer is that the ascension is more realistically described as the 'return to the Father', and in the normal way it would be natural to think that Jesus returned to the Father at the moment of his death. He came from the Father into the world, presumably at the moment of his birth, if any moment can be specified. Similarly, if any moment may be specified for his return to the Father it would be the moment of his death. But Jesus is saying on this day of resurrection that he has not yet ascended, i.e., in Johannine language, not yet returned to the Father. This cannot but mean that there has been purposeful delay. And it would seem that the delay has been undertaken for the

---

286   Marsh, 633.
287   Ibid, 637.

sake of establishing the necessary continuity between the earthly Jesus and the glorified Christ. What Jesus is doing and saying to Mary can be summed up thus: She is to cease from holding him, because the new relationship between the Lord and worshipper will not be one of physical contact, though it will be a real personal relationship. He has appeared to her in a form that while it was evidently different from that in which he had been known in the days of his flesh had sufficient elements in it to enable Mary to satisfy herself, and persuade others, of the identity of the Jesus who was, with the Lord who would for evermore be.[288]

Barclay's conclusion to the directive to Mary is this "...Jesus sent Mary back to the disciples with the message that what He has so often told them was not about to happen – He was on His way to His father; and Mary came with the news, 'I have seen the Lord.' In that message of Mary there is the very essence of Christianity. A Christian is essentially one who can say: 'I have seen the Lord.' Christianity does not mean knowing about Jesus; it means knowing Jesus. It does not mean arguing about Jesus; it means meeting Jesus. It means the certainty of experience that Jesus is alive."[289]

About this verse Tasker writes, "The full life that the good Shepherd has laid down for the sheep has been laid down for each separate sheep; and His resurrection life is now available for every single believer – but under conditions different from those to which Mary has hitherto been accustomed. When she tried to cling to her Master and keep Him at her side, she is accordingly told that she must cease touching Him, for the satisfaction of her desire would frustrate the ultimate purpose of the crucifixion and resurrection. Jesus suffered and rose again, in order that He might ascend to the Father, and in virtue of His finished work of Calvary intercede for all who would draw His finished work on Calvary intercede for all who would draw nigh unto God through Him. There is no record in this Gospel of the physical ascent of Christ into heaven. But the cross is often spoken of as His supreme glorification, and His death is viewed as the means of His return to His Father.

---

288 Ibid, 637-638.
289 Barclay, 316.

His being lifted up on the cross is in fact regarded as the beginning of the ascension. Jesus is therefore to be thought of as in the process of ascending to His Father when Mary meets Him. She must not therefore try to prevent Him from completing this ascent and from entering fully into His rightful inheritance. She must return to the rest of the little flock with the news that Jesus is now crowning the triumph of His earthly mission by returning to Him, whose will He has so unceasingly obeyed – His Father and their Father. But the Son of God does not return to His Father exactly as He had come forth from the Father. Having taken upon Himself human nature He goes back with that human nature, still bearing the wounds inflicted upon Him when He was 'bruised for our iniquity'. 'As life is present in His death', so 'the note of death is still to be heard in the midst of life'."[290] Tasker also points out that "the verb translated I am not ascended is in the perfect tense, and implies, "I have not yet completed my ascent.'" The second use of the word ascend, Tasker asserts, "should be taken as a continuous present 'I am in the process of ascending.'"[291]

Morris writes that "references to ascending are not completely clear." He continues, "It is not easy to see what difference the ascension could make to Mary's clinging to Jesus. Some point out that, whereas we use 'the Ascension' as a technical term, this was not so in the New Testament days." Regardless of how the word ascend is taken Morris continues, "it clearly refers to a decisive parting as Jesus returns to His Father. Part of the thought appears to be that Jesus was not simply returning to the old life. Mary was reacting as though He were. As he had not yet ascended He could appear to her, but she must not read into this a simple return to the former state of affairs. But part of the thought also will be concerned with the fact that the ascension was as yet future." As already indicated above, Morris believes the present tense of the verb "I ascend" is in reference to a future action, but one that will certainly come within a very short period of time. This conclusion Morris sums up in his transliteration, "Stop clinging to Me. I have not yet ascended to My

---

290   Tasker, 221-222.
291   Ibid, 225.

Father, it is true. But I shall certainly do so. Tell this to My brothers."[292] Concerning the word "brothers" or "brethren" here, Morris affirms that the term is a reference to his disciples, and not to his kinfolk.[293]

In similar manner, the Interpreter's Bible records the quote of Marcus Dods on this matter: "'For I have not yet ascended to my Father,' implying that this was not His permanent return to visible fellowship with His disciples, Mary, by her eagerness to seize and hold Him, showed that she considered that the....'little time' of 16:16 (John 16:16) was past, and that now He had returned to be for ever with them. Jesus checks her with the assurance that much had yet to happen before that. His disciples must at once be disabused of that misapprehension." Mary's mission, according to Arthur John Gossip, is thus engaged![294]

The conclusion of this author concerning the envelopment of Mary and Jesus in each other's arms finds its genesis in the circumstances of the Fall, and in the intense love and regard the two prime characters have for each other on Easter morning. In this chapter much exegesis and interpretation of the text has been provided. What this author thinks have been missed is the symbolism of Paradise restored and the pure human emotion and drama between the two lovers under the rising sun. In Jesus, God comes softly into another garden and re-embraces Eve and her children. Mary Magdalene is the symbol of Eve's restoration and the promised fulfillment of eternal relationship. We must not miss, however, that this encounter and embrace is a highly charged emotional moment for the two of them. The pain, ordeal, and agony of Jesus' passion is but only hours in the past. The terror and abject sorrow Mary experienced in the dark night of her soul has only been reversed a few split seconds ago. The clutching of the two is not from some sort of selfishness, but a time of extreme catharsis needed by both. The mysterious experience of Jesus in Sheol aside (Luke 23:43), this is the first physical contact Jesus has experienced since the hands placed upon him by his executioners –

---

292   Morris, 840-841.
293   Ibid, 842.
294   Gossip, 794.

and this is the first positive human fleshly contact since his arrest. If there were ever two people who needed to share in a long embrace, it is these two! Jesus only reluctantly breaks it off because he is due elsewhere. His verbiage to Mary assures her that she will soon be in his company again. He ends the embrace by assigning to her the most joyous news report of all time – He has, indeed, risen!

15

The Missing Time

"I bought a ticket to the world, but now I've come back again…. Oh, I want the truth to be known!"

(Gary Kemp/"True" by Spandau Ballet)

During my 38-year career conducting youth ministry, I always practiced, enjoyed, and shared self-deprecating humor. I repeatedly announced to the marvelous youth God permitted me with whom to minister, that I was completely void of talent. Many were the jokes at how terrible my singing had become. Many were the jokes about my inability to sing, dance, and perform certain athletic skills. Of course, this did not stop me from singing, dancing, and performing in front of, or with, the youth. My big break came when, Michael Zeiler, the Highlands High School musical director, and a youth group alumnus, asked me to perform a cameo appearance in his high school musical. I played the role of a clergyperson conducting a wedding and spoke, a whole eight or nine words. As I left the stage after the final performance, at the age of 56, I said to the play producer, Mrs. Debra Shank Lehew, "Well, this ends my first high school musical!" To which she said, "And your last high school musical!" In the musical, "The Wedding Singer", the 1983 song "True" by Spandau Ballet was performed as background music. As I listened to the music some of the words, listed above, came back to me. These words reminded me of Jesus, and I started to think about what Jesus might have been thinking and doing immediately after he walked out of (or was transported out of) the tomb. No one talks about it, but it seems to this author that there is some unaccounted time in the story and a missing Jesus. This is the time following the flight of the Roman pickets, the arrival of the women, the coming of John and Peter, and the second arrival of Mary Magdalene. How much time is involved here, I do not know, but it could not be too long. Since I believe that the Resurrection appearance to Mary Magdalene was primary and vital to the whole story of salvation history and is completely scripted, Jesus waits to appear to her first. Jesus waits to catch her alone. During this time period he cannot be too far away. Obviously, he remains in the area, allowing the women and Peter and John to discover the empty tomb before, by divine necessity, he reveals himself to Mary Magdalene. Again, this appearance to Mary Magdalene is no accident. It is in the plan!

So, what is Jesus doing as he waits for the comings and goings of the other human actors to set up his great encounter with Mary? It is the opinion of this author that Jesus is probably doing something quite human. He is in the vicinity of Joseph's garden, and presumably, the other gardens and groves adjacent to and around it. Perhaps he is walking about. Perhaps he finds a location just to be at peace, viewing the sights and sounds of the blooming colors of the morning. Perhaps he finds a place to sit down and reflect on what is now past and has transpired. It is, in part, for this very moment that he endured all the terrors of Friday past. After all the momentous events of his three-year ministry, the weeks leading up to Holy Week, the events of Thursday and Friday, and his presentation in Sheol, he finds himself, alone, for the first time. He takes some time for himself to digest the whole experience and quietly enjoy the victory and the new life he has won for God's own. Perhaps he breaks into a smile, and maybe even laughs, at the completely surprised individuals he is about to encounter. Maybe he thinks to himself, "This is going to be fun!" Fun, yes, but also highly emotionally charged as well! For Jesus there is a new sweetness in the air as he listens to the birds and feels the morning breeze caress his face, causing his hair to dance. He looks out over the expanse of land his eyes behold and he quietly contemplates the joy of his work being done.

I well remember the end of the third movie (actually "Episode VI") in the Star Wars multiple trilogy, "The Return of the Jedi". After Luke Skywalker, Han Solo, Princess Leia, and company vanquish the evil Empire's second Death Star, the victors share in a great victory celebration. Skywalker finds himself walking off for a moment by himself and quietly shares in a private quasi-spiritual moment as he reflects and revels in the hard-won victory. Only when he comes to complete terms with the cost and scope of the victory does he return to his fellow conquerors to celebrate socially. Is not that the way with us? Do not the greatest victories in life call for moments of quiet solitude to mentally, emotionally, and spiritually take it all in, come to terms with the victory, make sense of its importance, and to give thanks? Once again, I think of Mary Fahl's song, "Going Home" and the line "And I'll know what I've lost and all that I've won."[295] At times in our lives, we all need to take a time out, catch our breath, and reflect on the importance and value of certain events. I think that Jesus takes a walk in the gardens and revels in what he has won before he engages the "what next"! Jesus, as the incarnate God and the second Adam, walks in this garden not in the cool of the evening, but in the re-birth of a new day! And, he waits!

Jesus waits! Jesus is alone and waits. Let us not forget that the first Adam was also alone in a garden and was tasked with waiting as well. Both he, the first Adam, and the second Adam experience what I term

---

295   *Going Home,* sung by Mary Fahl from the album, "The Other Side of Time" was released in 2003. It is sung in the opening title sequence of Ronald F. Maxwell's 2002 film "Gods and Generals". The song was written by Mary Fahl, Byron Isaacs and Glenn Patscha. The movie's soundtrack album was composed by John Frizzell and Randy Edelman, including the song by Mary Fahl and another by Bob Dylan.

as "The Great Delay." In review, remember that Adam in Eden was probably alone for a long period of time. There was a sense that his task was great and he was in need of help. There appears also to be within him a sense of loneliness. God decides to remedy that, as God always planned it, by bringing forth Eve to Adam. Now we are in another garden with the second Adam on a rescue mission to redeem the first Adam, the first Eve, and their posterity. Mary Magdalene comes for a second time to the tomb. This time she is alone. The time is now. The staging is complete. Jesus walks into the heart of the garden. Mary Magdalene is at the tomb. The presentation is about to begin! In Eden, God presents Eve to Adam. Here, God presents himself, in Jesus, to Mary. When Eve is presented to Adam, Adam is absolutely ecstatic and overwhelmingly thrilled. Who is the person who is absolutely ecstatic and overwhelmingly thrilled in Joseph's garden? It is, of course, Mary, who spiritually and symbolically represents Eve. Jesus, as second Adam, brings to her the fulfillment of the promised salvation made millennia ago. Eve was informed that the remedy for sin would come. Mary, as the Eve in another garden, personally receives that remedy for humankind. Mary Magdalene, of whom some envision as the worst of the worst, was forgiven and made new and whole through Jesus' work of deliverance. As Eve is the representative of the initiation of sin for all of humankind, Mary now receives the grace bestowed by Jesus upon all humankind. And so, Jesus waits for Mary Magdalene, alone, just as Adam waited for the coming of Eve.

It is amazing what all is happening here! Like Adam, Jesus is a stranger in paradise. Adam was created by God outside of Eden and placed in that garden. Jesus also comes from outside the garden and is placed within. The coming of Eve becomes a new beginning for Adam. The coming of Jesus to Mary initiates a new beginning – the perfect new beginning – for the divine/human relationship. Eve's sin inaugurates the garden ban. Jesus' appearance to Mary Magdalene reverses the ban and opens up re-entry to the garden. In that Jesus stands for Adam and Mary for Eve, we have now come full circle from the events of the Fall and the prophecy of remedy in Eden. Eve and her children, represented by the New Testament Eve, Mary Magdalene, have been redeemed and the relationship with God restored. The one disgraced, cast out, and victimized by evil and sin, has now been retrieved, rescued, and restored. The garden circumstances have been reversed. Mary Magdalene, in a symbolic sense, now becomes a type of spiritual mother of all the adopted sons and daughters of God. They follow in the wake of the revelation she receives into a sinless future, as if sin had never entered the picture in the first place, and imbibe in the great reward of the eternal garden. Theologically, this eternal garden is known as the "Eschaton", which makes its appearance in the time following Christ's second physical coming to planet earth.[296]

As potentially the children, in a spiritually symbolic sense, of the New Testament Eve, we need to embrace the happenings in Joseph's garden and the significance of the empty tomb. Jesus' call to embrace him as Savior and Lord goes out to a lost and hurting world. Mary, upon seeing Jesus, runs to him. The question we all have to answer is, will we do the same?

---

296   Revelation 21 and 22.

16

"The Voice of One Calling in The Wilderness"

"I know you're out there somewhere!"

(Justin Hayward of the Moody Blues)

"One word can make a huge impact!", exclaimed a member of the Natrona Heights Presbyterian Youth Group staff in a Bible discussion one evening. How often is one little word or an expression of a simple phrase, transforming?

The Prologue of John (John 1:1-18) is much about the birth and infancy narrative of Jesus from a very different perspective. "In the beginning was the Word, and the Word was with God, and the Word was God. He was with God in the beginning. Through him all things were made; without him nothing was made that has been made. In him was life and that life was the light of men. The light shines in the darkness, but the darkness has not understood it." (John 1:1-5). The Prologue of John introduces us to the divine logos or Word. The Word, who is the agent of creation, is also the incarnate Savior. The Word represents the creative speech and action of God. The Word is God's creative power, purpose, reasoning for all things, wisdom and providence. The Word represents the eternal purpose of God who gives meaning to being, existence, and life. The Word grants an understanding of the cosmos. The Word represents the law, wisdom, and the thoughts of God prior to creation. God spoke (Genesis 1:1ff) and creation took place. The story of Jesus begins with the Word. The Word is divine being Himself and that which is begotten has the same nature of the begetter (as the Father's nature is eternal so is that of the Son). The Word is not some afterthought, but whose rightful place and home has always been with God. The Word is life and grants the first gift of creation, light. The Word brings insight and understanding to the universal struggle with which humanity endures. In the midst of that struggle, verse 14 declares, "The Word became flesh and made his dwelling among us." This speaks to the Incarnation. God puts on our human nature completely, taking up residence with us for a while. The word "dwelling" means to "tent" or "tabernacle". The remainder of verse 14 expresses to us the uniqueness of the Word made flesh in the person of Jesus the Christ. Jesus becomes the real body and physical tent of God. The good news is that into our darkness comes the Christ, shining a light that cannot be overcome and obliterated; the purpose of which is to bring comprehension and apprehension of the new life the coming of God offers.[297]

Mark's Gospel does not offer us a nativity narrative either from an earthly or divine perspective. Mark's Gospel begins with Jesus' fore-runner, John, known as the Baptist, echoing Isaiah's prophecy (Isaiah 40:3) of "a voice of one calling in the desert (wilderness....)" (Mark 1:3). Mark immediately recounts, briefly, Jesus' baptism and desert tempta-tion (Mark 1:9-13). And so, Mark begins with the movement from the desert to the garden; from the wilderness to paradise. Mark picks up the

---

297   John Marsh, *The Gospel of Saint John* (Harmondworth, Middlesex, England: Penguin Books Ltd., 1968), 93-112.

story of salvation history where Adam is left off; exiled and banished to the wilderness from the garden. It is here that Jesus begins. It is here that Jesus picks up the narrative and brings it around full circle. As the story progresses to its completion, we see the impact of Christ's calling upon people. In the four Gospel accounts, the reader experiences the tremendous power of Jesus' words, declarations, and even the employment of one word that "can make a huge impact."

What is in a name? Our name is much our identity. In reflection upon my full name it testifies to family history down through many generations all the way back to the Perth and Dundee area of Scotland, and honors an individual, though outside our family genetic line, who acted as a savior type figure for some of my ancestors.[298] My wife's name is Laurie. She hates it when she is referred to, or her name is pronounced as, Lori. Laurie loved my father who always pronounced her name properly and also spoke the correct inflection. I find myself chastised by her when I pronounce her name, or the first syllable of her name, in a lazy manner, "Lor" instead of "Laur"! Jesus' exclamation of Mary Magdalene's name, as recorded in John 20:16, must have had some unique character to it which revealed for Mary the identity of the mysterious stranger with whom she was engaged in conversation. This, however, should not come as a surprise to the reader. Not only was there something in the way Jesus spoke her name that connected voice to identity, but also what John records about the Good Shepherd in John 10:1-18, 27-29. John 10 informs us of Jesus' final recorded public address. It represents the 14th movement and seventh discourse in John's Gospel. The Good Shepherd imagery of which Jesus speaks picks up the Old Testament relationship between God and God's people – the image of shepherd and flock. Jesus chastises the Pharisees here for being bogus shepherds and the spiritually blind leaders of Israel. Jesus, the Good Shepherd, calls out and draws out his own. Jesus knows them by name and leads them out of the wilderness darkness. The sheep follow the Good Shepherd because they know his voice. In knowing the good shepherd's voice, they will never follow another. Mary Magdalene knew

---

298   His name was Cameron,

the voice of her leader, Lord, and guiding light. Note what Jesus says in John 10:27, "My sheep listen to my voice; I know them, and they follow me." Notice what he says next and apply it to Jesus' encounter with Mary Magdalene at the tomb, "I give them eternal life, and they shall never perish; no one can snatch them out of my hand." (John 10:28).

Jesus' exclamation of Mary's name is all about comprehension and apprehension. Mary's spoken name is weighty with meaning as we shall see. This moment in salvation history reminds me greatly of a similar incident in Jesus' life just two or three weeks prior that is also recorded in the Gospel of John.

The raising of Lazarus in John 11:1-57 is a significant event which prompts Jesus' enemies to speed up their movement to eliminate him. It is also the most important "sign" of his divinity in the Gospel of John leading up to his ultimate "sign", his own resurrection.[299] In the opinion of this author, it foreshadows the meaning of Jesus' great encounter with Mary Magdalene on Easter morning. Chapter 11 in John's Gospel is the 15th movement in the book, is the seventh sign, and contains, by my count, the ninth and greatest "I am" statement.[300] Lazarus, Martha, and Mary of Bethany are among Jesus' greatest supporters and within his circle of best friends. The name Lazarus means, appropriately, "God helps". Lazarus becomes gravely ill. The sisters send word to Jesus that their brother is sick. This is a plea for Jesus to come and help. By the time Jesus receives the news of Lazarus' illness, he already is aware of the fact that Lazarus is dead. Death, however, does not take Lazarus out of the sphere of the operation of God's power and grace. This pow-

---

299   There are 9 "signs" which point to God at work in the Christ and also speak of Jesus' divinity in the Gospel of John. They are: the changing of water into wine at Cana in Galilee (John 2:1-11); the healing of the official's son (John 4:41-54); the healing of the lame man (John 5:1-18); the feeding of the 5000 (John 6:1-15); walking on water (John 6:16-24); the healing of a man born blind (John 9:1-41); the raising of Lazarus (John 11:1-44); the miraculous catch of fish (John 21:1-14); and the resurrection of Jesus himself which is the greatest and ultimate sign (John 20:1-31).
300   This author counts 15 "I am" (ego eimi) statements in the Bible. They include: the Messiah (John 4:26), Bread of Life (John 6:35); From Above (John 8:58); Light of the World (John 8:12 and 9:5); The Door (John 10:7); Good Shepherd (John 10:11); Son of God (John 10:36); Resurrection and Life (John 11:25); Lord and Master (John 13:13); The Way, Truth, and Life (John 14:6); True Vine (John 15:1); Alpha and Omega (Revelation 1:8; 21:6; 22:13); First and the Last (Revelation 1:17); the Living One (Revelation 1:18); and Beginning and End (Revelation 2:6; 22:13).

er and grace also flows through Jesus. In what appears to be an act of callousness, Jesus remains in his present location for two more days. In essence, Jesus is employing Lazarus in ministry for a great demonstration of God's love, grace, mercy, and power. Some might think that Lazarus is being abused by Jesus. The truth of the matter with Lazarus, as it is with all those whom God calls to acts of ministry and service, is that God's employment of human agents is for a number of great divine purposes and reaps for those who heed the call much blessing. The plan is to save Lazarus from his temporal death. The ultimate plan is to save Lazarus from eternal and spiritual death. Lazarus has "fallen asleep", which in Greek is a reference to his death. In Jesus, death, while an enemy of humankind, presents no real danger to one of God's own. The real danger presented here is to die without knowing or owning a relationship with God, through the person of the Christ. In the account, Jesus finally clears the air with the 12 and notes that Lazarus' death is a gift that will deepen their belief in his person and power.

According to Jewish culture, the soul of an individual who dies remains in a state of suspended animation and does not depart the body until after three days.[301] Jesus enters the scene in Bethany on the fourth day. It is more than obvious that Jesus, in his grand demonstration, is communicating to all the witnesses that Lazarus' return to life is a true resurrection, and not just a resuscitation. Jesus is Lord of all life and death. Raising a person back to life is obviously impressive, but a greater demonstration is to come. Self-resurrection will capitalize the title, "LORD OF ALL LIFE AND DEATH!" This is the greatest sign of deity of which Mary Magdalene is the first to sample and witness.

Martha, being the eldest of the sisters, is the prime individual in the household to conduct the responsibilities of hospitality. When she hears, however, of Jesus' approach, she sallies forth to meet him. Martha expresses a deep and concrete faith in Jesus in verse 21, but perhaps her faith is limited to the events of this sphere of operation only. Verse 22 must be compared to verse 39, wherein Martha appears to make a state-

---

301   Wilbert F. Howard, *The Interpreter's Bible in Twelve Volumes: The Gospel According to Saint John*, vol. 8, ed. George Arthur Buttrick (Nashville: Abingdon, 1982), 642.

ment that Lazarus is beyond restoration as decomposition of the body has already set in.[302] When Jesus responds in verse 23 that Martha's brother will rise again, Martha affirms her faith in the coming bodily resurrection (resurrection in the Jewish culture was always physical and not simply a soulish or spiritual occurrence)[303] in the last day.[304] Jesus then makes presentation of the greatest "ego eimi" ("I am" statement of divinity) in John's writings. "I am the resurrection and the life. He who believes in me will live, even though he dies; and whoever lives and believes in me will never die. Do you believe this?"[305] The declaration Jesus makes to Martha is a startling one in the Jewish culture. Jesus not just declares resurrection and life, he is the actor who performs it in and of and through himself. In response in verse 27, Martha makes one of the three or four greatest Christological statements in the Gospels.[306] "Yes, Lord. I believe that you are the Christ, the Son of God, who has (is coming) come into the world." The Greek here (note above in parentheses) indicates a continuous coming of Christ into and upon the world. In other words, Jesus is still in the process of his revelatory work and action, continually making an impact on this sphere. Martha's profession of faith here is a high affirmation and sets the groundwork to properly understand not only what is about to take place with her brother but, in days, what is about to happen to Jesus as well. Mary comes next, repeating Martha's words and falling at Jesus' feet. She perhaps is expressing not only sorrow at the loss of her brother and relief that Jesus is now present to help and comfort but also engaging in an act of worship.

The title, "the Jews" noted several times in the story can mean those who doubted Jesus' person, the enemies of Jesus who were present, and professional mourners.[307] Context is important in this chapter to make possible identification of which group is meant. When Jesus (verse 33) sees Mary shedding tears, and the professional mourners, who came

---

302   Howard, 642.
303   Walter Martin, *Essential Christianity* (Santa Ana, CA: Vision House, 1962), 60-64.
304   Howard, 643.
305   John 11:25-26.
306   Peter: Matthew 16:15; Mark 8:29; Luke 9:20, and Thomas: John 20:28.
307   Leon Morris, *The Gospel According to John, The New International Commentary on the New Testament* (Grand Rapids, Michigan: Wm. B. Eerdmans Publishing Co., 1979), 547, 562-564.

along with her to meet Jesus prior to entry to the town and the dwelling, shedding tears as well, he is "deeply moved in spirit and troubled." The phrase can be understood that Jesus "groaned" and/or was in the rage of a deep anger. His disquieted, and even resentful, spirit here speaks volumes concerning the nature of our God. Present in this passage are many possible reasons as to the anger of Jesus. He may be angry at those who doubt his abilities as we see in verse 37. Many might have supposed that his powers, which were known to be great, were limited. It is the opinion of many that Jesus reveals the "paracleting" nature of his divine/human personage here. His sympathy for the sorrow and plight of his friends is great. As they sorrow and weep, he feels their pain and anguish even though he knows the outcome his coming work will secure. He cannot help but be touched deeply by it. Perhaps his anger is targeted at the fact of death itself and what sin has wrought from Eden to the present. Maybe he is contemplating his own death and the anguish it will cause for the many who witness it. Another possibility is the fact that he is wrenching Lazarus out of Paradise. The question remains: Was this resurrection a positive thing for Lazarus, personally? There is a tradition in the Christian Church that Lazarus, experiencing "Paradise" or "Abraham's Bosom" as the saintly location and state of Sheol was known, lived a melancholy life until the end of his life whether by natural causes or his murder by the enemies of the Christian movement. There is some evidence that he fled Palestine due to persecution and ministered elsewhere in the Mediterranean region for many decades.[308]

In verse 34, Jesus asks for the location of the grave site. Verse 35, which is often mentioned as the shortest verse in the Bible, is also one of the most powerful – "Jesus wept." The Greek word employed here is a different word than previously used. While Martha and Mary's crying might have been a quiet sobbing, here Jesus is represented as wailing. Jesus' love is richly demonstrated here. Jesus is an action agent. He moves not only to deal with the circumstances of death

---

308   William Steuart McBirnie, *The Search for the Twelve Apostles* (Wheaton, Illinois: Tyndale House Publishers, 1973), 273-279.

in this story, but also foreshadowing his coming work that will ultimately make death obsolete.

Verse 38 repeats Jesus' emotional and personal state as he takes full command of the situation initiating a gift of divine grace. His actions appear to be much like a superhero ready to engage the enemy. Engaging the enemy, he does (1 Corinthians 15:26)! Jesus commands the removal of stone covering the entrance to the cave tomb (verse 39). Jesus then looks up,[309] speaking to the Father so that people might make proper identification with his person. In verse 43 he speaks the quickening word, "Lazarus, come out!" The action taking place here is not a set up or a faked performance. It is not an action of the sleight of hand. It is not the work of a magician or a wizard pronouncing some incantation. Neither is he breaking or casting a spell. The dead man hears the voice of Jesus and is restored to life both physically and spiritually. As many here have noted, there is a miracle within the miracle. The main miracle here is not that Lazarus comes back to physical life, but that he hears the voice of the Son of God and lives. This too, should not be lost when thinking about Jesus' one-word proclamation, "Mary!"[310]

The formerly deceased manages to come out of the tomb bearing the wrappings of Jewish embalmment. Jesus commands attendants to remove the strips of linen and the head cloth, and Lazarus is restored to his family, friends, and associates.

Jesus calls his own to new life. His call went out to Lazarus in a very dramatic way. His call went out also to Mary Magdalene in a way that was even more dramatic and meaningful. In the case of Lazarus, and also in the case of Mary Magdalene, the affirmation of John, chapter 10 is true; God's own know the voice of the Good Shepherd and to that voice they respond![311] What is in a name? When it comes to Jesus' interaction and relationship with us, much!

---

309 The Jews practiced many prayer positions. Many of these can be revealed in the Parable of the Pharisee and the Tax Collector in Luke 18:9-14 and in the story of Jehoshaphat in 2 Chronicles 20. Note that Ken Bailey makes reference to the "accepted posture for prayer in the Temple in his books, *Jesus through Middle Eastern Eyes*, on page 348.
310 John 20:16.
311 John 10:4, 27.

17

"Up from The Grave 'She' Arose"

"Once upon a time. Once when you were mine.... Once upon a time in your wildest dreams!"

(Justin Hayward of the Moody Blues)

We now come to one of the most enlightening concepts I advance to you concerning Mary Magdalene and the events of Resurrection morning. It is my assertion that the Bible is a book of themes that are set out primarily in the first three chapters of Genesis and rake through its 66 books, culminating in the last three chapters of Revelation. Whoever stated that the "Bible has bookends" is certainly correct. One must understand the thematic nature of the book in order to glean its interpretive material.

Both Jesus and Mary Magdalene are at the epicenter of the great themes of the Word as they play out in the Passion and Resurrection of the Christ. Mary is at the cross and witnesses the death of Jesus. As

I stated above this is very significant. She, whom I have termed as the New Testament Eve, is watching "the heel being bitten and the head being crushed" (Genesis 3:15). The morning of the Resurrection, Jesus, like the Spirit in the creation story (Genesis 1:1,2), is "hovering" in and around Joseph's garden, walking in the cool of the morning. In terms of Resurrection morning, I have noted in passing comments by people, including both clergy and laity, concerning the chaos evident that morning. There is, however, no chaos with the Christ. Jesus is always in control and now he is ready to demonstrate, first to Mary Magdalene and then to others, that the chaos wrought in Eden is over. He is now ready to raise up humanity above all the chaos of death, hell, sin, and Satan, that we have brought upon ourselves.

Was the tomb where Jesus' body was laid empty? The answer is no! We have already identified that it was occupied by graveclothes and an angel or two. From time to time, it was also occupied by human visitors. The angels were visitors to the tomb. John and Peter went into the tomb. Perhaps some of the women entered its narrow confines. Most assuredly the authorities examined the internals of the tomb later that day. The tomb was never completely empty. Many people came and entered into it, looking around this carved edifice. There is much here that I think is significant. Christ came not to leave us empty but to occupy. The word *occupy* means to take possession of; to hold possession of; to take up; to fill up. Adam and Eve were the only humans of the Adamic line who originated in a state known as original righteousness. From the beginning, they had a relationship with God and knew little, if anything else (Adam, who was created outside the garden would have some limited knowledge of reality beyond Eden). As we have seen, they became alienated from God through their own choice. From that time on, all their descendants, that is us, are born in what is known as a state of original sin. In part, that means that we are born outside of a relationship with God. In reading the late Abie Abraham's books on the situation of the American soldiers during the Death March and death camps in the Philippines during World War II, Tech. Sgt. (and Butler, Pa. native) Abraham records the observations of his fellow American GI's, noting that something is very wrong with humankind, this world, and people.[312] What is wrong is that we are created for a relationship with God Almighty. Unless we are "occupied" by the Spirit of God, a vacuum exists in our lives. Everyone notices and is aware of the vacuum. We all know that something is just not right! People attempt to fill this vacuum with many things, all of which are harmful and self-destructive. Only God can satisfy the human spirit. We all have a hole in our lives that only God can fill. Ultimately, we will have no peace or find rest unto our souls unless we find our home in God.

The Resurrection appearances of Christ were from an empty tomb in order to occupy an empty soul. This occupation begins with Mary Magdalene. This is part of what the encounter between Jesus and the Magdalene was all about! In one of the most tender moments in the Bible, the appearance of Jesus to Mary displays both relationship and occupation. From that moment on, no one who truly encounters the resurrected Christ is ever the same again. This is what God, in the person of Jesus, has come to do in the lives of His own – to occupy, to take up residence with us, to allow us to experience the fullness of the "with me" God forever. Jesus moves from the empty tomb to the occupied soul!

The tomb, however, is not empty. Jesus rises and leaves the tomb. There is, however, another resurrection that takes place. In the text of John 20:10-18 a second resurrection occurs on Easter morning. Notice in the text the one who is outside the tomb and the one who is inside the tomb! The one outside the tomb and at a little distance from the sepulcher is Jesus. It is the second Adam's purpose to engage an encounter with Mary Magdalene and to bring her up from the grave. The one who is in the grave – the one who is entombed is Mary. The symbolism speaks to this writer that Mary Magdalene, who represents the second

---

312   Abie Abraham wrote two books about his experiences as a POW on Bataan in the Philippines, the "Death March", and the sufferings at Camp O'Donnell, Cabanatuan, and Bilibid Prison. His books are titled: *Ghost of Bataan Speaks*, (Greenville, PA: Beaver Pond Publishing, 1971); and *Oh, God, Where Are You?* (New York, NY: Vantage Press, Inc., 1997). Please note pages 130, 168, 175, and 300 of this second book. Both books must be read in their entirety to capture the real depth of human depravity, the essence of human hope and willingness to believe in God and goodness amid circumstances akin to hell, and the remarkable spirit of a Godly man.

Eve, is now to be delivered from the curse of her sin. She is raised from death to life! Eden's folly has now come full circle, and the hope of the ages is about to be fulfilled. The circumstances that fell upon Eve have been lifted, and the realization of that is now to be demonstrated. The death Eve's transgression has wrought is now to be fully reversed. It is Mary Magdalene who now comes out of, or from, the tomb. By bending over and looking in, she is physically within the confines of the grave. By speaking her name, Jesus is calling her, like Lazarus, to come out and come forward. There stands Jesus, fully clothed in the righteousness of God, calling forth Mary, to wrap His righteousness around her. In calling Mary out of the clutches of death, he raises her to the reality of new life that his work of salvation has wrought. She, representing Eve, is now clothed with new life. The nakedness of death is over. In Jesus, Mary and all of God's spiritually adopted children that she represents are now clothed in new life as well. Jesus rose from the dead, and now brings Mary out from the tomb. She, and all of Christ's own, are now raised up to eternal life.

This moment for Mary had to have come as a complete shock and a tremendous surprise. In the opinion of this writer this has to be the most shocking and startling surprise in human history. Jesus is alive and has conquered death, hell, sin, and Satan. The revelation of this is, however, not the "out-resurrection" (Philippians 3:11) of Jesus himself, but that of Mary departing the grave! "Up from the grave" Mary arises. Eve has been forgiven, rescued, and restored. The paradise that once was lost has been found once more! Terminal life, has now become eternal once more.

18

The Marriage of Jesus and Mary Magdalene:

It's Not What You Think!

> "Never gonna give you up. Never gonna let you down. Never gonna run around and desert you. Never gonna make you cry. Never gonna say goodbye. Never gonna tell a lie and hurt you."
>
> ***(Stock Aitken Waterman/Rick Astley)***

There has long been speculation that Mary Magdalene and Jesus were involved in an intense love affair. Our culture, throughout my lifetime, has suggested a boyfriend/girlfriend link between the two often involving some sort of illicit sexual physical contact if not outright marriage. The fact of the matter is that these suggestions and assertions in our culture are correct, but not in the way advertised. Mary Magdalene is a profound character in the Bible. She is, in the estimation of this author, one of the top five personages depicted in Scripture as previously advanced. The story of salvation in the Bible begins with two human characters and ends with two human characters. Mary Magdalene represents Eve in Joseph's garden. Once more the story revolves around two gardens and two people in each garden. We have the first Adam and Eve, and we have a garden with a second Adam. The second Adam needs a second Eve to complete the pattern of the story. It seems to this author that one cannot have a second Adam without a second Eve. Mary Magdalene becomes the second Eve. She is the redeemed and restored Eve. Jesus, upon the completion of his work to accomplish what the first Adam failed to secure, sacrifices himself to save both the first Adam and the first Eve. In an astounding way, this is demonstrated in the Resurrection by Jesus coming back to the tomb and bringing forth, out of the subterranean edifice, Mary Magdalene. This is a highly symbolic moment in salvation history which has been missed by the Christian Church. In the first Resurrection appearance, Jesus has a date to bring Eve forth from the grave of death and wash away, through the mercy, forgiveness, and grace of God, her sins (both original and actual). The sentence of death for her sin has been satisfied and Eve has been justified! Mary Magdalene, as potentially Jesus' best female friend (perhaps, best friend, period!), with her background of imprisonment of spirit, her role in his life and ministry, and her sheer delight in her new estate, is the perfect candidate to play this role. Banished from Eden, angels guarded against re-entry.[313] At Joseph's tomb, angels (cherubim) are present and do not bar the way from walking back into another garden.[314] Eve emerges from the death sentence and rushes into the embrace, once more, of Adam. A second Adam demands a bride, and Mary Magdalene completes the story as the second Eve. Keeping the parallelism of the story, you cannot have a second Adam without a second Eve. The "relationship of one" has now come full circle with eternal benefits which follow in the train, as we will soon explore. Mary Magdalene is the bride of Christ. This author suggests that she is the first and principal member of the great New Testament theme of the Church

---

313   Genesis 3:24.
314   John 20:12; Matthew 28:2-7; Mark 16:5; Luke 24:4-7.

as the bride of Christ.[315] For after all, are not all who believe and have found faith in Christ the spiritual children of the second Eve? Do not all the redeemed follow in her wake? Yes, Jesus and Mary Magdalene were a real item, but it is not as some think. What has been missed in the back and forth debate about their persons and relationship is the middle ground. What the New Testament presents is a marriage, but one only symbolic in nature. It is the opinion of this author that all the speculation about the two has blinded people to what really has taken place in Joseph's Garden and the mastery of the universe's great story weaver. Humanity has missed what the late Paul Harvey used to call, "the rest of the story!" One wonders how we could have missed it! The "rest of the story" for the five principal people of the Bible, and by extension for us all, is portrayed as of first order on Resurrection Day. The whole rationale behind the set up and playing out of the first Resurrection appearance is "all about Eve." The movement of Mary Magdalene coming from the tomb and into the arms of Jesus speaks volumes and says it all! In Joseph's garden, Jesus, the groom, comes for his bride!

We should not be surprised by this, especially in the Gospel of John, considering how the Jewish wedding scene ranks as a significant component in the story of Jesus as the "with-me God". Does not Jesus' public ministry, as portrayed in John, begin with the wedding celebration at Cana in Galilee?

According to the late John Marsh, John 2:1-11 represents the third movement in John's Gospel. The passage, interestingly enough, begins with the statement of a wedding taking place on the "third day". Marsh recognizes and believes that this is no accidental or coincidental statement.[316] He believes it is figurative and points to the work of the Messiah and his coming Resurrection. Marsh also believes that the third day is the day of marrying a virgin.[317] John Marsh and Tony Campolo, among others, affirm the wedding celebration as a reference to the Kingdom of

---

315   Ephesians 5:21-33; Revelation 19:7; John 14:1-6; Matthew 25:1-13.

316   John Marsh, *The Gospel of Saint John* (Harmondworth, Middlesex, England: Penguin Books Ltd., 1968), 141-143.

317   Marsh, 148.

God and is an earthly reflection of the heavenly celebration, including the coming "feast of the Lamb." The Jewish wedding celebration goes on for several days and is the most joyous occasion celebrated, helping to break up the dull village life experience for many. As Tony Campolo points out, Jesus utilizes the wedding celebration as the best image he can employ of "the party" that is heaven.[318] We discover, in verse 3, that the wine has run out. The failure of not stockpiling and providing enough wine for the lengthy celebration is a huge failure in terms of hospitality and a terrible social embarrassment for the host. Marsh also interprets the failure of the wine to refer to the former divine communion with Israel which has now run out.[319] There is apparently nothing the host can do to save himself and the party at this juncture, and so Jesus' mother, Mary, hints in conversation with Jesus that they need his help. Jesus is not yet ready to inaugurate his ministry which ultimately reveals himself as "the Lamb of God which takes away the sin of the world." While his mother's concern and his primary concern are not the same, he sees her immediate anxiety and the dilemma of the host and moves to remedy the situation. Marsh writes that the 6 stone jars employed in this, Jesus' first sign of divinity in the Gospel of John, symbolically represent the inadequacy of Jewish religious rites--six, being less than seven, the perfect number![320] Jesus tells the servants of the host to fill six empty jars standing nearby, used to contain water for ceremonial purification, to the brim with water. They do so! Then Jesus tells them to take a sample of the contents to the master of the banquet. The master of the banquet tastes the water in which Jesus had turned into wine and commends the bridegroom for serving the quality wine, not at the beginning of the feast, but enhancing the feast as it continues. Neither of them knew about Jesus' act of transformation. Symbolically, according to Marsh, Jesus is the bridegroom whose work is going to transform, not water into wine, but people from sin to salvation.[321]

318   Tony Campolo, *The Kingdom of God is a Party* (Dallas, Texas: Word Publishing, 1990), 9, 28-29, 36.
319   Marsh, 144-148.
320   Marsh, 145.
321   Marsh, 146-148.

Jesus, as the second Adam, comes for his bride, to transform her from the death of sin to the life of salvation. Much more can be referenced here through the writings of many commentators, but the next time the Jewish wedding scene appears in the Gospel of John is in the all-important "farewell discourses"[322] of Jesus, John 14:1-7.

These seven verses form one of the most famous and beloved passages in the entire Bible. It is referenced and read many times and is the text for many sermons and funeral meditations. There are a number of Biblical themes which intersect in this pericope, including, but not exclusive of: the quest for a permanent residence; the journey through life accompanied by the Good Shepherd; the coming of the groom for his bride; and the celebration that is heaven.

The beginning of John 14 picks up the conversation in the Upper Room following Jesus' predictions of Judas' betrayal and Peter's denial. The eleven are intently listening to Jesus as he begins to speak to them about his departure. They are confused and mystified trying to make sense of the rapid pace of information Jesus is sharing with them. They are anxious and far from relaxed and tranquil. Jesus calls upon them to abandon themselves to a state of complete confidence in God and in himself.

The quest for a home is one of the major themes in the Bible. Humanity was banished from its first home in Eden. It could be understood that all humanity is homeless due to our exile from Eden! It is at this point that the theme of journey is introduced in the Bible as God's people strive for a return to paradise. Much of these dual themes of a quest for a home and the journey to find it are inaugurated with Abraham in Genesis 12. Suffice it to say, that as the Bible moves through this quest for a physical abode granting complete "shalom", there develops within its pages a sense of a spiritual quest as well. We should not be surprised at this development for it revolves ultimately around the reason for our creation – relationship with God. The quest for a permanent abode becomes a spiritual quest in the Bible. A permanent home is longed for as we come to understand and wrestle with this

---

322   John 13:1-17:26.

impermanent world. We come to desire an incorruptible home and one that is not tarnished by earthly demise and the ravages of time. We want a home that lasts forever. Jesus, it seems to me, spoke often about our quest, for it was his quest as well. As God incarnate, it appears that he longed to return to the Father's abode. As the Son of God, he came right to where we live, joining us and leading us in this quest.[323] John 14 becomes one of the most revealing texts about finding our way home again. As with much of the Bible, this passage has a depth of meaning to it often unknown to many people.

"In my Father's house are many rooms", says Jesus as recorded in verse 2. In that era of culture in Palestine, when a man took a wife, often a new habitation was constructed adjacent to or near the family of origin. Frequently the groom would construct a new dwelling connected to or right by, if possible, his father's house. Many of the Palestinian houses were set around an open courtyard known as an "insula."[324] In this courtyard the family would cook and prepare meals in the open air.[325] Here they would often dine, play, accomplish chores, ply their trade, share story time together, celebrate, and converse. It was a place of celebration, joy, and, at times, feasting. The space could also be a place of beauty (to recapture a sense of paradise), rest, and repose. On all sides of the courtyard, housing complexes would rise as it was the son's duty, upon engagement and marriage, to construct an addition so that eventually a whole series of dwellings would encompass this interior place.

When two individuals were married in those days there existed an entire procedure containing several parts or processes that had to be followed. Information about this is readily available in book form and online. What this author is suggesting is a reasonable outline of the

---

323 John 1:14.

324 The word, *insula*, is Latin for "island." In architecture it is a group of separate dwellings, or connected dwellings. In terms of Palestinian housing these dwellings tended to wrap around a courtyard. There is a significant architectural difference when employing the term to refer to Roman buildings.

325 Msgr. Charles Pope, "What Were Typical Homes Like in Jesus' Time?", *Community in Mission, WordPress* (March 21, 2017), blog.adw.org/2017/03houses-like-time-Jesus (accessed April 15, 2019).

events. When it came to the engagement of a young man and a young woman, often as young as 12 or 13, the families of the potential bride and groom would initiate the betrothal.[326] The young man may make his preference of a particular young lady as a wife known to his parents. His parents may, or may not, agree! The prospective bridegroom would then go from his father's house to the home of the prospective bride. At this time, a negotiation would be engaged with the father of the young woman and a specific price (mohar) would be determined that he, the groom, must pay to purchase the bride. Once the bridegroom paid the price or agreed to pay a certain price over a specific period of time, depending upon the circumstances and whether or not he had the cash on hand, things could proceed. This payment was known as the "bride's price". Its purpose was to compensate her parents for the cost of her care in raising her, to compensate them for her value to the family in terms of her departure, to provide contingencies for her in case of the young man's demise or other complications, and as an expression by the young man as to the value of his affection for her. All of this was to be part of the "ketubah" or marriage agreement or covenant. This agreement was a binding contract. "Ketubah" literally means "written". It includes the groom's obligations to the young woman to provide for her, care for her, to be loyal to her, and to honor her. Once agreed upon the bride was declared to be set apart or consecrated exclusively for her prospective groom. A symbolic action reflecting this agreement was the pouring and drinking from a cup of wine in which both partook. The young man would pour wine into a cup and present it to the young lady. If she agreed to accept the proposal, she would drink from the cup. This cup represented the covenant. It was a blood covenant. If she drinks from the cup, she is announcing her acceptance of the young man and his proposal. At this point, they would be betrothed.[327] To summarize, mutual promises were made by the contracting parties before witnesses

---

326   E. Cockrell and Carmen Puscas, "Ancient Jewish Wedding Customs and Jesus Christ, His Bride, the Church," *Rapture Bible Truth* (2014). https://www.rapturebibletruth.com/ancient-Jewish-wedding-customs (accessed 4/15/2019).

327   "Jewish Wedding Customs and their Place in Jesus' Teachings," *Wildolive* (February 16, 2013). www.wildolive.co.uk/weddings.htm (accessed 4/15/2019).

at a betrothal ceremony, and a benediction is pronounced. At this point, the young man gifts his bride and prepares to take his leave. Before going, the groom announces that he is going away to prepare a place for her and that he will return for her when everything is proper and ready. The bride, on her part, was to make herself ready for the groom's return. She was to keep herself pure and make herself as beautiful for the groom as possible. During this time, she would wear a veil to show to everyone in that society that she was spoken for ("purchased with a price"). It would be customary for her to keep a lamp, the veil, the wedding clothes, and other implements needed for the marriage, beside her bed.[328] Her attendants would also be prepared in waiting and have a ready supply of oil for their lamps.[329] This is portrayed in the Parable of the Ten Virgins in Matthew 25:1-13. During this time, the couple would not live together or engage in the "act of marriage". It was understood, however, that their union was real and could only be broken by an act or decree of divorce. Infidelity on the part of either party was considered adultery.

The usual practice at this stage of the process was for the young man to go to his father's house and build a dwelling (the honeymoon room) for their lodging adjacent to or near the father's dwelling. This dwelling is symbolized by the "Chuppah" or canopy characteristic of Jewish weddings. The son, wanting to consummate the agreement, might be in a hurry to finish the house. He was not permitted to go and collect his bride until the father indicated that all was prepared and the house finished. If people inquired as to the date of the wedding, all the young man could do was indicate that his father only knew the time frame! Usually the time frame for the betrothal was around one year.[330]

The parable of the Ten Virgins or Bridesmaids is important here. It is the first of three parables of judgment included in Matthew 25, along with the Parable of the Talents in verses 14 through 30, and the parable of the Sheep and Goats in verses 31 through 46. The bridegroom

---

328   Ibid.
329   Ibid.
330   Ibid.

in the story represents Jesus. This parable describes his return. In the prophets, we learn that God pictures himself as the husband of Israel. We find this in the minor prophet Hosea, in chapters 2 through 4, but particularly in Hosea 2:19 and 20. In terms of the major prophets, we find this designation in Isaiah 54: 1-8 and in chapter 62. In the Gospels we find Jesus as the bridegroom of the Church in Matthew 9:15, Mark 2:19, 20, and John 3:27-30. The Church as the bride of Christ is stated in Ephesians 5:25-32. In this parable of the Ten Virgins the bridegroom and his friends go in grand procession to the bride's house. This usually occurred around dusk. They would carry torches or lamps. The lamps would contain a small oil tank and wick. If the light were a torch it would be a stick with a rag soaked in oil. Both could require either refilling or re-soaking. The torches acted like wedding invitations. Without a torch, it was assumed that one was attempting to "crash" the wedding or attempting entry for other nefarious purposes. Five of the bridesmaids were properly prepared. Five were not! When the groom arrives at an unanticipated time, the five who were unprepared are refused entry.[331]

The text in John goes on! When the dwelling was ready, the marriage could proceed. Granted permission by the father, the bridegroom, with his friends accompanying him, would go to the location of the bride's house. As they made their way in this torch light processional they would announce their coming, with a shout and often with the blowing of a trumpet (shofar – an ancient musical instrument which was usually a ram's horn). This, of course, was to announce to the bride and her maidens to get ready. The groom would then gather his bride. In a grand processional, he would take her to the prepared place. It was to the father's house they would go. This was the location of the wedding feast. At the father's house, wedding guests would be assembling. Special wedding clothes would be worn. A special ceremony would be prepared. And a special supper would be readied. The parents of the bride and groom, along with family and friends, would bless the couple,

---

331   S. Michael Houdmann, "What is the Meaning of the Parable of the Ten Virgins?" *Got Questions Ministries* (February 14, 2019). https://www.gotquestions.org/parables-ten-virgins.html (accessed April 15, 2019).

and the special marriage contract would be noted. The couple would then be escorted to the bridal chamber (huppah). The bride and groom would enter the prepared place and consummate their covenanted marriage by entering into physical union. The best man would act as a sentry at the door, waiting for the bridegroom's signal that the marriage had been consummated (proof of which was the bloody bedsheet indicating the brides' purity and representing the blood covenant). When he heard the signal (the voice of the groom), the news would be passed and the reception would begin and could last up to seven days or so. In fact, the wedding guests feast for seven days while the couple engages in a seven-day honeymoon. Once the seven days are up, the couple emerges from the prepared place. The bride's veil has been removed and now all can properly focus their gaze upon her to congratulations from their guests. At this point, the marriage supper would begin.[332] This reception was a joyous one. It was the most wonderful, marvelous, and happy celebration that the Jewish people at that time enjoyed. It was so joyous and fun that Jesus related the wedding reception to the marvels and glory of heaven. The marriage feast was the closest thing on earth to the party, as Tony Campolo refers to it, that is heaven. We must remember that just as Jesus turned the water into wine to keep the party going at Cana in Galilee, while at the same time improving the quality of the wine, so heaven is one massive enduring celebration which never ends with Jesus constantly improving the character of the feast. Throughout the New Testament parables and teachings of Jesus, heaven is depicted as a grand celebration. A Godly eternity of a grand reunion, ecstatic celebration, and everlasting joy is what the coming new paradise, the eschaton, is all about. The eschaton is the location wherein Christ's bride, the Church, is taken to enjoy the goodness of the embrace of God forever. It is Mary Magdalene who first experiences that embrace!

Jesus is the bridegroom who paid the price and purchases us from sin. This is the meaning of being "bought with a price" as stated in 1

---

332   Kenneth E. Bailey, *Jesus Through Middle Eastern Eyes* (Downers Grove, Illinois: InterVarsity Press, 2008), 269-275.

Corinthians 6:20 (see also, 1 Corinthians 7:23, Acts 20:28, Romans 12:1, 1 Peter 1:18, 2 Peter 2:1, and Revelation 5:9). The bride, and the Church, and each believer has been purchased at a very costly price! The good news is that the bridegroom wants us. The Father also wants us to share His house. "In my Father's house are many rooms." The word for house can mean "dwelling", "temple", "treasure house", and "palace".[333] Early Christians also employed the word as a place for gathering and fellowship. The Father's house also carried the idea of a heavenly resting place for the "earthly afflicted disciples" of Jesus. This concept reminds me a great deal of the Emerald City in the movie "The Wizard of Oz". In the Emerald City, Dorothy and her companions got what they needed after their harrowing journey to that refuge. They were washed and cleaned, refreshed and renewed, and put back together again! After the journey of this life, will we not need much the same?

The word "rooms" has often been translated by the word "mansions".[334] This word, however, has many meanings including "dwelling place", "resting place", "abodes", "homes". This author has also heard and read where the word is translated as "lodge", "watch house", and even "hunting blind."[335] It also carried the idea of "hospice".[336] This would be a permanent hospice. As a hospice, it would be a home for God's people wherein they are cared for, tended, watched over, and have their needs met after their earthly sojourn and journey. In the era in which Jesus lived, the "kataluma" or "guest room" of a common Palestinian house was a room well prepared by the host for the arrival of guests. These guests were often relatives. As members of the family, great provisions were made. Usually guests stayed a long time. The design of the room and adjustments to the room were made according to the perceived

---

333   Walter Bauer, *A Greek English Lexicon of the New Testament and Other Early Christian Literature*, trans. & ed. William F. Arndt and F. Wilbur Gingrich (Chicago: University of Chicago Press, 1957), 562-563.

334   R. V. G. Tasker, *The Gospel According to Saint John, Tyndale New Testament Commentaries* (Grand Rapids, Michigan: Wm. B. Eerdmans Publishing Co., 1980), 171.

335   This author cannot document these translations, but they have been heard in presentations and seen in print over the expanse of two or three decades.

336   Wilbert F. Howard, *The Interpreter's Bible in Twelve Volumes: The Gospel According to Saint John*, vol 8, ed. George Arthur Buttrick (Nashville: Abingdon, 1982), 699.

likes and tastes of the visitors. This tradition, of course, has been carried down even to this very day. God knows our particularities. In the Jewish wedding scene, the groom's father knew the particularities of the bride and attempted to express them in the design and decorative essence of the house the son proceeded to build. Eternity has a unique character for each person in relationship. It is not at all characterized by uniformity and a socialistic value. The idea of "many rooms" indicates that within God's realm there is plenty of space and vacancy. God's people are not lost or overlooked; rather, each one in relationship with the Christ has a special place in the Fathers' heart.[337] "Mansions" are probably not individual houses in most understandings of the word. Elder and lay preacher, Laurence E. Weed advances that the concept that the idea behind "many rooms" or "mansions" is more like the former manor houses and estates of yesteryear. The rooms or houses of which John 14 speaks are individual components of a complex. They are rooms around the "insula" or courtyard. They are beautiful yet utilitarian. They are spacious while at the same time meant for fellowship and gathering. They have both a private and public persona or character to them. What is the idea here? The image offered of the place prepared for us is one where we all gather and celebrate new life and the new eternal paradise together. Family orientation is much the essence of the new heaven and new earth to come. The emphasis is on relationship! Mary Magdalene, once more, was the first individual to catch a real glimpse of what was to come. The groom came for the bride in Joseph's garden and inaugurated the new reality of the new paradise that will be given. The quest for permanency in both relationship and place was over. The journey which began with the banishment of Adam and Eve from the garden had now come full circle. Thomas in John 14:5 asks a question of Jesus, revealing that he has no definite knowledge of either the process or the goal Christ is pursuing. Jesus, as the second Adam, states in the eleventh "I am" statement (once again, my count) that he personifies "the way, the truth, and the life." Jesus does not just show the way. He

---

337   Arthur John Gossip, *The Interpreter's Bible in Twelve Volumes: The Gospel According to St. John*, vol. 8, ed. George Arthur Buttrick (Nashville: Abingdon, 1982), 699.

is the way! Jesus is truth. He not only secures truth, but he, himself, is utterly dependable and completely reliable. Jesus as life is both life itself, and the source of life for us as well. All of this comes into complete fruition and is amply demonstrated when he, the groom, comes for his bride, in Joseph's garden.

After all the centuries of speculation and theorizing about the relationship between Jesus and Mary Magdalene, we have a marriage between them after all! C. S. Lewis spent a good bit of time and brain power contemplating the afterlife. One of the questions with which he wrestled was the concept of marriage and sexual union in the heavenly state and eschaton to come. Lewis affirmed that, when rightly practiced, the united joy of the act of marriage and the composite unity it affords, if not a part of the resurrection state and life of eternity, would have to be replaced by a greater joy, yet unknown to us, by God. Lewis affirmed that God would not leave such a vacuum in eternity.[338] Whatever this may be, such an experience, perhaps, was engendered and first expressed when Jesus came for and embraced Mary. Yes, in the way this author understands and takes seriously the themes of the Bible; Jesus and Mary were a real item!! It is just not how we think about it today!

---

338   C. S. Lewis, *Miracles* (New York, NY: Macmillan, 1947), 160.

19

The Embrace of Eternity

"Close your eyes, give me your hand, darling. Do you feel my heart beating? Do you understand? Do you feel the same? Am I only dreaming, or is this burning an eternal flame...Say my name sun shines through the rain. A whole life so lonely. And then you come and ease the pain. I don't want to lose this feeling, oh...Am I only dreaming, or is this burning an eternal flame?

(Billy Steinberg, Tom Kelly, & Susanna Hoffs/The Bangles)

In the musical, "Jesus Christ Cosmic Star", which my youth group developed and performed, we had a young lady named Sarah Tady play the role of Mary Magdalene. Not only did she do a commendable job, but along with Jesus, performed by Benjamin Grove, they enacted John 20:10-18 as I have scoped it out in this book. A long time prior to any idea of writing and producing a musical (performed only in the sanctuary of the Natrona Heights Presbyterian Church), I imagined the song lyrics listed above as representative of Jesus holding Mary, and

Mary holding Jesus, outside the tomb. "An eternal flame" is truly what is burning between Jesus and Mary Magdalene in their great encounter on Easter morning. This song - "Eternal Flame" - is one of my all-time favorite ballads. It is a marvelous love song written by Susanna Hoffs, Billy Steinberg, and Tom Kelly. The song was in The Bangles' 1988 album "Everything". It was released as a single in 1989 and hit No. 1 on the charts in the United States and around the world. The Bangles desired to be the female version of the Beatles. Billy Steinberg commented that this song was something like "the Beatles meet the Byrds." The song was inspired by two eternal flames: the light for Elvis Presley at Graceland witnessed by the band, and a little red light described as an eternal flame in the synagogue Billy Steinberg attended as a child in Palm Springs. This pop rock band formed in Los Angeles in 1981. Band members Vicki Peterson, Debbi Peterson, Michael (Micki) Steele, and Susanna Hoffs performed the number. The tone and the mood of the song speaks well of the human desire for a love that burns, truly, forever. It is one of the most tender and soul filled songs ever written. It is marvelous in its simplicity, communicating volumes about the human desire for a relationship that is never ending.

This author is convinced that Mary Magdalene and Jesus launch into a full embrace the moment Jesus reveals himself to her. Ryleigh Hendrickson, of the NHPC youth group, was once overheard saying that what we need to do is "embrace the eternal", which is exactly what Mary is doing when she rushes into Jesus' arms. Jesus, following his Resurrection, now represents the sum total of eternity and personifies it in his person. Mary Magdalene is the first person in human history to embrace it when she embraces him, whether she had an idea of that going through her mind or not!

Imagine this scene in Joseph's garden, if you will! There is Jesus and Mary in a full embrace on Resurrection morning. Mary is the first human being to see Jesus alive. Mary is the first human being to embrace him. To me, this speaks volumes. We often play with images in our mind and culture of two lovers in the moonlight. Here we have two lovers with the backdrop of the rising sun. One is the lover of our souls and persons. The other one has found completion and fulfillment in the embrace of none other than God Himself. In the portrayal here is the idea that the sun is rising on eternity. The sun is rising on a new reality. The sun is rising on a new human hope and expectation. The sun is rising on a completely new era for humanity. The sun is rising on a renewed divine/human relationship. The sun is rising on a new eternal paradise.

Seven centuries before Jesus' birth, the prophet Isaiah employed an image of light and shadow to foretell the coming of a Savior for Israel. "The people who walk in darkness will see a great light. Those who live in a dark land, the light will shine on them…for a child will be born to us, a son will be given to us." (New American Standard Bible, Isaiah 9:2, 6a). The last phrase of Isaiah 9:2 can be translated either as "a light will shine" or "a light has dawned." Both translations have great meaning. "A light has dawned" portrays well the Resurrection of Jesus. It is a reminder not only of the time of day during which he arose, but all the brilliance we can imagine with his bursting forth from the tomb and the dazzling presence of the angels. It is also what his light ultimately points and lead us to – the darkness of our sin and the evil world being portrayed and dealt with in Christ's passion on the cross. In that very bloody happening, the darkness which could not extinguish the light was overcome by "the light of the world."[339] Darkness is apparently a nothing. It is only the absence of the light. The light now bursts forth illuminating all darkness for what it really is. Isaiah indicates in his prophecy that the coming of this light will be a cause of great rejoicing and lead us to an increase of joy.[340] Mary is the first human being to embrace the light. We can only imagine the ecstasy she experienced in that moment and in her continuing reflections on the meaning of that moment. From God rushing as if in a storm through the garden of Eden after Adam and Eve sin,[341] to this embrace of Jesus and Mary in

---

339   John 1:4-5; John 9:5.
340   Isaiah 9:2-3.
341   Genesis 3:8.

the quiet and peace of another garden, the message is clear: the storm that has enveloped the relationship between God and humanity is now over! What a sense of complete shalom this must have been for the two of them! The light of a new creation, a glorious re-creation, has finally dawned. The time for a complete universal transformation has occurred, and the testimony of this truth is exhibited in this new garden by the second Adam, with Mary Magdalene encircled and encompassed about in his arms.

Mary rushes into the arms of Jesus. The embrace is undoubtedly a long one if we properly understand Jesus' eventual response to her. This embrace, in reality, is both final and everlasting. In a deeply spiritual sense, Mary, as the second Eve, will never again leave Jesus' arms. Jesus is God. Mary, in the affirmation of this author not only represents Eve, she represents all of humankind. Mary represents us. Here in this embrace we see how God really feels about us. God embraces us. The work of Jesus Christ, the second Adam, is over. The work Adam was called to perform has been accomplished, and Jesus, as the perfect sacrifice, has gone to the cross as the propitiation (Romans 3:25) for our sins. Our sins and their penalty have been taken away and satisfied. We have been justified (made right before God). All this has been accomplished. Now our own personal resurrection after our own physical death, a permanent relationship, and life eternal is, for us, the reality of Christ's victory. Our resurrection and forever life is sure! Jesus' embrace of Mary is a welcoming expression to new life. What is witnessed in that garden on that particular morning is truly the embrace of eternity. For Mary to lovingly embrace Jesus in this manner becomes the greatest act of worship, an indicator of permanent relationship, and an expression of eternal love. The mission of the cross and the victory over the grave has been fully completed and now demonstrated. God has kept the promise of his prophetic word as pronounced to the serpent in Eden (Genesis 3:15) as the relationship between the divine and the human has been restored once again! This embrace has a sense of finality to it. It is a welcoming to new life with all the terrors of the past done, gone, and over! It is a re-embracing of the divine identity and God's purpose in creation. Never in history, has a hug or an embrace meant so much!

"Is this burning an eternal flame?" is the question the Bangles ask in their song. The good news is that the "eternal flame" and the embrace of eternity is meant not just for Mary!

20

The Ultimate Moment
in Human History

"Children play in the park, they don't know. I'm alone in the dark, even though. Time after time again I see your face smiling inside. I'm so happy that you love me. Life is lovely when you're near me. Tell me you will stay, make me smile. Living life is just a game, so they say. All the games we used to play fade away. We may now enjoy the dreams we shared so long ago. Oh, my darling, got to have you. Feel the magic when I hold you. Cry sweet tears of joy, touch the sky. Now I need you more than ever. No more crying...we're together. Tell me you will stay. Make me smile!"

(James Pankow/Chicago's part 1 of "Ballet for a Girl in Buchannon")

What is the ultimate moment in human history? Rich are the suggestions of many scholars, academics, writers, thinkers, historians, commentators, and observers of the times. Up for consideration could be these happenings along with many more from all over the world: the American Revolution (July 2-4, 1776); the Industrial Revolution (circa 1760); Gutenberg's Printing Press (circa 1440); Luther Posting the 95 Theses (October 31,1517); Karl Marx's "Das Kapital"(1867); the Fall of the Soviet Union (December 26, 1991); VE and VJ Day (May 8, 1945 & August 15, 1945 respectively) ending World War II; Caesar crossing the Rubicon (January 10, 49 BC); Waterloo (June 18, 1815), Columbus "re-discovers" the Western Hemisphere (October 11, 1492); The Renaissance (14ᵗʰ through 17ᵗʰ centuries); the Enlightenment (circa 1730's); the development of Judeo Christian thought and spirituality from the Skygod Religion through Abraham, Moses, and Christ; the genesis of Islam (circa 609 AD); the Scientific Revolution (1543); The Chinese Great Proletarian Cultural Revolution (1966-1976); the Pax Romana (27 BC through 180 AD); the Apollo 11 Lunar Landing (July 20, 1969); The British Slavery Abolition Act of 1833 (1772 & 1807); and Lincoln's Emancipation Proclamation (September 22, 1862 & January 1, 1863).

It is the opinion of this writer that the ultimate moment in human history occurred on April 5, AD 33, with the resurrection of Jesus Christ.[342] More specifically, the moment Jesus calls out to Mary Magdalene, and departing the tomb she rushes into the embrace of the second Adam! This is the one defining moment in history wherein everything, both planetary and cosmic, changes. This also makes the penultimate moment in human history (both the second most critical moment and also the worst) Adam and Eve's Fall and banishment from Eden. These are the book-ends of the main drama of salvation history! The embrace of eternity is the climax of the Bible. It is the climax of divine/human history! It is the moment that the story of the Bible comes full circle! Everything that follows it, in the opinion of this writer, is the denouement or working out of the consequences of this one great moment. The saints, both militant and triumphant, are still living in the era of the denouement with the expectation of the eschaton to come!

Often the only significant historical importance that people give to the encounter between Jesus and Mary Magdalene is the social relevance

---

342   April 5, AD 33 is now widely acknowledged as the date of the Resurrection of Jesus. Much information referring to this date can be found in writing and online.

that Mary, a female, is the first person to witness the resurrected Christ. Historically, this encounter does help establish the legitimacy of the text. Simply put, if you were making up the story of Jesus' Resurrection, you would not have a female being the first person to encounter him. Females, at that time, were considered inferior to men mentally and given to, it was believed, great flights of fancy. Their testimony in a court of law was considered suspect and unreliable.[343] It is possible that the authentication of the account is part of the reason for Mary being the first person to witness the resurrected Jesus, but this author thinks it is subordinate to the greater symbolism and meaning thematically presented here as a significant part of salvation history, which is the message granted here in terms of eternity and what the interaction between Jesus and Mary communicates here about the future of God's own! Mary Magdalene represents the Eve of Eden. Eve has now been forgiven. A new Paradise will be given, and she will be granted entry. Not only that, if Mary Magdalene symbolically represents the forgiven Eve and comes to represent a type of spiritual mother of all of God's children in Christ, we not only learn how God really feels about us (through the embrace), but that the time of acceptance and transformation of Eve's children has come as well! The Revelation 21:5 statement, "Behold I make all things new!" (KJV) is a key verse not only for Eve and the second Eve, but for all of God's own. Our old selves (Colossians 3:9) in Adam have been replaced with our new selves in Christ. It is the "with-me" God's time-honored promise for all of the second Eve's spiritual offspring as Jesus reassuringly declares at his Ascension, "Lo, I am with you always". (KJV, Matthew 28:20b). What has been wrought by the Christ event has a ring of permanence to it and is meant to be understood eternally.

Just imagine this significant moment on Resurrection Sunday if you will! Mary is convinced that the body of Jesus has been relocated. She is in much distress and anguish over the prospect of Jesus' body being disrespected. Imagine the shock, awe, stunning surprise and revelation,

---

343   Josh McDowell, *The Resurrection Factor* (San Bernardino, CA: Here's Life Publishers, Inc., 1981), 73-74.

along with the staggering emotion of the discovery, that Jesus is, in fact, alive![344] What follows for Mary Magdalene, and for us, are the ramifications and consequences of such a divine act. This is the one moment in history wherein everything changes. What has been true before, has been altered by a new and glorious understanding of the outworking of the rest of what God has in mind!

Commentators and writers often like to point out the confusion that is evident during the Day of Resurrection. We have the confusion of the Roman guard, the religious elite, the women, and the disciples and followers of Jesus. In reality there is no confusion at all, at least not on the part of God. Everything plays out as scripted. All the apparent confusion evaporates and is made clear the moment the encounter with Mary Magdalene is engaged.

What we have here between Jesus and Mary Magdalene I like to call "the perfect unveiling." One could also refer to it as the "perfect presentation". What is the perfect unveiling or the perfect presentation from the divine perspective? In writing the history of the Natrona Heights Presbyterian Church and its people, I am reminded of the story of the late Dorothy Jane Murphy Gestner Hazlett. During her childhood, Dorothy's father made a grand presentation to his family on Christmas morning. When all was ready, he would gather his family in the foyer, fling open the double doors of the main room in the house, and allow them to gaze at a magnificently decorated Christmas tree and family room, with all the holiday presents wrapped up and carefully placed underneath. This became a cherished tradition for the family and one that Dorothy dearly recounted both with a smile upon her face and a tear in her eye. I know of other families who have similar traditions. One family would gather all of their children on the top upstairs step on Christmas morning, only permitting them to descend and celebrate when all was in readiness for a grand reveal. In my childhood we always let Saint Nicholas take care of decorating our tree. With high expectations, my sister, brother, and I would run down the stairs to see the look of the living room and dining room

---

344   Paul Little, *Know Why You Believe* (Wheaton: Scripture Press, 1967), 68-69.

with all its festive décor! In terms of the perfect presentation, many people would regard the moment of the presentation of a bride in her elegant dress on her wedding day as she appears at the opening of the door in grand processional. When it comes to the perfect unveiling, whether it is expressions of romance, celebration, surprise, and the pleasantries of mystery, the manner of the presentation matters! Gifts matter, of course, but what often makes them special is the way they are given. I remember my wife's comment after I took her on one romantic, mystery, get-away weekend some years ago, saying to me as we traveled home, "What was important to me this week-end was not the gifts you gave me or the things you planned for us, but that you put so much thought into it!" Presentation matters! Presentation is a big part of the beauty of gifts, gift-giving, and relationship.

In thinking about God's interactions with humankind, I think His majesty has blessed us with three marvelous presentations or unveilings, with a fourth one yet to come as a part of divine/human history. The first perfect unveiling or presentation was the gifting of Eden to Adam. This perfect revealing or disclosure, it seems to me, has two parts. The second phase of Eden was the gifting and presentation of Eve to Adam which I find hugely significant in the Bible,[345] perhaps far more than Christian society realizes.

A second perfect unveiling or presentation in the Bible is what we call the Christmas story.[346] The events surrounding the Nativity of Jesus becomes the most fabulous divine act since Eden. The incarnate God was gift wrapped for us in a way. Jesus is God wrapped in human flesh.[347] He came as a gift to rescue us from our plight and sinful selves. God could have wrapped Himself in a mind-boggling display of power and theatrics, lighting up the entire sphere in a celestial light show. Instead, he chose to wrap himself with the human essence becoming one of us. He became no stranger to our struggles and the terrible vicissitudes of life. He experienced denial, betrayal, rejection, opposition, persecution,

---

345   Genesis 2: 8, 15, 22-25.
346   Matthew 1:18 – 2:12: Luke 2:1-20.
347   John 1:14.

temptation, false accusation, public shame, misunderstanding, human limitations, pain, sorrow, broken heartedness, separation, and physical death. He can identify with us. He knows our pain and how difficult life, from our perspective, can be. As a result, we can come before him with a sense of confidence because he has a heart exercised toward us knowing the vile circumstances of this world and life from an experiential point of view. In him we can find the grace, mercy, love, and forgiveness we need amidst the necessities of life and throughout our disappointments, frustrations, vile happenings, and foibles. He came wrapped in swaddling clothes and was placed in a feeding trough which was a perfect presentation and unveiling for those characters in the story of the Nativity.[348] They entered into the big plan and, knowingly or unknowingly, were part of the symbolism and the messaging of the tale. There was joy that night in the house wherein Jesus was born and throughout the little village of Bethlehem. Please do not discount that God afforded two marvelous light shows, after all, in the humbleness of the birth. We have the amazing presentation drawn out over more than a year of the presentation to the Magi[349] and a wonderous proclamation to the shepherds.[350] God has the perfect touch, whether his revealing and disclosure is to the individual or to the multitude! It is always just right! The angelic manifestation to the shepherds was but a forerunner of the unveiling or presentation yet to come. As Dieppe was a trial run for D-day during World War II, the announcement of God's personal, physical entry to planet Earth was but a foreshadowing of the global announcement of his coming "re-entry".[351] Our God is the master of the unveiling. He is the master of the presentation. He is also great at setting up that which He plans to divulge and announce in the future. While Philippians 2:1-11 deals with the "Kenosis theory"[352] and has been much debated and questioned, in whatever way God stripped

---

348   Luke 2:7.
349   Matthew 2:1-12.
350   Luke 2:8-20.
351   The Second Coming
352   Sinclair B. Ferguson, David F. Wright, J. I. Packer, eds., *New Dictionary of Theology* (Downers Grove, Illinois: InterVarsity Press, 1988), 364.

himself of the divine in the person of Jesus, the total unwrapping of God's gift was on display affixed to a cross.

The cross leads to the third divine unveiling or presentation in the estimation of this author. This is God's ultimate unveiling or presentation. However glorious was Eden and the giving of Eve to Adam, and however glorious was the incarnation and virgin birth, the resurrection of Jesus is the ultimate perfect unveiling! It is significant to note that while Jesus goes into the tomb naked, he is represented as fully clothed when first presented to Mary. In his Resurrection, we find our nakedness before God fully clothed as well. The Resurrection of Jesus is both the unwrapping and the clothing of the cosmos. In the resurrection stories, starting with Mary Magdalene, God's perfect unveiling of sins forgiven and eternity secured is fully displayed. These stories are God's marvelous displays of new life, love embraced, and liberty (from sin and everything evil) ensured.

God's fourth unveiling or presentation is yet to be experienced, but the foreshadowing of it occurs with Mary Magdalene in the early morning embrace in Joseph's garden. This is why it is the ultimate moment and climax of human history. There will come a time, of which only the Father knows, when Christ's "re-entry" to planet earth[353] will be the actual final outworking of the end of all the diabolical operations of evil in this world. Jesus, as the Messianic King, will, at once, be in charge of everything and everyone. "Every knee shall bow... and every tongue shall confess that Jesus Christ is Lord...."[354] (Living Bible), whether they are one of his own or not! The second phase of this revealing and disclosure is the complete destruction of evil, and evil beings, on and around this planet and throughout the cosmos. The great cosmic war will terminate and all enemies will come to complete defeat. Following our own bodily resurrection (coming back into the physical as humans are meant to live)[355] and the great revealing or evaluation of our lives (known as the

---

353   "Re-entry" is a term coined by John Wesley White (forward by Billy Graham) for Christ's Second Coming, and is the title to his 1970 Grand Rapids, Michigan, Zondervan Publishing House book of the same name.
354   Philippians 2:10-11; Romans 14:11.
355   1 Corinthians 15:1-58.

Judgement),[356] the delivery and gift of the eschaton (which is the new Eden, the new paradise, the new heaven and the new earth and with the new Jerusalem) will be unveiled.[357] The genesis of it all is initiated in all its glory in that moment of personal revelation and embrace shared between our resurrected Savior and his beloved Mary!

If it is, as this author surmises it to be, that God would not let Adam and Eve go. His intention was to rescue them specifically and personally based primarily on His "relationship of one" with them as a composite unity in the concept of marital union. This displays great significance according to God's nature, person, and character. The good news is that the relationship and salvation engendered here is broadened to include many more. The moment that changes everything for humankind (the embrace of Mary and Jesus) is repeated again and again. Jesus greets the children of Eve as they too depart the tomb of death into the new life which Christ offers. The children of Eve are his children too! The embrace of eternity is not a one-time historical event. It is personally offered with arms wide open and received with arms enclosed in tight affirmation. There is no other moment in human history like it! This is the defining moment for God and for us all in Christ Jesus!

---

356   Acts 10:42; Romans 14:10-12; Mark 8:38; 1 Corinthians 4:5; 1 Thessalonians 1:5-10.
357   Revelation 21 and 22.

21

The Perfect Celebration

"Joy to the world! the Lord is come; Let earth receive her king...."

(Isaac Watts)

Consider the word, "celebrate"! The word means a number of things. It means to remember. It means to honor publicly. It means to recognize formally. It means to mark a happy occasion by engaging in some enjoyable activity. It usually means to observe in great or significant numbers, or if by family – the totality of a person's loved ones. Frequently it means to perform a ceremony marking the occasion with delight and a joyful countenance. Once I attended a celebration in which some people, it became quite obvious, had too much to drink. One woman spoke loudly about her faith in Jesus Christ to several others. She shouted to the little group that encircled her saying, "I am a Pres-by-God-terian! I don't care what the rest of you are, just do the Jesus thing!" That is precisely what the perfect celebration is all about – doing "the Jesus thing"!

For many people, the holiday season (Advent, Christmastide, and Epiphany; including all the liturgical festival dates, New Year's celebrations, and Twelfth Night festivities) is the "most wonderful time of the year". The season reminds us all of the events of Christ's nativity. It marks the spectacle of a divine birth. Our celebration has been encrusted with centuries of ethnic and cultural expressions of unique imagination and local reflections, some of which took on regional, national, and international awareness and sharing. It is believed that as early as the pontificate of Telesphorus, who held the papacy from 126-137 AD and is considered to be the seventh Roman bishop after Peter, a decree was issued about how to celebrate the Lord's birth, believed by some to be December 25th by this time. All churches were to mark this occasion with special celebratory services with specific Scriptural readings and sing the words spoken by the angels, "Gloria in Excelsis Deo". Some accredit Telesphorus with the institution of the Christmas midnight mass, the celebration of Easter on Sunday, and the establishment of a seven-week period for Lent.[358] The fact of the matter is, regardless of the alleged decree of Telesphorus, for nearly 1500 years the observation of the birth of Jesus was little recognized. When it was, it tended to be a clergy event with rituals and music that we would consider today to be quite dull, lacking life, and rather boring! It has been recorded that Telesphorus' decree was pursued by many churches within his charge, and that by the third century it held a special appeal. It was not, however, universally practiced. Regardless of this fact, as noted by many, few if any nativity songs were elicited that attempted to describe the joy that the world should feel with the coming of God in human flesh! Biblically, there is joy and celebration throughout much of the nativity accounts in Matthew and Luke. Five songs of great rejoicing have been identified and considered in Luke: the joyful song of Elizabeth; the thankful rejoicing of Mary; Zechariah's song of praise to God; the angel's spoken words, "Gloria in excelsis Deo"; and Simeon's time-honored praise of God. While there is a most definite "dark side of Christmas",[359] we might begin to envision the real experience of joy that

---

358 "Pope Telesphorus." *Wikimedia Foundation, Inc.* (September 28, 2018). https://en.wikipedia.org/wiki/Pope_Telesphorus (accessed April 16, 2019).
359 Matthew 2:1-23; Luke 2:34-35.

the characters shared in Christ's marvelous birth if we would remove the story from all the cultural baggage and the Biblical misconceptions that have become encrusted around and believed to be part of the story. It all starts with the fact that, as we now know, Jesus was born in a common house which contained a dug-out stable.[360] This gave protection to the household animals at night as well as provided additional warmth to the interior. The idea of the late-night arrival of Mary and Joseph and the birth of Jesus is both myth and a literary construction. Mary and Joseph travelled to Bethlehem prior to the end of Mary's gestation period and lodged with relatives as was the common practice and tradition. Joseph and Mary had plenty of relatives in Judea. If Joseph was unable to find relatives to house the couple, they could always stay with Elizabeth and Zechariah, who would be nearby in tiny Judea. Each common Palestinian house at that time possessed a "guest room". In the story, Luke informs us that the guest room was already occupied, and so the family invites Mary and Joseph to reside with them in the common area.[361] Jesus is either delivered in the stable area or near the stable area, as the carved feeding trough for the animals is employed to secure the baby Jesus. The birth, in this way, depicts Mary and Joseph surrounded by family who rejoice at the successful delivery and arrival of a son. We also know, in that particular culture, everyone in the small village would learn of the birth and come to visit and celebrate the arrival. There would be many smiling faces. All would be happy! The angelic appearance to the shepherds and their visit (Mary, Joseph, and Jesus would be easy to locate) adds greatly to the joy. We must note here that Luke records the fact that the shepherds find everything positive and in good order.[362] They return to their responsibilities praising and glorifying God because all was well with the baby and his family. We also must note that village life was quite boring. The townspeople would employ any excuse to celebrate. Those who knew something more about the

---

360   For more information please access all the books, articles, lectures, and videos of the late Dr. Kenneth Bailey, particularly Dr. Bailey's Christmas drama entitled, *Open Hearts in Bethlehem,* first published on May 1, 2005 by InterVarsity Press Books, June 5, 2013.
361   Luke 2:7.
362   Luke 2:20.

nature and destiny of the child would experience an even greater joy. The birth of Jesus was accompanied by light, well-being, and love. The story is warm, bright, happy, and joyful. To a family, and to an extended family, a child has come. To Mary, Joseph, the shepherds, Anna, and Simeon, this was not just any child. This child is the "anointed one" who would somehow save humanity from "death, hell, and sin."[363]

In the history of the church some monks, writers, and musicians realized that the Christmas story was not being properly celebrated and ought to be attended by joyful worship and uplifted countenance. Hence came hymns of joy like "Angels from the Realms of Glory", "Angels we have heard on High", the "First Noel" ("noel" meaning a joyful shout expressing delight), and Isaac Watts' "Joy to the World." Due to the influence of many, including Queen Victoria, many of the beloved street carols found their way into the worship setting as well. One of the songs of the Christmas season that is exceedingly celebratory is "God Rest Ye Merry Gentlemen". It is a song that tells the Christmas story which English commoners began singing over 500 years ago. At first it was not welcome or admitted to public worship. Eventually it found its way into church singing. Today, however, people do not know what to do with the song because its title and first verse are now strange to us. When "God Rest Ye Merry Gentlemen" was written, words like "merry" and "rest" meant something different than they do to us today. Also, a comma is needed following the word, "merry"! The word "rest" formerly meant "keep" or "make". We should understand the title as saying, "God make or keep you merry, gentlemen." The word, "merry" today is generally understood to mean "happy" or "celebrative". This word, however, formerly meant "great" or "mighty".[364] Put it all together and the song declares, may "God make and keep you mighty, gentlemen." The purpose of the song is twofold: it is for men and women to experience the greatness of God and God's salvation; and to make us

---

363   Luke 1:26-56; Luke 2:8-40.

364   Note the use of the term "merry" in Old English. Robin Hood's "merry men" were "mighty men" to be feared. The expression "Merry Old England" refers to a nation of power and might. The phrase, "eat, drink, and be merry" is a reference to soldiers during times of war when engagement in combat was always on the horizon.

God's mighty people.[365] Our joy comes in knowing that God, through Jesus, has lifted us up to become something more, something other, something greater both now and in the eternal future. God in Jesus has granted us a mighty salvation. We who embrace the salvation God offers us are now God's mighty women and men. Perhaps the expression, "Merry Christmas" should be understood by what it means to have a "mighty Christmas".[366] A "mighty Christmas" is both the individual and corporate response we can exercise due to the coming of God in Jesus as second Adam and the work of salvation he has wrought.

The reason, of course, for all this discussion of Christmas celebration is due to the fact that Jesus, who gave up his earthly life on the cross, rose from the grave three days later. If not for the Resurrection, Christmas would hold no meaning! We know that the seasons of Advent and Christmastide can be a difficult time of year for many people, particularly for those who have suffered the loss of loved ones. We grow up with certain Christmas traditions celebrated in family. When we are younger they seem set in stone. Life, however, is constantly changing. The disappearance of people through illness, aging, and death forever alters our traditions because these celebratory practices always are centered and revolve around certain personages in our lives. The earthly physical loss of loved ones through death is magnified during holidays, and most certainly at Christmas. It is a fact that we have difficulty in accepting and rendering that our celebrations will never be the same!

To this day the greatest image of Christmas celebration I know personally came from the lips of Alice Ruth Maharg Purvis, one of the most esteemed individuals I ever had the pleasure to meet and get to know. Alice, whose family and greater family once owned much of

---

365   Ace Collins, *Stories Behind the Best-Loved Songs of Christmas* (Grand Rapids, Michigan: Zondervan, 2001), 53-57.

366   Please note that there are those who challenge the depiction above countering that "merry" refers to "companion in arms" in terms of a band of soldiers. When referring to England, the word "merry" refers to "bountiful" or "prosperous." The phrase "eat, drink, and be merry" is noted in Ecclesiastes 8:15 and Luke 12:19 and is a reference of "a sense of joyfulness." Also, Isaiah 22:13 should be noted. Information on this contrarian view can be found in an online article: David Mikkelson, "Fact Check: God Rest Ye Merry Gentlemen", *Snopes Media Group Inc.* (December 5, 2013), https://www.snopes.com/fact-check/god-rest-ye-merry-gentlemen. (accessed April 16, 2019).

the land in and around Succop Nature Park of the Audobon Society of Western Pennsylvania in Butler County, joined the church triumphant in October 2001 at the age of 95. At the death of her husband John Stanley Purvis in 1994, her family lamented that the Christmas season would no longer be nearly as marvelous or joyous for them due to his loss. How could they possibly be celebrative? This is when Alice, one of the most solid and dearest Christians I have ever met, said, "No, this Christmas is going to be the best Christmas we have ever known because now we have a reason to really celebrate! Stanley has received the gift of eternal life. A gift is not a gift until it has been received! This will be, truly, the best Christmas!" "A gift is not a gift until it has been received!" I do not know if Alice was quoting a statement she heard or learned during her life, or if she coined the assertion herself! When she repeated this story to me I immediately scribbled it down and have employed it many times in sermons and essays during my career. To me, it ranks right up there with Dickens, and others, in the hall of fame of great Christmas season declarations and assertions. Of course, what Alice was communicating to her family was the fact that now the meaning of Christ's coming truly has significance. This is due to the fact that the purpose and reason for Jesus' birth now has been experienced in a direct way by her family. The gift of sins forgiven and life eternal is the gift that has now been received in a very tangible way. This is the prelude to, as the late Walter Martin referred to it, the ultimate "hope of the ages!"[367] In that the gift of life eternal has now been personally and directly received and applied, the family can rejoice because of the Christ event's great declaration that death is not the end – that there is more, much more – and the reunion awaited with our loved ones in Jesus is a big part of it!

Christmas joy, however, is not, and cannot, be the perfect celebration! The perfect celebration is related to the ultimate moment in human history. The perfect celebration is that very moment when the gift that is given is received. In terms of both the Bible and salvation history, the perfect celebration is the precise moment when Mary

---

367   Walter Martin, *Essential Christianity* (Santa Ana, California: Vision House, 1962.), 89-101.

Magdalene understands that the person with whom she is in conversation is Jesus, leaves the tomb, runs toward and embraces the Christ. At this moment of realization and reception, for both Mary and humanity, the gift extended to us by the victorious Christ becomes the ultimate in celebration. It is a celebration that has the imprint of eternity upon it! It is a celebration which is unending! It is a celebration which grows in magnificence, scope, and meaning with the continual inclusion of our loved ones and all of God's own!

As the reader knows now, it is the affirmation of this author that the ultimate celebration in human history is the revelation of the risen Christ to Mary Magdalene, accompanied by their heartfelt embrace. Mary Magdalene is representative, in my estimation, of all of elect humanity. I have tried to imagine this moment in my mind, playing it over again and again in wonderment about the emotions elicited by both Mary and Jesus. The good news is that the impact of this representative moment in human history is played out again and again, each in its own personal way. The perfect celebration continued as Jesus appeared to his disciples, faithful followers, family, and relatives during his 40 days of Resurrection. The perfect celebration continues when each person becomes personally aware of the identity and reality of the person of Jesus Christ and embraces him as both Savior and Lord. The perfect celebration continues with our advent to the "intermediate heaven",[368] our initial awareness of the presence of the resurrected Jesus with us, and the reunion with Christ's own (our own) we will share there. The perfect celebration continues with the reception of all those who follow us into Christ's more immediate presence, having been liberated from the grave. The perfect celebration continues beyond the second coming with the resurrection of the dead (our embodiment in our new glorified, both spiritual and physical, bodies) and the glorious eschaton (the new Eden or Paradise) that God brings into fruition. The perfect celebration redounds with the "marriage supper of the Lamb";[369] the quality of which both grows and continues on forever!

---

368   Randy Alcorn, *Heaven* (Carol Stream, Illinois, Tyndale House Publishers, Inc., 2004), 41-45.
369   Revelation 19:9.

Christmas is not the perfect celebration. It does shout out a clarion call that our time of great joy is coming, and that this coming joy will most surely come about! The birth of Jesus points to that one ultimate moment when Jesus himself, who came out of the grave, calls Mary Magdalene from the grave as well. In terms of this ultimate moment in human history, we can truly express to each other both a "Mighty Christmas" and a most "Mighty Easter" as well.

22

Regarding Mary

"And then along comes Mary."

(Tandyn Almer/The Association)

It is the contemplation of this writer that Mary Magdalene ought to be considered by the Christian churches to represent the "New Testament Eve". There is perfect symmetry in her consideration as such. Beyond the reflection of two Adams, two gardens, and two women, Eve, who is banished from Paradise and given the sentence of death, is symbolically and spiritually retrieved from her state of sin and death and embraced again by Jesus following his passion and bodily Resurrection. The theme of judgment and sentencing, followed by the substitutionary atonement granting reprieve and new life, is unmistakable. It is the opinion here that this portrayal cannot be ignored and simply cast aside.

There is, however, another powerful and impressive candidate for the designation of "New Testament Eve". This candidate is well attested in the annals of church history and has been a major subject of church thought, discussion, and debate for the past two millennia. I am, of course, referring to Mary, the mother of Jesus.

This chapter has been included to examine the only substantive objection some people might have to the thesis of this book that Mary Magdalene figuratively, symbolically, and thematically qualifies for the designation New Testament Eve. Since there are many in the Christian community who grant this title to another, their reasoning and rationale must be considered. This chapter is included to examine their claim. It is the position of this writer that their objection must be stated and analyzed. The chapters that follow this one, delve into the joyous news of the theme practically applied. If this chapter is of no interest to the reader skipping to chapter 23 and beyond is recommended.

The song "Along Comes Mary" by the late 1960's musical group The Association is thought to have featured the idea of a "disgruntled" youth encountering a new person who provides him with newness and joy. Of course, people read into the song the idea of marijuana use and a religious reference to Mary, the mother of Jesus. Whatever the background meaning to the song, the historical advent of the Biblical Mary brings with her a significant change in humanity's outlook. "And then along comes Mary" initiates a whole new perspective for humanity.

Mary is a critical figure in salvation history. The plan of salvation and its outworking in history belongs entirely to God. He owns the ideas, the means, and the methods. What God includes, and has determined to exclude, is by God's sovereign choice. It is God's marvelous declaration that human beings are permitted and called to be incorporated in God's earthly operations. Since the creation of humanity, certain people have been called by God to perform specific tasks and to embody specific roles in God's rescue strategy. Some of the key people in salvation history include Abraham, Moses, David, Elijah, John, Peter, James (known as "the Just", the brother of Jesus and bishop of Jerusalem) and Paul. Millions, and perhaps billions of the faithful, throughout history have also been included in God's work. Mary, the mother of Jesus, is not least among these figures. She is not least among anyone else in history.

In fact, she is much the focal point of the conduct of God's salvific invasion of planet Earth. Everyone who is God's own possesses a unique relationship with God. There are those, however, whose relationship with God must be regarded as superlative. I would include Mary in this category. I would also include Eve and Mary Magdalene. All three share a very elevated, unique, and special relationship of love and wondrous regard with God. Each of these relationships shares different dynamics, circumstances, tasks and roles. Mary, as the mother of the incarnate Son of God, is most special, indeed! In all the discussion and debate Christians have advanced about her precise personage, much of it a quite legitimate academic enterprise I might add, we must not let it diminish her character and the prodigious, through grace, relationship with God she embodies. This writer feels much the same way when it comes to Eve and Mary Magdalene. Each, in her own way, inspires a sense of awe and the presence of the numinous. While there are many other great women in the Bible and in salvation history, these three, without a doubt, are most special, which is the opinion advocated here, in the heart of God.

Mary is remarkable for what we know about her and with what we can probably credit her. It is rightly pointed out that unlike Eve, when visited by a supernatural being (Gabriel in the case of Mary, and Satan, the tempter, in the form of a serpent, in the case of Eve) that she readily accepted and embraced her role in the incarnation, virgin birth, and as motherly protector of God's Son. She was obedient to God and the charge God placed upon her. She bravely and boldly performed the responsibilities with which the Lord entrusted her, especially in the light of Simeon's distressing prophecy (Luke 2:34,35). Those who see a reversal of Eve's disobedience in Eden make a valid point with which to consider! It is believed here that she not only was one of Jesus' followers even prior to his passion, but that she blessed the Church as the keeper of the nativity narratives. As Luke records in Acts 1:14, she and her other sons (referred to as "his brothers" in the text), were present with the early Church of Jesus Christ in the days following Jesus' Ascension and prior to Pentecost. She had to be a key person in the early church even though this reference is the last one concerning her person and personal activity in the sacred Writ. It is the opinion of this author that both of the nativity stories originate with her. She would have had the opportunity for a great deal of contact with Matthew, and we know that Luke spent a lot of time in Jerusalem with Paul's 2-year imprisonment there and in Caesarea. Luke, by necessity, and what to this writer is more than obvious in the first two chapters of his account to Theophilus, had to have interviewed Mary and received from her this treasured and storied history of the first Advent. It was probably only after Jesus' Resurrection that Mary opened her heart to the things secretly treasured there (Luke 2:19 and 2:51) and revealed them to the faithful.[370] One account is more reflective of Joseph (Matthew) and the other of Mary (Luke). If, as it is believed, that Joseph was deceased by the start of Jesus' ministry (which may or may not have been the fact, see John 6:42) his side of the story had to have come from Mary. Each writer would have chosen the material he viewed as important to the themes of their accounts. Perhaps these writers were aware of the writing endeavors of the other. In terms of the Nativity, the second one to write may have intentionally included more of the "rest of the story" as it fit their theme and thesis.

It is precisely here that we must be honest about the task we face when it comes not only to the person and life of Mary, the mother of Jesus, but the entire Bible itself. There is a great deal about which we cannot be completely certain. Over my career, I have read many articles, commentaries, and books on various aspects of the Bible and the life and times of the people it documents. While many conclusions can be rendered with complete certainty, there is also much that falls into he category of assumptions, opinions, suppositions, creative constructions, and eisegesis (eisegesis can best be understood when compared to exegesis. Exegesis is the attempt by a commentator to identify and draw out the precise meaning of a text as intended by the author. Exegesis is highly objective. Eisegesis is highly subjective. It is the process of

---

370   J. Gresham Machen, *The Virgin Birth of Christ* (Grand Rapids, Michigan: Baker Book House, 1982), 265-266.

reading something into the text which may or may not be intended by the author. In doing so, one's own presuppositions, ideas, and biases can be revealed. The conclusions rendered by eisegesis may be accurate and prove to be helpful. The conclusions rendered by eisegesis may also take one far afield.). It seems to this writer that much that is written by commentators (including early church fathers, prelates, and esteemed personages) through history present enough information to suggest certain positions, but not enough validity to actually know something for certain. This writer also admits that he falls into the same boat, particularly with some of the things written in this very book! Ultimately there are many things we will not know for certain until we learn the truth ("the rest of the story") in the eschaton. It seems to me that our task is to continue to research the evidence, employ reason, present our thoughts, examine the evidence and positions of others, agree to disagree at times, and to hold some things in tension as possibilities until we can know for certain. It would certainly be helpful to admit that there is a complete world of unknowing out there. Part of what it means to be human is to keep growing and learning. I think God understands that. I also think that throughout eternity God will feed the expansion of our knowing. It will be fun to learn what thoughts and positions we maintained and advanced that were accurate, and perhaps humbling to learn the what and why of the positions we took that were inaccurate.

A good example of eisegesis and pure supposition is that of Pope John Paul II, who suggested that Jesus (John 20) employed the time after his exit from Joseph's tomb and before appearing to Mary Magdalene to first present himself to his mother, Mary.[371] There is nothing by which to establish this claim as true. It certainly has everything to do concerning his high regard for Mary and, perhaps, wishful thinking. It is most likely (again we cannot know with complete certainty) that Mary was among the followers of Jesus whom Christ visited that first day of Resurrection.

---

371   Pope John Paul II reflected on a possible initial visit by Jesus to Mary, his mother, at the General Audience of May 21, 1997. April 3, 1996 has also been cited as the Pope's first expression of a possible visitation of the risen Jesus with his mother during the time prior to his recorded appearances.

We can imagine a very heartfelt reunion. We do not, however, have any record of it.

What is important, in the consideration of this author, is to keep the focus on the 66 canonical books of the Bible. While the opinion of the early Church fathers, for example, is important to reference and regard when it comes to the subject of Mary the mother of Jesus, yet these are the thoughts of men and not inspired Scripture. In seminary, under the tutelage of the late Dr. Ford Lewis Battles (1915-1979), we were assigned to scrutinize the early Church fathers and to either recommend them for an imaginary Christian Church "Hall of Fame" or a "Hall of Anathema". I remember struggling over a few characters, no one more than Origen (184-253). There was much in the personhood and writings of the early Church fathers to recommend them. There were a few rare aspects and positions taken that caused me to give pause. This author also highly regards Church reformers, particularly those of the Protestant Reformation. At the same time, it must be remembered that what they wrote is not inspired Scripture. There is much to admire about them, but they, as men, were not perfect or infallible.

What is also of a critical nature to note is that which might be attributed to the work and operation in history of the Holy Spirit. Some people might be tempted to refer to certain Church movements, positions, and traditions as coming from the leading of the Holy Spirit. In this they may be correct. My enthusiasm for this defense of the working out of certain church dogma is tempered by the position that many liberal Protestant denominations have taken to advance certain agendas. When exact Scriptural validation for certain "new" positions could not be found or worked out in the Bible, the Bible is simply jettisoned (or considered wrong and invalid) with the oft repeated cry that "the Spirit is doing a new thing in our day." A good argument can be made for the "closing of the canon (the 66 authoritative and inspired books of the Bible)". To advance that "God is doing a new thing in our day" is tantamount to advocating "new revelation". This appears to be an anchorless position to take, allowing the advocacy of just about anything including any new permissive societal and cultural norms. It reminds me of certain cults and cult leaders over the expanse of my lifetime. Just because the mantra of "God doing a new thing" is oft repeated and the ideas it advocates are voted into being by an ecclesiastic legislative body does not make it something that has originated from the Holy Spirit. We must be careful in that which we affirm as being of the movement of the Holy Spirit. I have witnessed much in my life that others claimed was of God, only to be proven most wrong, sometimes with disastrous results. In my life, I have experienced the movement of the Holy Spirit (particularly in helping me with my counseling ministry), but beyond a micro awareness of the Spirit guiding me I hesitate on anything with a more macro aspect to it. What I have experienced in my personal relationship with God, including God's guidance, is nothing that would speak to or be interpreted as new revelation. I am also very suspicious of anyone who says to me, "God told me this or that" (while still affirming God's communication with us)! Certainly, any position that cannot be validated in the Bible should be rendered as highly suspicious, if not spurious.

One of the things I admire are those Christian communions which staunchly advocate the virgin birth of Jesus Christ. As an advocate of this essential doctrine, I take complete exception with those Christian communions that have waffled on this doctrine and their willingness to give it up or consider it irrelevant. One commentator I greatly admire, though with whom I have some significant disagreements, is the late William Barclay. A member of the Church of Scotland and Professor of Divinity and Biblical Criticism at the University of Glasgow, Barclay, in his Daily Study Bible Series concerning the virgin birth, indicates that the Church of Scotland, "does not insist that we believe in this doctrine." He presents two reasons for accepting the doctrine, one of which, I find, is very weak on his part. He then presents four reasons for rejecting the virgin birth. He notes the genealogies of Jesus in both Matthew and Luke, tracing Jesus through Joseph commenting, "which is strange if Joseph was not His real father." He then makes reference to the temple Passover story in Luke 2:48, wherein Mary employs the name "father" when speaking to Jesus in regard to Joseph. Thirdly, he notes the repeated references to Jesus as Joseph's son (Matthew 13:35 & John 6:42). Of course, all of this can be easily explained with an appeal to the Hebrew culture of the day. His fourth reason to reject the virgin birth is that "the rest of the New Testament knows nothing of the Virgin Birth." He does make reference of Galatians 4:4 wherein Paul refers to Jesus as "born of a woman." His explanation for the rise of the doctrine if we choose not to take it literally is, in his words, as follows: "The Jews had a saying that in the birth of every child there are three partners – the father, the mother and the Spirit of God. They believed that no child could ever be born without the Spirit. And it may well be that the New Testament stories of the Birth of Jesus are lovely, poetical ways of saying that, even if He had a human father, the Holy Spirit of God was operative in His Birth in the most unique and special way. In this matter we may make our decision. It may be that we will desire to cling to the literal doctrine of the Virgin Birth; it may be that we will prefer to think of it as a beautiful way of stressing the presence of the Spirit of God in family life."[372] In his commentary on Matthew he refers to Jesus being "born of a virgin mother" as a "crude fact".[373] His commentary here on the role of the Holy Spirit in the nativity is, however, worth consideration.

This author soundly rejects any form of the "adoption" theory or any other alternative to a literal virgin birth of Jesus by Mary. That is my position based on a clear reading of both Matthew and Luke. The first question, which becomes relevant for a discussion of both Eve and Mary, the mother of Jesus, postulated by many as the second Eve, is on the circumstances of the virginity of both women.

There are those who draw a comparison between Eve, who they assert was a virgin at the moment of "The Fall", and Mary's virginity at the moment of the birth of Jesus. Early church leaders such as Irenaeus (125-202), Tertullian (155-240), and Justin Martyr in his "Dialogue with Trypho" in 135 all assert that Eve was a virgin. Am I the only one who

---

372   William Barclay, *The Gospel of Luke, The Daily Study Bible Series* (Philadelphia, PA: The Westminster Press, 1956), 6-7.

373   William Barclay, *The Gospel of Matthew, vol. 1, The Daily Study Bible Series* (Philadelphia, PA: The Westminster Press, 1958), 13.

finds this assertion curious? This idea must be based on the location of the statement in Genesis 4:1 which reads, "Adam lay with his wife Eve, and she became pregnant and gave birth to Cain." I would agree with those who may assert that it appears that Eve did not become pregnant until after the Fall and the banishment from Eden. The text does not indicate, however, that this action in becoming pregnant was the occasion of the surrender of her virginity. A more suitable occasion for the physical union of Adam and Eve would appear to me to be at or shortly following the introduction of Eve to Adam by God. As a person who considers the time frame reference of the stories of creation and human inauguration to be worth serious contemplation, we do not know how long it was between the introduction of Eve to Adam and the actual fall to temptation. It must be admitted here that this is a matter of opinion without any factual basis. Is this any different than the position of these early church leaders? That Eve was a virgin at the moment of her sin is also in the realm of supposition and opinion. The Interpreter's Bible does comment that Genesis 3:20 and 21 could possibly indicate that children were born to Eve prior to the expulsion from Eden.[374] There is nothing even close to substantiation, however, in their scholarship. Others have opined that Genesis 3:16 suggests that Adam and Eve had no physical union prior to the Fall. The reasoning advanced here is based on the words "Your desire will be for your husband, and he will rule over you." Does this mean that prior to the Fall Eve's desire was solely concentrated on her relationship with God and not upon any physical union with her husband? This statement by God may be one of degree rather than a failure to engage the command to "be fruitful and increase in number." There is not enough information here with which to say for certain. While there may be many parallels between Mary and Eve, and while the "recapitulation" theory[375] between the two may

---

374   Cuthbert A. Simpson, *Genesis, The Interpreter's Bible*, vol 1, ed. George Arthur Buttrick (Nashville: Abingdon, 1982), 513.

375   The Theory of Recapitulation can refer to many things including the atonement of Christ due to Adam's sin and theories in evolutionary biology. In terms of Eve and Mary, the mother of Jesus, this theory indicates that Jesus' mother repeats aspects of the life of Eve reversing her disobedience and rebellion in Eden.

have some validity, the notion of dual virginity as part of the parallelism cannot be maintained as absolute truth.

In terms of the scholarship concerning Mary, the mother of Jesus, this author does not subscribe to the "all or nothing" approach that might be advocated by some defenders of classical Mariology. Just because one does not affirm every position advanced about Mary by certain churches does not mean that one is doing a disservice to her person and violating the sacred. While it is not the purpose of this chapter or book to do a complete examination of the topic, some dogmatic aspects of thought about Mary must be pointed out in terms of the main thesis of this writing. I have heard it said by several professors and prelates in my life that Protestants do not regard Mary as much as they should, and that Roman Catholics may esteem her too highly. This statement may be regarded by some as hostile. As a Protestant, I find on the surface of my study that there might be much more about Mary Biblically than most Protestants know or would even recognize. If the 66 canonical books of the Bible are the rule which informs our evaluation, we might be surprised at what can be found within about Mary. It is the opinion here that some things advanced about her might not be out of the realm of possibility, but which cannot be fully substantiated. Some things about her might be true. Some things we may just have to hold in tension as possible. There are some other things which this author affirms are highly unlikely. Some aspects of thought here will be examined. Other aspects of thought concerning her will only be referred to and pointed out for the reader. Either way there is much written about this subject. It is an expansive one! Anyone seriously interested in the subject would be well advised to engage their own study!

Another question I would like to advance regards the evidence for the concept of the perpetual virginity of Mary. What is the evidence for the concept of the perpetual virginity of Mary? The idea that Mary was a virgin when she gave birth to Jesus is absolutely supported here. It is what comes after her time of cleansing that must be considered, especially in reference to Matthew 1:25. The verse reads, "And he knew her not until she bore a son; and he called the name of him Jesus". The

NIV renders the text, "But he had no union with her until she gave birth to a son. And he gave him the name Jesus." Some translations (KJV) render the verse, "And he knew her not till she had brought forth her firstborn son: and he called his name Jesus." According to R.V.G. Tasker there is solid ancient manuscript evidence that the word "firstborn" was not in the original text and was added from Luke 2:7 where the text reads "and she gave birth to her firstborn, a son." Tasker also notes that "some scholars would also omit the words, 'and knew her not till' on the evidence of an old Latin MS and the Sinaitic Syriac, arguing that the presence of the words is unnecessary, and that they were added to prevent misapprehension about the virgin birth."[376] Tasker does note that Alan Hugh McNeile (1871-1933) makes reference to Greek grammatical construction rendering the meaning that the consummation of the union of Joseph and Mary was not engaged until after the birth of Jesus. Tasker also notes that those who assume the idea of Mary's perpetual virginity point out that the idea of "firstborn does not necessarily imply the birth of other children" and only reinforces the notion that Mary was a virgin at the time of Jesus' birth.[377] Tasker does assert, that the "prima facie meaning of this verse would seem to be that after Mary's firstborn son was born, Joseph had normal sexual intercourse with her...."[378]

The Interpreter's Bible states that Matthew 1:25 "does not support the theory of Mary's perpetual virginity...."[379] References are made to Matthew 13:55, 56 and Mark 6:3 indicating that Jesus had brothers and sisters. The names of his brothers, James, Joseph (Joses), Simon, and Judas are listed in both texts.

It appears that the strongest appeal based on literary evidence for the perpetual virginity of Mary comes from the Protoevangelium of James. This apocryphal (a document that was widely circulated whose

---

376   R. V. G. Tasker, *The Gospel according to John, Tyndale New Testament Commentaries* (Grand Rapids, Michigan: Wm. B. Eerdmans Publishing Co., 1980), 36.
377   Ibid., 36.
378   Ibid., 36.
379   Sherman E. Johnson, *Matthew, The Interpreter's Bible,* vol. 7, ed. George Arthur Buttrick (Nashville: Abingdon, 1980), 255-256.

origin and authenticity are highly questioned) and pseudepigraphal (a falsely attributed work wherein the real author claims the writing's origin comes from a prominent historical figure of the past) work is also known as the Gospel of James and the Infancy Gospel of James, among other titles. The author is purportedly James, the brother of Jesus. It is clear to scholars, however, that he could not have been the author. There are many, you will discover if you look deeper into this writing, who doubted and denied the authenticity of the text in the first few centuries of the Christian Church. This writing of the mid-to-late 2nd century is a prequel to Matthew and Luke. It concerns the origin and youth of Mary, and attempts to give more details prior to, during, and following the birth of Jesus. It is the first and oldest writing outside Matthew and Luke to assert the virginity of Mary. It not only asserts her virginity, but her perpetual virginity as well. The text claims that Joseph was quite her senior and whose only purpose in the marriage was to be her protector. He is not pictured as her lover. It is a marriage without engaging the "act of marriage". The book claims that the siblings of Jesus were the children of Joseph by a former, deceased wife. These children were older than Jesus and came not from Mary's womb. The late Dr. Kenneth Bailey, in speaking about this writing, simply and summarily dismissed and dispatched it, in its entirety, as "a novel."[380]

The three main prophecies which concern the advent of the Christ (Messiah) are Genesis 3:15, Isaiah 7:14, and Micah 5:1-5. From the off-spring of Eve comes a woman who gives birth to the one Paul refers to as the second Adam who "crushes" the head of the serpent. From Isaiah 7:14 we learn (supported by the commentary of both Matthew and Luke) that the young maiden is a virgin. The woman of Isaiah 7:14 is the virgin mother of the one referred to as Emmanuel (a reference to the "with me" God). This young maiden is the one "who is in labor" who gives birth in Bethlehem of Judea in this announcement of the coming Messiah. The Isaiah passage is vitally linked to the famous chapter 9 announcement of a coming child who carries the titles of "Wonderful Counselor", "Mighty God", "Everlasting Father", and "Prince of Peace".

---

380   This statement was shared in conversion by Dr. Bailey with the author.

Isaiah 7 and 9 appear to refer to the coming of the Messiah. It appears that both reference the same child. Isaiah 7 may (or may not) support the idea of the virgin birth. A young maid may conceive a child, while a virgin. She may remain a virgin throughout her gestation period. As a possible virgin, she delivers the child. What I do not see any evidence for in this passage (or the others) is the concept of perpetual virginity! Likewise, I find no vow or reference to perpetual virginity in the Luke 1:34 statement of Mary to Gabriel. When Mary is informed by Gabriel of her coming pregnancy she inquires saying, "How can this be since I am a virgin' (NIV). Or as the Greek Interlinear refers to is as, "How will be this since a man I know not?"[381] To "know not a man" is a reference to her current condition at this precise time in her young life. To extrapolate from this comment the idea that she is informing Gabriel of her life long commitment, or previously declared vow of perpetual virginity, seems to me to be difficult to establish. Yes, it might be possible, but from this comment alone, how would we know this? Early church fathers and current scholars might advocate Mary's perpetual virginity, but the evidence to know this in certainty is very suspect and very speculative, in my opinion. Mary is betrothed to Joseph. The time for their complete union is not readily at hand considering cultural circumstances. Mary interprets from Gabriel the understanding that she will be found to be with child very rapidly. She discerns that being found with child is not a reference to the future natural and human consummation of her union with Joseph. Perhaps (or perhaps not) she makes quick reference to the prophecy of Isaiah 7:14 in her mind. Gabriel's response in verse 35, however, underlines both the immediacy of the conception and that this conception is the creative action of God. Regardless of any classical or modern view favoring Mary's perpetual virginity, the actions and concerns portrayed in both Matthew and Luke mitigate against it. Once again, why marry at all if one has taken such a vow? Reason, the cultural setting of the day, and the circumstances of the text do nothing to support the perpetual virgin theory. In fact,

---

381   Alfred Marshall, *Greek-English New Testament* (Washington D. C.: Christianity Today, 1976), 165.

it seems to this author to be a twisting of the evidence to attempt to fit the advancement of this theory. What is the purpose for the concept of perpetual virginity anyway? Mary can still be highly esteemed and many of the things ascribed to her by scholars can still be valid and true without the addition of this conviction of perpetual virginity!

During my career I had the privilege of engaging in both a large and successful youth ministry and counselling ministry. The youth groups I organized and led, and the counselling sought out by those in need dominated much of my pastorate. Both areas were overshadowed by issues and tensions over pre-marital sex and marriage tensions, which included sexual relations. Growing up in the 1960's I witnessed the "Sexual Revolution", wherein sexual relations went from something sacred between a man and a woman in marriage to a recreational activity. While society poked fun and decried Christian standards of morality in terms of sexuality, I found myself frequently dealing with the devastating results borne by teenagers and men and women of the "new morality". It was not pretty! While sexuality was often treated in a comic and cavalier way by many, numerous were the men and women, especially teenagers, who came to my office quietly and alone, crushed by the circumstances and results of the new moral code. My most heart rending counselling moments came from those who felt they were used and cast aside, unwanted pregnancies, the development of STD's or venereal disease, and all the emotional, psychological, and spiritual issues that attend the violation of Biblical sexual morays. To this day, I find the Billy Joel song from the album "The Stranger", entitled "Only the Good Die Young" to be quite offensive. The single, released in May 1978, claims not to be anti-Christian or "anti-Catholic", but in the words of the artist himself, "pro-lust"! When this song, with a very catchy beat, comes on the radio, I turn it off in protest as to what the true meaning of human sexuality is as ascribed Biblically, particularly in the creation account, the Song of Songs, and New Testament teachings. The value of virginity is both a protective measure from some of the worst circumstances in life, but also the provision of something most extraordinary and valuable safeguarded in the marital union of a man and a woman.

Roman vestal virgins and cultic virgin mythology aside, virginity is meant to safeguard a full emotional, spiritual, mental, psychological, and physical depth of union and intimacy between a man and a woman in marriage which speaks to the very relational nature of the Trinity. Perpetual virginity has its place, as the New Testament teaches, to those so anointed with the gift of chastity in order to serve God. Primarily, however, virginity prior to marriage is to enhance and maximize the marital union and what can be learned from it in terms of our relationship with God. It is the opinion of this writer that Mary, the mother of Jesus, was not denied this great divine favor!

In Luke's infancy narrative, there is much in the Annunciation (Luke 1:26-38) which speaks very well of the person and character of Mary. Wherein both Eve and Zechariah (Luke 1:18) doubt either the veracity of God or Gabriel, Mary refrains from doubting the words of the agent of God. In turn, she only inquires as to the method and manner this great declaration will be fulfilled. When the explanation is given, she courageously, faithfully, and humbly submits to the Lord's will! In the temptation in Eden, Eve was reaching for a great benefit unto herself. Mary, who expresses both awe and perplexity concerning the visitation and announcement of the divine messenger, embraces the communication as fact and is ready to selflessly obey her God, who will lead her along this new road in which she will travel. Unlike Eve, it appears that her intention in embracing the Lord's will is not for her own glorification and elevation but for that of God and the purposes of salvation for many. I think that part of the heroism of Mary depicted here is in placing herself in the complete disposal of God (verse 38). Obedience means major life complications with her family, with Joseph, and with the community. She is not yet fully married in the Hebrew cultural sense. There will probably be a very strong reaction from many to her being found with child. Embarrassment, shame, the termination of relationships, shunning, suffering, and, though highly unlikely, even death were possible outcomes she might have to endure. Through it all, as Geldenhuys points out, she remains "most sober-minded", "modest", and free of "hysteria".[382] There is nothing in the text, however, that indicates that she took a vow of perpetual virginity. Both the Interpreter's Bible and Morris indicate that support for such an idea is "a reading into the text"[383] and a "difficult exegesis".[384] Such an idea also raises the question as to the plan to marry Joseph if she had taken such a vow. As questioned above, why be betrothed at all if she planned to remain a life-long virgin? The explanation of the Protoevangelium of James is dismissed here as being non-historical, thus irrelevant. As to the fact (Luke 1:28, 30, and 31) that she is "highly favored" or "full of grace", according to Morris and Geldenhuys, does not mean that she herself is full of grace and favor being a source to confer it upon others. It is, rather, that God has given her a gift of God's free grace and upon her person it rests. The moment of the conception and the fact of its completed action is not advanced in the text. The emphasis at the conclusion of the text is upon the attitude of servanthood toward God of Mary and her faith in the Lord and God's call upon her![385]

When it comes to Marian Doctrine it appears that advocates have made a connection between Luke 1:28 and the Immaculate Conception. Gabriel's sudden and startling appearance before Mary is accompanied by the words (NIV), "Greetings, you who are highly favored! The Lord is with you." Two critical Greek words appear in the text: chaire and kecharitomene. Chaire can be translated as "rejoice" or "hail".[386] Kecharitomene can be translated as one "having been favored."[387] (A fuller rendering of these words both in Greek and in the context of the passage is worth the time and study). This latter word appears to refer to an individual who has been previously transformed by God's

---

382   Norval Geldenhuys, *The Gospel of Luke, The New International Commentary on the New Testament* (Grand Rapids, Michigan: Wm. B. Eerdmans Publishing Co., 1979), 75.

383   Leon Morris, *The Gospel According to Luke, Tyndale New Testament Commentaries* (Grand Rapids, Michigan: Wm. B. Eerdmans Publishing Co., 1979), 73.

384   S. MacLean Gilmour, *The Gospel According to St. Luke, The Interpreter's Bible*, vol. 8 ed. George Arthur Buttrick (Nashville: Abingdon, 1982), 39.

385   Geldenhuys, 78.

386   Walter Bauer, *A Greek-English Lexicon of the New Testament and Other Early Christian Literature*, trans. and ed. W. F. Arndt and F. W. Gingrich (Chicago: The University of Chicago Press, 1957), 881.

387   Ibid., 885-886.

grace. Gabriel's words to her as recorded in Luke 1:30 seem to reinforce the idea that she is an object of God's favor and that grace has been bestowed upon her prior to this coming birth announcement. The employment of a similar word, "echaritosen" from the verb "charitoun" or "charitoo" is found in Ephesians 1:6, 7. The idea employed by Paul is that believers in Christ have been transformed by the grace of God. The text appears to be informing Mary (and the reader today) that she has already received God's marvelous redemption from sin. The text does not inform us when and where this came to be, only that she has already found "favor" or "grace" in the providence of God. This author finds no difficulty in Mary being redeemed by God prior to the work she has been selected to perform. In that she has found grace, or that grace has been bestowed upon her, seems to imply that God has dealt with and taken away her sin. A salvific transformation has been granted to her. There is no evidence that this grace was actualized in an "immaculate conception" or that it implied a perpetual virginity. Concerning the Immaculate Conception, the *New Dictionary of Theology* indicates:

> By the beginning of the Middle Ages it had come to be believed that Mary had lived without sin. But when had she been delivered from sin? Anselm held that she was born with original sin (Cur Deus Homo? 2:16). Bernard of Clarivaux held that she was conceived with original sin but purified before birth (Ep. 174). This view was also held by Thomas Aquinas and the Dominican school. It was Duns Scotus who popularized the idea that Mary was conceived without original sin. This new idea did not meet with universal acceptance and Pope Sixtus IV in 1485 and the Council of Trent in 1546 both left the matter undecided. But eventually Duns Scotus'view prevailed and in 1854 Pope Pius IX proclaimed it a dogma in his bull Ineffabilis Deus: 'We declare, pronounce and define that the most blessed Virgin Mary, at the first instant of her conception was preserved immaculate from all stain of original sin, by the singular grace and privilege of the omnipotent God, in virtue of the merits of Jesus Christ, the savior of mankind, and that this doctrine was revealed by God and therefore must be believed firmly and constantly by all the faithful.' This doctrine was proclaimed on the basis of the unanimity of the contemporary church. There was no scriptural basis for it. It

was asserted that this doctrine had always been held in the church as a revealed doctrine. But this is not so much an appeal to tradition (which does not support the doctrine) as the triumph of dogma over tradition. The definition of the immaculate conception is rightly seen as a 'trial run' for the doctrine of papal infallibility, to be defined sixteen years later at the First Vatican Council.[388]

Eventually in any discussion of Mary, the mother of Jesus, representing the "New Eve", we must get around to God's narrative in Genesis chapter 3:8-19. The key verse in this pericope is 15. In this section of the Genesis account, we get what many believe to be the first indication by God that a plan to redeem those who have fallen will be put into play. Often, Genesis 3:15 is referred to as "the Protevangelium" (also known as the "protoevangelium" and "protoevangelion") or "first Gospel proclamation". The Protevangelium is God's declaration to Eve's tempter (the serpent), after the fall of Eve and Adam to sin, that the woman's seed would ultimately crush his (the serpent's) head. This follows the almost comical (if it were not so tragic) "passing the buck" blame game to which God endured after storming into Eden and locating the offending couple. In his encounter with God, Adam immediately blames Eve (verse 12). The way in which he suggests that Eve is the culprit sounds as if he is attempting to stick God with the ultimate responsibility for the situation. "The woman you put here with me – she gave me some fruit from the tree, and I ate it." This to me almost sounds like an elementary school visit to the principal's office after being taken in for a playground infraction! Eve, on her part, squarely places the blame on the serpent (verse 13). While the serpent shares in the culpability, is Eve attempting to re-route a part of the blame, like Adam, toward the very loving and caring Father who made the creatures of Eden in the first place and populated the garden with them?

God then addresses the serpent without making an inquiry with the talking reptile. There is no reason for any conversation or dialogue

---

388   Sinclair B. Ferguson, David F. Wright, and J. I. Packer, eds., *New Dictionary of Theology* (Downer's Grove, Illinois: InterVarsity Press, 1988), 415-416.

with this articulated monster for God already knows his identity and the reasoning behind his creation of chaos in this otherwise pristine environment. The serpent tempter is none other than the leader of the cosmic rebellion, Satan. In verses 14 and 15 of chapter 3, God curses the monster. This chapter explains, in part, the reason for the chaos, discord, and anarchy characteristic of human reality throughout history. Adam and Eve are the responsible human actors for the advent of sin on planet Earth. Sin, however, was prevalent cosmically prior to their ill choice and resident in Satan. There exists an external sin agent in the story, and this factor seems to be one which plays a role in God's consideration of the discouraging event. The Bible maintains, whether people are comfortable with the notion or not, that Satan is an individual creature and personal entity possessing volition. This being has chosen to be the universal supreme antagonist to God and everything fine, good, and wonderful relating to God's handiwork. His goal, if not to replace God as the master of the universe, is to spoil and bring ruin to everything God has created. Revelation 12:9 identifies the serpent in Genesis 3 as "that ancient serpent". John also refers to him as "the great dragon." Revelation 20:2 records the following: "He seized the dragon, that ancient serpent, who is the devil or Satan, and bound him for a thousand years." Jesus is recorded by John in his Gospel (8:44) as saying this about Satan: "You belong to your father, the devil, and you want to carry out your father's desire. He was a murderer from the beginning, not holding to the truth, for there is no truth in him. When he lies, he speaks his native language, for he is a liar and the father of lies." Paul refers to Satan in 2 Corinthians 11: 3 and 14 masquerading as an "angel of light." Paul indicates in Ephesians 6:11 that the devil is a schemer. In his final exhortations in the book of Romans, Paul notes in 16:20 that "The God of peace will soon crush Satan under your feet." The curse that God lays down upon Satan in Genesis 3:14, 15 is a prophetic announcement of his sure and fast future fate in "the hands of an angry God." Satan's predetermined and ultimate doom is the subject of Revelation 20: 7-10 (and is also mentioned in the Parable of the Sheep and the Goats in Matthew 25:41).

The prophecy of Genesis 3:15 not only reveals the total demise of Satan, but also all those in league with him. God reveals that the seed or the offspring of the woman would vanquish Satan and his seed or offspring. The key concept in the passage appears to be a proper understanding of what is meant by "seed"! The word represents the idea of offspring, family descendants (Genesis 9:9), and ethnic line. In Rabbinical Judaism, the concept of seed was understood to represent a plurality. The "seed of the woman", applied to humankind in Adam,[389] is prophesied to take on and "crush the head" of the serpent and his cohorts. It appears to represent two groups: all those who, of their own free volition, rebel against God and align with Satan; and those who are God's own. Satan's seed also share in his destruction, though the focal point of the prophecy appears to be the complete ruin of Satan himself. There exists an uncompromising antagonism and belligerency between the two groups which can never be negotiated into an armistice, peace treaty, or compromise. It is a fight to the end. It is a conflict unto death. The "enmity" that enjoins the battle in the physical realm is much about spiritual warfare and becomes part of the cosmic struggle. The question we need to answer is the precise identity of the woman's seed. While the primary focus appears to be Satan and not his seed in the prophecy, it appears to be the reverse for the woman and her seed. The central point that dominates the prophecy seems to be, not Eve or "the woman", but her seed. It is the seed that engages the warfare to obliterate Satan. The seed represents a descendant of Adam and Eve. The "he" of the line, "he will crush your head", represents singularity. Cain, Eve's first child who appears immediately in verse one of chapter 4, is not the one who fulfills the prophecy. It is another. References to the seed or descendants of Adam and Eve are picked up and referred to often in the account of Abraham in Genesis. They all represent (Genesis 12:7; 13:15,16; 15:3,13,18; 17:7-10,12,19; 21:12; 22:17,18) plurality. The seed promise, however, has much to do with the Abrahamic covenant and

---

389   Uri Yosef, "The 'Seed of a Woman': A Kernal of Deception – Gen. 3:15," *Noahide – The Ancient Path* (November 20, 2011). Noahide-ancient-path.co.uk/index.php/Judaism-articles/2011/11the-seed-of-a-woman-a-kernal-of-deception-genesis-315/ (accessed April 22, 2019).

is carried down the line of the patriarchs (Abraham, Isaac, Jacob). The one who does the crushing is not only represented by singularity, but also by masculinity. The "he" is masculine, and any rendering otherwise is incorrect. The identity of the "seed of the woman" with Jesus Christ is evident in the writing of Irenaeus, the second bishop of Lugdunum, or Lyon, France, who lived from 130-202 AD. It was on the cross, according to Irenaeus, that Jesus crushed the serpent's head, with the idea of the serpent's lethal bite represented by the nails through Christ's feet pinning him to the tree. Wayne Jackson in his article in the Christian Courier, "Crushing the Serpent's Head: The Meaning of Genesis 3:15", provides illumination about the bruising and the crushing.[390]

In the common versions, the term "bruises" is twice found. Satan bruises the Seed's heel; the woman's Seed bruises the serpent's head. Some translators prefer to render the first instance as "bruise" or "strike at" (NIV) while rendering the latter term by "crush". The reason for the difference, in the minds of some scholars, is twofold: Some contend that the Hebrew verb swp ("bruise") occurs twice in this verse, but that contextual considerations suggest a varied rendering. A man can "crush" a snake's head, while the snake can only "bruise", or wound, the man's heel, without the action necessarily being permanent. The translation should conform, they suggest, to the nature of the circumstances.[391]

Jackson refers to Dr. Harold Stigers, among others, who see a "play on two Hebrew words" here. The word "bruise" (suph) and "crush" (saaph) come from the same root word.[392] Jackson quotes Atkinson who writes, "Whatever the exact meaning of the verb, the picture seems to be clear. To bruise the head is a picture of fatal and final destruction. To bruise the heel is a picture of damage, which is neither fatal nor final."[393]

---

390   Wayne Jackson, "Crushing the Serpent's Head: The Meaning of Genesis 3:15," *Christian Courier* (2019). www.christiancourier.com/articles/1571-crushing-the-serpents-head-the-meaning-of-genesis-3-15 (accessed April 22, 2019).

391   Ibid.

392   Ibid.

393   Ibid.

The apparent conclusion of it all, in light of the advent of Jesus the Christ and his Passion, is that the fulfillment of this prophecy resides in Christ's atoning death on the cross paying for the sins of humankind. Though he is wounded in his work by Satan (remember the bodily resurrection), Jesus, the victorious Christ, achieves the final, permanent, and ultimate triumph! Satan's defeat is actualized, even if it is not completely realized, until later in the story of salvation history. Based on the "Suffering Servant" passages of Isaiah (the other accompaniment of Messianic prophecy along with the Kingly version), particularly Isaiah 52 and 53, we get a most detailed and pointed account of the coming injuries of the prophesied Christ whom Peter (1 Peter 1:18-20) states, in supralapsarian terms, was established by God before the foundation of the earth.[394]

Jackson notes that the allegations of myth in reference to the serpent in the story of the temptation and Fall, are based on "anti-supernatural presuppositions." He notes both archeological evidence, and cultural references wherein the serpent has been "associated with the destruction of human immortality." He also notes that "Paul viewed the episode as strictly historical" (2 Corinthians 11:3).[395]

While the seed of the woman implies human birth and the coming of a human being to take on the task of crushing the serpent's head, the idea of the "woman's seed" is an interesting concept. From what I understand and can find, the term "the seed of woman" appears to be unparalleled and unprecedented in literature. In usual references to conception, the idea is that the male provides the seed. In the creation story of Genesis 1:27, both the male and female appear to be created at the same time. The soul or spirit of the woman appears to be resident in Adam. When God took a portion from Adam's side and formed Eve, this might also reference the passage of Eve's soul or spirit being placed within her newly made frame. Eve is never an afterthought in the creation story. She is neither an afterthought in the judgement God renders in Genesis 3. In a primary sense, Eve appears be the woman of

---

394   Ibid.
395   Ibid.

the prophecy in Genesis 3:15. In every other use of the term, "woman" in Genesis 3, the person identified is Eve. One individual who has been a life time student of the Bible, in conversation with me, identified the woman as Israel. It is out of Israel, according to this gentleman, that the Seed, Jesus, is derived. He also asserts that the prophecy of Genesis 3:15 is much about what is found in Revelation with the final battle between Christ and the Antichrist. He affirms, however, that while the woman represents Israel, an actual woman, Mary, from Israel, is employed to bear Jesus. While asserting that Mary derives from the "seed of man" and being a sinner is still in need of salvation, she must, however, be pure (a virgin) to bear Jesus. Jackson concludes, as we have seen, that the "'seed of woman' implies humanity". Jackson writes, "There are tremendous reasons for the necessity of the Redeemer being human, not the least of which is the fact that a spirit being cannot die a physical death." In Jesus, God took on human flesh (John 1:14 and Hebrews 2:14), but does the "seed of woman" imply a virgin birth? Jackson points out that the seed (descendants) of Hagar in Genesis 16:10 do not represent a virgin birth, and neither does the seed (offspring) of Rebekah in Genesis 24:60. His conclusion, referring to Jack Lewis in his work, "Exegesis of Difficult Passages", is that prophecy in Genesis 3:15 "does not exclude a virgin birth, but the grammar alone does not establish it."[396]

There is also some thought presented that since Jesus twice refers to Mary as "woman" in John 2:4 and John 19:26, that this could be a link with Genesis 3:15 and the terminology of the "seed of woman." Morris notes that the term, "woman" is an expression of both affection and respect.[397] Jesus is, once more, not "reproving his mother."[398.] Morris, however, believes calling Mary "woman" and not "mother" could indicate "a new relationship between them as he enters on his public ministry."[399] Morris points out that Mary knew five things about Jesus: She knew that he was very resourceful; She knew he was incredibly special

---

396   Ibid.
397   Leon Morris, *The Gospel According to John, The New International Commentary on the New Testament* (Grand Rapids, Michigan: Wm. B. Eerdmans Publishing., Co. 1971), 180.
398   Tasker, 59.
399   Morris, 180.

based on the angelic message; She knew she had "conceived Him while still a virgin"; She knew that "his whole manner of life stamped him as different"; and she knew him "to be the Messiah."[400] Morris believes that at this point Mary comes to the realization that "things between them are not the same."[401] Mary, however, knows his ability, his concern for others in need, and his resolve to help. She subsequently acts upon what she knows is true of his person.[402]

While the connection with Jesus' reference to Mary as "woman" to Genesis 3:15 may be interesting to note, it is not conclusive. Yet from the New Testament perspective looking backward: the seed of woman is directly interpreted by Paul as Christ (Galatians 3:16); the virgin birth of Jesus to Mary is firmly established; it is the seed of the woman, not the woman herself, who conquers; and the woman at enmity with the serpent may have a larger meaning. It appears that it may personally represent Mary as an actress on the stage of salvation history, at least in part, (note Revelation 12 which is a highly symbolic passage fraught with interpretive difficulty wherein Mary may be represented as a part of a greater definition of the chapter's use of terminology), by being the vessel of the all-conquering and victorious seed.

So, who then should we designate as the "New Testament Eve"? At first glance we need to remind ourselves that the term "Second Eve", "Last Eve", or even "New Testament Eve" is not found in the Bible. Unlike Paul's employment of the terms "Second Adam" or "Last Adam", "New Testament Eve" is a human made formulation and designation. Perhaps we can employ it to help aid our understanding of salvation history. Maybe this whole exercise is purely academic without any real substance in interpretation. It has been noticed, however, that certain parallels exist between Eve and Mary, the mother of Jesus. In terms of comparison, this author finds that there are also many parallels that can be demonstrated between Eve and Mary Magdalene. Parallelism is defined as a state of close resemblance. It is a state of similarity wherein

---

400   Ibid., 179.
401   Ibid., 182.
402   Ibid., 182.

a counterpart, a match, a likeness can be drawn. Comparisons between both Eve and the two women in the New Testament appear to exist. One theory I have encountered has been loosely called the "Recapitulation theory". This is not the same meaning of the term when, historically, it has been employed by some (erroneously) to refer to the precise nature of Christ's work in life culminating on the cross. Rather, this designation, where it has appeared, has been used to draw some comparisons between Eve and Mary, the mother of Jesus. Recapitulation can be defined as a repetition of a story wherein certain developments are restated, duplicated, reiterated, renewed, or reappear. Recapitulation is a twice-told story employing a certain amount of repetition to complete a tale or bring a story around to a proper conclusion or a satisfactory ending. As such, there are many parallels that apparently exist between Eve and Mary, the mother of Jesus. It also appears that Mary is a complement to Eve completing her story. Mary, in short, succeeds where Eve fails. What follows is a listing of some of the classifications of similarity, parallelism, and completion that make Mary a good candidate for the title of "New Testament Eve".

There is what I call the Grace Factor. Some might want to refer to this as the Creation Factor. Eve started life in a state of Original Righteousness. She possessed no stain of sin. While some believe that Mary began her life in an immaculate state, which is very much in doubt here, by the words of Gabriel it is reasonable to believe that a state of grace was bestowed upon Mary by God prior to her call to divine servanthood. In both cases, whether created or bestowed, grace from God was a major factor in both of their lives in terms of the issue of sin. One could say that God took care of the sin issue in both similar, yet different ways for both women.

Another parallel between the two is the Centrality of the Tree. The Tree of Life and the Tree of Knowledge were located centrally in the Garden of Eden. The cross, also referred to as a "tree" in the New Testament (Acts 5:30, Acts 10:39, Acts 13:29, Galatians 3:13, and 1 Peter 2:24), holds the central focal point of God's redemptive plan in Jesus. Eve touched and ate from the tree. Mary found herself at the foot of the tree on Calvary. Trees shape the central focus of the story for both Eve and Mary.

There is also the Virginity Factor, which the two shared to one degree or another as discussed above. Eve may or may not have been a virgin at the time of the Fall. Mary was a virgin at the time of the birth of Jesus. Neither of them lived life as "perpetual virgins" in the opinion arrived at here. Others see this as a major parallel between the two as already referenced.

Both Eve and Mary shared what I would call superlative "Divinely Originated Relationships". Both were chosen to engage in, possess, and exercise superbly intimate relationships with God Almighty in unique ways. Both were chosen to perform certain tasks and to relate to God in ways shared by no other.

Eve and Mary parallel and complement each other when considering Alien Encounters. Both women received non-human visitors which interrupted their lives. In terms of Eve, her encounter was Satanic in person and nature. Mary experienced the angel Gabriel as God's divinely appointed messenger. While Eve failed in the face of temptation, Mary succeeded in embracing God's plan for her. Mary rightly reverses Eve's disobedience. Both women share in the "Enmity Issue" when it comes to Satan. In the cosmic struggle with the "evil empire", both women engage significant roles.

As such both women are Causal Agents. In terms of the Causality Factor, both help to produce an effect. Eve's sin aids greatly in the totality of complete human failure in regard to disobedience toward God. Mary's willing acceptance of her mission aids greatly the plan of salvation redeeming God's chosen from both original and actual sin. While both Adam and Jesus are the main agents in the failure of the divine constitution and its remedy, both Eve and Mary share what we might call in the world of sports, an assist! It is not the view here, that Mary acts as a Co-Redemptrix, the viewpoint from a Roman Catholic perspective which is explained in the *New Dictionary of Theology* (which refers to the Second Vatican Council's Dogmatic Constitution on the Church) this way:

> Some had hope that Mary would be proclaimed 'Co-Redemptrix' at Vatican II, but this did not happen. But while the term was avoided, the concept is clearly stated. Mary plays a (subsidiary) role in Christ's work of redemption. The incarnation could not occur without Mary's permission or 'fiat' (Luke 1:38). Mary 'gave life to the world' (53); 'Death through Eve, life through Mary' (56). She suffered grievously with Christ at the cross and 'lovingly consented to the immolation of this Victim which she herself had brought forth (58). She 'was united with [Christ] in suffering as he died on the cross' and co-operated 'in the Saviour's work of restoring supernatural life to souls' (61).[403]

The advocacy that it took two to bring down the human race and that it takes two to restore it says too much. Mary is a major participant in the drama of salvation, but she is not a Co-Redemptrix. While she may have suffered much personal pain and anguish at the foot of the cross that is precisely the point that needs to be advanced. Mary is at the foot of the cross. She is a witness and spectator like Mary Magdalene, John, and the other women. She herself is not on the cross. Her personal suffering at the death of Jesus is not salvific! Jesus does the work of atonement and he accomplishes it alone! However, if the concept Co-Redemptrix (depending upon how you understand the prefix) refers to a personage in fellowship with and aiding the Redeemer historically in the accomplishment of this work (who accomplishes the work of redemption solely by himself as stated above) then this terminology might have some validity. That is if, and only if, it is understood that Mary is not, in any way, a fellow or real actress in the remission of sin. If the latter is the case, the terminology can certainly be viewed as confusing and possibly, even unintentionally, deceptive.

While it may be tempting to draw a contrast between the origin of death due to Adam and Eve and the restoration of life from Christ and

---

403   Sinclair B. Ferguson, David F. Wright, and J.I. Packer, eds. *New Dictionary of Theology* (Downers Grove, Illinois: InterVarsity Press, 1988), 416.

Mary, the view in mind here is that we are dealing with four deaths and four renewals of life. Jesus died on the cross and his life both physically and spiritually was restored. This effort was to procure the conquest of the grave and grant new life for and to (in a primary sense), Adam, Eve, and Mary, although some might speculate, through the development of the dogma of the Assumption of Mary, that Mary shared the same destiny of Jesus. The idea advanced in this speculative thinking is that Adam and Eve's destiny was the grave, while Jesus and Mary did not succumb to the grave but were translated to the intermediate heaven. While the idea of the Assumption of Mary is possible in the providence of God, there is no Biblical warrant for such a belief as well as no historical substantiation. The fact of the matter is that Jesus did die and was buried. It is likely that Mary succumbed to physical death and was buried as well. The good news is that because Jesus lives, the remaining three, as well as God's chosen, will live, too. Death does involve all four! Life involves all four as well! Concerning the Assumption of Mary, the *New Dictionary of Theology* says this:

> In the fourth century there arose the legend that Mary had been assumed into heaven, like Enoch and Elijah in the Old Testament. During the early Middle Ages it came to be generally believed. From the seventh century there was pressure for its definition as a dogma and this finally took place in 1950. Pope Pius XII defined it in his apostolic constitution, Munificentissimus Deus: 'Since [Jesus Christ] was able to do [Mary] so great an honour as to keep her safe from the corruption of the tomb, we must believe that he actually did so…The majestic mother of God… finally achieved, as the supreme crown of her privileges, that she should be preserved immune from the corruption of the tomb and , like her son before her, having conquered death should be carried up, in body and soul, to the celestial glory of heaven, there to reign as Queen at the right hand of her Son, the immortal king of the ages.'[404]

The *New Dictionary of Theology* further states, "Again the basis for the definition is said to be its theological suitability and the consensus of

---

404 Ibid., 416.

the contemporary Roman Catholic Church. It should be noted that the doctrine concerns more than an (alleged) episode in Mary's personal history. It is the basis for belief in her as Queen of Heaven and as mediatrix."[405] While this author finds some merit and Biblical substantiation in the claims for Mary as "Daughter of Zion", and possibly a parallel between the Old Testament Ark of the Covenant and the virgin birth (neither of which are developed here), the idea of Mary as Queen of Heaven and Mediatrix probably goes too far. While a cultural case (and possible Old Testament references) in terms of the Hebrew royal society can be made for Mary as "Queen Mother", the *New Dictionary of Theology* notes that Nestorius warned "his hearers to 'beware lest you make the Virgin a goddess.'"[406] The *New Dictionary of Theology* states, "This warning was timely in that the cult of Mary burgeoned during the Middle Ages. She came to be seen as Queen of Heaven, a title that enjoys no favour in Scripture (Je. 7:18; 44:17-19, 25)."[407]

In terms of Mary as Mediatrix, it is also worth noting what the *New Dictionary of Theology* records about it: "In the Middle Ages the practice grew of praying to saints. Mary became especially popular. There was a tendency to see Jesus Christ as stern and unapproachable and so the faithful were directed to Mary as a sympathetic figure who could mediate between the believer and Christ. This view of Mary as mediatrix was forcefully stated in 1891 by Pope Leo XIII in an encyclical: 'Nothing is bestowed on us except through Mary, as God himself wills. Therefore, as no-one can draw near to the supreme Father except through the Son, so also one can scarcely draw near to the Son except through his mother.' The Second Vatican Council reaffirms Mary's role of mediatrix, but states that it should be so understood as 'neither [to] take away from nor [to] add anything to the dignity and efficacy of Christ the one mediator.'"[408]

While additional parallels between Eve and Mary, the mother of Jesus, probably exist and have not been included or examined here,

---

405   Ibid., 416.
406   Ibid., 415.
407   Ibid., 415.
408   Ibid., 415.

a final one for our consideration is the concept of motherhood. Both Eve and Mary, it can be said, share in what I call Human Classification Leadership. Adam, who has Eden naming rights, identifies his wife by the name Eve. The name "Eve" apparently refers to the concept of life and means "living, lively, and enlivening". She becomes, Genesis 3:20, the "mother of all the living". Mary is often regarded as the mother of all those redeemed and regenerated in Christ. The concept of the motherhood of Mary appears in Luke 1:43, wherein Elizabeth exclaims to her niece or cousin, "Why am I so favored, that the mother of my Lord should come to me?" From this Scriptural rendering, the idea of "theotokos" was advanced. Theotokos means "one who gave birth to God". It is often translated and referred to as "mother of God." As indicated by the *New Dictionary of Theology*, the term was employed to safeguard the concept of incarnation and Deity of Christ. Historically, Nestorius preferred the term "Christotokos", "mother of Christ", but "theotokos" became the preferred terminology for Mary in order to counter the possible advocacy of the theory of adoptionism concerning Jesus.[409]

A prime reference for the advocacy of Mary being the mother of all those in Christ, is often linked to John 19:25-27. This is the scene of the crucifixion in John's Gospel. Tasker, Barclay, and Morris all note and comment upon the four "faithful women" who stand near the foot of the cross. Morris compares the four "believing women" over and against the "four unbelieving soldiers" who make up the execution detail.[410] The disciple John is also there standing among Mary, the wife of Clopas, Jesus' mother, the unnamed sister of Jesus' mother Mary (probably Salome, the mother of James and John), and Mary Magdalene. Barclay comments that these four women are "not unimportant and unnoticed". Mary of Clopas is often identified as the wife or daughter of Clopas (often spelled Cleopas or Cleophas). Possibly she is the mother of James, son of Alphaeus. While nothing is really known about her, she is apparently related to the family of Joseph and Mary. Obviously, she is a follower of Jesus and acutely interested in his person

---

409   Ibid., 415.
410   Morris, 810-811.

and the events surrounding him. Barclay comments that the love that these four women had for Jesus outweighed any risk to their persons in being there. Jesus' mother is present out of both love for her child and the special loving knowledge she has about him, which is much her life's story. If Jesus' mother's sister is Salome, the mother of the sons of Zebedee, she is an individual Jesus once chided. As Barclay comments, Salome accepted Jesus' rebuke and loved him with an "undiminished devotion." Mary Magdalene owes Jesus everything. He rescued both her soul and person. As Barclay comments, "her love for him could never die" and neither could she "forget what he had done for her." Each and every one of these women probably represent, in a deeply meaningful way, the variety and special depth in terms of relationship that can be known and embraced with the Christ. John, most likely of course, is a cousin of Jesus and the one whose own self-designation of the deeper relationship with Jesus is termed as "the disciple whom Jesus loved."[411]

As Jesus hangs on the cross he concludes both his family responsibilities and missional activity as portrayed through his last recorded statements. In terms of his mother and John, he deals with both the immediacy of the present time and the future. As presumed here, that Jesus is the eldest son of Joseph and Mary, he discharges his duties vis-à-vis his mother. As Barclay writes, even amid the cosmic struggle swirling around him "he never forgot the simple things that lay near home." Barclay further states, "to the end of the day he was thinking more of the sorrows of others than of his own."[412] Jesus charges John, his most loyal and reliable disciple, assigning him the task of both the provision and care, as well as the protection, of his mother. This charge is to be understood concerning the immediacy of the moment (verse 27b), and quite possibly extending into the future ("from that hour on" or "from that time on"). Jesus' brothers, to whom this task would rightly fall, were not present, nor were they believers in Jesus' person and mission. This, of course, would change following the Resurrection

---

411   William Barclay, *The Gospel of John, The Daily Study Bible Series,* vol. 2 (Philadelphia, The Westminster Press, 1956), 297-299.
412   Ibid., 299.

(the Bible indicates that Jesus spent significant time in Galilee during the days of Resurrection; he appeared to James – 1 Corinthians 15:7; and his brothers were present with believers as recorded in Acts 1:14). Perhaps due to the location, the professional responsibilities of his brothers and Mary's vital connection with the centrality of believers, John was charged with taking responsibility for her. This committal of Jesus is also a "two-way street". As Barclay points out, there is mutuality in their care for each other.[413] Tasker points out, that in his opinion, this is the beginning or "birth" of a new "Christian fellowship."[414] So, what exactly is "born" here? While Marsh typically reads into the text a multitude of potential meanings, he does make reference to the nourishment Mary can provide John in terms of his faith which can be "found in and from her who bore him."[415] The concept of motherhood for the Christian fellowship and community found in Jesus' words, "Behold your mother" and "Behold your son" is what has given Biblical impetus, or substantiation, in the rendering of some, to the mother-hood of Mary concerning all those who live in Christ. Is this saying too much? Is this what is intended exegetically in the passage, or are we dealing with eisegetical supposition here? Again, is this saying too much? While the Bible states that Eve is the "mother of all the living" (Genesis 3:20), there is no specific statement saying the same for Mary. This, of course, does not necessarily negate the concept or the designa-tion! If John is to regard Mary as his own mother, which appears to be a personal and individual dynamic, how can this notion be extrapolated to the entire Body of believers? Where is the evidence in the text for every follower of Christ to regard her as mother? While not completely conclusive, there is some rationale for this concept as long as the con-notation "mother" does not take on the status of Deity or some lesser divine understanding. Mary is a human being. She is one of us. She is an individual created by God. She is a creature, not divinity, so she shares nothing of the essence of the Trinity. If, however, all those who

---

413   Ibid., 299.
414   Tasker, 210-211.
415   John Marsh, *Saint John, The Pelican New Testament Commentaries* (Harmondsworth, Middlesex, England: Penguin Books Ltd., 1974), 616.

have embraced Jesus Christ as Savior and Lord are understood to be unified with Christ the Head of the Body, and since Mary is the mother of Jesus Christ the Head, could it not be said, understanding the unity of the Head and Body, that Mary is our mother through the Christ? Chapter 12 of First Corinthians speaks to this type of arrangement. The concept of Mary as mother might have some legitimacy in the light of Jesus' words in Mark 10:29-31. If Revelation 12 personally represents Satan, Mary as the woman in the text, and the woman's child as Jesus, a reference is made in verse 17 to the "rest of her offspring." If members of the Body of Christ are in reference here as Mary's other "seed", then it may be considered, in a spiritual and symbolic way, that she is the spiritual mother of all in Christ.

While this author does not concur with everything indicated about Mary, the mother of Jesus, in the early church by the early church fathers, historically down through the centuries including the Reformers, or in recent times (from the 19th century onward), the designation of Mary as the "second Eve" is plausible and has enough evidence to support the position's legitimacy. There is, however, that other contender for the title "the second Eve" as stated at the beginning of this chapter. Let us now turn to examine the evidence for the parallelism and recapitulation of another candidate for the designation, "the Second Eve." Let us now consider the candidacy of Mary Magdalene.

Before we consider my lengthy list, let us remember that Mary Magdalene was also present at the foot of the cross. She was among the "faithful four" pointed out by Tasker, Barclay, and Morris. She also, from the Resurrection onward, apparently, shared an intense friendship, enjoyed close fellowship, and participated in a residential arrangement with Mary, the mother of Jesus, and John. The close communion of the two Marys should not be missed or discounted! Their relational life circumstances may hint at something quite interesting to consider!

The inauguration of the story of the human dilemma in the Garden of Eden with Eve seems to find its solution in the Garden of Joseph of Arimathea with Mary Magdalene. On the one side is Genesis chapters

2 and 3 which detail the problem. On the other hand, we have John 20, which is the story's resolution and restoration.

In Genesis 2:21-23, God does something quite extraordinary. God creates the woman and brings her to the man. The setting is quite interesting. Adam, much like a surgical procedure, is placed in a state of unconsciousness by God. God performs some sort of surgery on him in the creation of the woman. The text indicates that God does not place Eve with Adam, God brings her to Adam as if she is physically created nearby and walks toward her husband much to his delight. There is a presentation by God of Eve to Adam here in this text. A presentation of this great gift is given! In John 20, Jesus and Mary Magdalene are represented as being in proximity to each other but still separated by a short distance. Jesus stands outside the tomb facing the sepulcher. Mary Magdalene comes from inside the entrance of the crypt and apparently runs into the embrace of Jesus after she comes to an awareness of his identity. Eve experiences life and becomes a wonderfully celebrated gift for Adam. Mary Magdalene experiences new life and receives the wondrously marvelous gift of eternal relationship in Jesus. The movement in the twin tales is of Eve walking forth and encountering Adam, along with Mary Magdalene running toward and embracing the Christ.

Such movement illuminates another action. In the story of Eve, following the Fall, she figuratively, with Adam, runs away from the presence of God. "They hid from the Lord God among the trees of the garden" as it recorded in Genesis 3:8. Both Eve and Mary Magdalene take to flight in their respective gardens. Eve flees from the presence of God. Mary Magdalene runs toward God's incarnate presence. Eve is fearful and afraid of God's presence. Mary Magdalene desires to embrace God's presence.

In the flight by their respective persons, we note that Eve embraces the lie (Genesis 3:2-5) while Mary Magdalene runs to embrace the truth (John 20:17). Eve is ultimately disobedient. Mary Magdalene will have nothing to do with that which tempted Eve. She obediently embraces the one in whom she has placed all her trust!

In the saga of the tension between obedience and disobedience, we find that Eve is captured by the devil and comes under the curse of death, both physically and spiritually. Mary Magdalene finds herself freed from the devil, not only through her personal deliverance from demonic oppression by Jesus during his ministry but ultimately from the inherited curse of the lineage of Adam and Eve. Eve, in her story, enters death. Mary Magdalene, in her story, enters life. The good news is that the story of Jesus' encounter with Mary Magdalene redounds to the ultimate restoration of Eve, to which, in the opinion of this author, is symbolized in the person of Mary Magdalene.

In Eve, Satan brilliantly succeeds in his deception and goal of ruining God's creation, most specifically God's ultimate creation of life formed in God's image. In Mary Magdalene we discover the first tangible proof, outside of Jesus' Resurrection itself, of the permanent and ultimate failure of Satan's diabolical cause.

Both Eve and Mary Magdalene experience Satanic encounters. Eve experiences, in the temptation through the serpent, Satan up close and personal. While Mary Magdalene may never have experienced the personal Satan firsthand, she did experience his demonic and evil empire through her possession entertainment, as well as by being a witness to the sufferings of Jesus.

In terms of Satanic encounters, both Eve and Mary shared in Alien encounters. Eve with Satan, of course, and the fierce guardian to the entrance of Eden, and Mary with the angels within Joseph's tomb. One encounter led to death and banishment. The other encounter was a sign of life.

In the garden of Eden, it is revealed that humanity, in Adam and Eve, move from a figurative atmospheric calm into a major storm. God arrives in thunder and fury as he pronounces judgment on those culpable for sin (Genesis 3:8ff). In the Gospel accounts, Jesus takes the storm upon himself and, weathering it, brings a calm to Joseph's garden. Mary Magdalene finds that the storm that she has experienced has been totally calmed by Jesus, both in terms of her own personal history and in the history of humankind which she comes to represent. In Jesus God truly walks in the garden "in the cool of the day". It is the cool of a new day! Where the time in Eden probably represents the end of the day. Jesus' appearance to Mary Magdalene represents the dawn of a new day!

The story of the need for salvation originates in Adam. The resolution of the problem for Adam, Eve, and all humanity is found in Jesus. He restores the salvific state and does the totality of the work. Mary Magdalene is the first person to experience that restoration. In Jesus' encounter with her, God has fulfilled the hope of God's promise to Eve.

With the circumstances of the Fall reversed, we now find that "Paradise Lost" is Paradise found or restored. Eve is a major player and witness of that which has been lost. Mary Magdalene is a major witness and, by grace, the first and prime recipient of the news and reality of the restoration.

Both Eve and Mary Magdalene share the centrality of the tree. The tree of knowledge is central in the story of Eve. The tree of the cross is central in the story of Mary Magdalene.

There is also a type of virginity factor present in the stories of Eve and Mary Magdalene, though not as prominent a symbol and reality as with Mary, the mother of Jesus. Both women started life as virgins. While the surrender of Eve's virginity has nothing to do with sin and is part of God's wonderful plan for humanity, Eve still succumbed to sin. Mary Magdalene also succumbed to sin and, perhaps, the surrender of her virginity as a part of it. This we do not know because we have no record of her life prior to her deliverance by Jesus. We do not know if her life once included prostitution. We do not know if her life once included immoral sexual actions. We do not know if her life once included marriage and a husband. In all these things, we simply are subject to guesswork. What may be more likely is that she lived the rest of her life unmarried and chaste. Often in my youth ministry I picked up and utilized the term "secondary virginity" in presentation and discussion with teenagers concerning the illicit loss of their virginity through unmarried sexual acts. Mary Magdalene may be a person, after her deliverance or following the Resurrection of Jesus, who took the vow and lived the life of "secondary virginity" in terms of her commitment to the Christ. If people want to postulate on a virginal connection between Eve and Mary, the mother of Jesus, why not speculate about Mary Magdalene as well?

This writer also sees Eve and Mary Magdalene as representatives of class leadership. Eve is the original woman from which all humanity derives. Can not Mary Magdalene be the new representative of all those who embrace Christ? After all, it was to her that Jesus first appeared! Mary Magdalene is the first person to share an embrace with Jesus in the aftermath of the reality of the reception of new life. Mary Magdalene is the image and model of the redemption and restoration of Eve and her offspring. She is the receptor of new life for Eve and all humankind. The disaster that was Eden is now over. The circumstances have been dealt with and reversed. God has completed the rescue of God's own. It is as if it is Eve herself coming from the tomb. Eve is the mother of all the living. Mary Magdalene is the lead figure in all those who come to embrace Christ. Could not her person and example illustrate a type of new spiritual fellowship and, in one way of looking at it, a redeemed and spiritual motherhood?

What then can be made of all this? What conclusion can we agree upon? It seems to this author that if there are those who affirm that death (in terms of the women involved) came through Eve and life through the birth of Jesus to Mary, should not we at least conclude that Mary Magdalene has received both the promise and the outworking of the plan of salvation which involved the other two women? If Mary, the mother of Jesus, can be considered by some as the "bridge" between the two Testaments, and the connector between the events of the Fall and Christ's Passion and Bodily Resurrection,[416] can we not subscribe to Mary Magdalene, in Joseph's Garden, the concluding female personage of this great trilogy to whom all things come to completion? The life promised to Eve and born to Mary now bursts gloriously before Mary Magdalene as she hurriedly embraces its renewal. The story of the Bible

---

416   This concept of Mary, the mother of Jesus being a "bridge" or connector between the Old and New Testaments is a concept that this author has read and/or heard on a number of occasions throughout his career.

comes down to two men and three women and a very special God whose favor is magnificently bestowed on the five main Biblical protagonists. If Mary, the mother of Jesus, is considered the "New Eve" in terms of fulfilling the promise given to Eve by birthing the Christ, cannot Mary Magdalene be envisioned as the "New Eve" who walks away from the sentence of death and imbibes of life once more? There are some ways in which Mary, the mother of Jesus, is a perfect fit for the designation of "New Eve." There are some ways in which Mary Magdalene fits the picture. What if it takes two to complete God's salvific masterpiece? Personally, I see no tension here. I am happy to receive both women and the role they played in God's great design. Both women testify to the glory and magnificence of God. Both women, who are so inter-connected in the story of Christ, in the early church, and in the living out of life together, can mutually share the New Testament or Second Eve designation. Each played a significant role in the resolution of the dilemma caused by or which befell Eve. Both participated and shared in the glorious situational out-working and results! While it is the position of this author that the parallels between Eve and Mary Magdalene are too strong to dismiss a rendering of Mary Magdalene as the "New Testament" or "Second" Eve, also understood by the author is the advocacy and the case for Mary, the mother of Jesus. This author sees nothing inherently wrong for those who desire to hold the two in tension as long as Mary Magdalene is not erased from this designation. A fair criticism can be made here that I am contradicting my own thesis. The intent of this author is to give Mary, the mother of Jesus, the respect she deserved for her vital role in the drama, and to recognize the role played by Mary of Magdala that concludes the drama. Mary Magdalene, reprising the role of Eve cannot be discounted. In this, she has been greatly ignored. She is both the end of one story and the beginning of a new eternal one. Therefore, the designation of the "New Testament Eve" fits her well!

23

"Bye, For Now"

"In this world we're just beginning to understand the miracle of living. Baby, I was afraid before. But I'm not afraid anymore. Ooh, baby do you know what that's worth? Ooh heaven is a place on earth. They say in heaven love comes first… ooh heaven is a place on earth"

(Rick Nowels and Ellen Shipley/Belinda Carlisle)

Cemeteries have always held a sort of fascination for me. Growing up, my father, mother, and grandmother would take my brother, sister, and myself to "decorate" the graves on Memorial Day. Some of my relatives were veterans who fought in World War I. We would travel from cemetery to cemetery because the family was divided up among at least seven burial locations in four different counties. What always fascinated me were the older monuments one would find, and the inscriptions chiseled into them. Some inscriptions quoted the Bible and the hope of eternity. Some gave reference to the coming resurrection and the promise of the new heaven and new earth. Among my favorite "top ten" Bible quotations is the verse from Revelation 21:5 which reads, "Behold, I make all things new (KJV)!" I once found this verse inscribed on a tombstone and thought it most appropriate, especially in light of Paul's great desire to experience the "out-resurrection from the dead" (Philippians 3:11). One of the things I have always appreciated from the generations that preceded my own was the firm grasp, confidence, and expectation the truly faithful had in their own physical resurrection and ongoing extension of life in the coming eschaton. Death was not viewed as a tragic termination, but a step into the embrace of Jesus who ushers in eternality. The glorious expectation of resurrection and upcoming life in the confines of the "new heaven and new earth" was virtually a universal perspective looked upon, not with dread, but with joy. Separation from loved ones was never viewed as permanent, but a part of Christ's glorious ingathering of his own. One woman, whose memorial service I had the privilege to officiate, is named, Mary Bovard. Mary lived to be 101 years young. She was a marvelous individual who always lived in expectation of the next time she was in your company. Her expression at parting was "Bye, for now!" This phrase was not only meant for contemporary life, but it had an eschatological meaning to it as well. In my family, we adopted a phrase from my late cousin, Doug Atkinson, who always said when parting, "Catch you later!" As time went on, the phrase became one utilized at the translation of family members at the time of death. "Catch you later" took on an eschatological meaning for us as well. I have always linked Paul's race running imagery (Philippians 3:12-14, 2 Timothy 4:7) with those passages of the eschaton (Philippians 3:10, 1 Corinthians 15, and Revelation 21 and 22). In this life we are inexorably moving toward our final disposition. There are loved ones who precede us. There are loved ones who will follow us. From the eternal perspective, the brief time of separation, while it can be painful, is fortunately temporary. What matters is the end game! What matters is ending up in the state of permanent reunion. For the adherent to the Body of Christ, the phrase, "Bye, for now" becomes both confessional and prophetic. In imitation of the hope forecast in

Christ's Ascension, we confidently await the future God has declared we will one day inherit and with which we will eternally imbibe.

The embrace of Jesus and Mary Magdalene becomes the first indication that a whole new world and reality will be graciously ours. This embrace communicates that the reality that spoiled Eden is terminated, and a new and glorious paradise awaits us. The fullest description of this new paradise is found in that last chapters of John's Revelation.

As stated earlier in this writing, the Bible really does have a distinct beginning and ending. Somewhere during my pastoral career, as I referred to earlier, I heard someone say that "the Bible has bookends!" Whoever that individual is, he was certainly correct. In review, the first three chapters of Genesis introduce us the major circumstances, themes, and dilemmas to which the rest of the book addresses. The first three chapters of Genesis charts creation, the reason for our creation, the character and nature of God, and walks us into the problem that we still face, suffer through, and continue to endure. At the end of the Bible's 66 books, roughly the last three chapters of Revelation mirror, in reverse, those of Genesis 1 through 3. Revelation chapters 20 through 22 form the conclusion of the Bible. It charts the final consummation of the issue. Here God walks us out of the problem that humanity faces and endures. We experience from God the final resolution of the Christ event and the re-creation of all things unto the state of perfection desired by God for God's own.

Revelation 21 through 22:5 is the section of these three chapters which describes for the reader the coming New Heaven and the New Earth. One can divide this pericope into two subsections: Revelation 21:1-8 represents the New Creation; and Revelation 21:9 through 22:5 represents the New Jerusalem.

There are a number of significant things the reader learns about the coming eschaton from this text. One thing that is prominent in the book of Revelation and appears to be a major theme is the narrative employing the word "new". In Revelation there are five things that are declared "new": God gives us a "new song" in 5:9; God gives us a "new name" in 2:17; God gifts us with a "new heaven and a new earth" in 21:1;

God gifts us with the "new Jerusalem" in 21:2 (the coming of the city is declared in 3:12, but actualized in 21:2); and the greatest declaration of newness in the whole apocalypse is found in 21:5, "Behold, I make ALL THINGS new!" How are we to understand this newness? The Koine Greek holds the answer. The word for "new" here is "kainos", meaning "fresh".[417] The word "neos", which means "recent", is not utilized by the author.[418] The meaning is clear in the text. In the person of Jesus Christ, God gives everything, including us, a fresh start.

Another significant thing in our text is that the "Intermediate Heaven"[419] is replaced by the "New Heaven and New Earth." In the Bible there is movement in terms of the concept of "paradise" from Eden, to the place of paradise in Sheol (otherwise known as "Abraham's bosom"), to the intermediate heaven where the departed spirits of the righteous currently inhabit, to the eschaton's final disposition of the "new heaven and new earth". Paradise lost in Eden is paradise found once more. Paradise, which once was Eden (according to some, such as the Reasons to Believe group in California, a tiny location now at the bottom of the Persian Gulf to the south and west of the Straits of Hormuz),[420] now encompasses the whole sphere of planet earth. The "new heaven and new earth" is Eden restored but significantly enlarged and enhanced to the "nth degree". It is not the same Eden – not by a long shot!

Another thing we must reckon with in the text is that the readers then, as well as us today, must understand that the reality of the new heaven and new earth is a rejection of any concept of philosophical dualism. Flesh and the physical creation is not something which is evil of which we need to escape. Our physical countenance or bodies, particularly our coming glorified bodies, are understood, counted by, and referred to by God as being "good". As we discussed previously, God's initial declaration of God's human creation is in fact designated

---

417 Walter Bauer, *A Greek-English Lexicon of the New Testament and Other Early Christian Literature,* trans. and ed. William F. Arndt and F. Wilbur Gingrich (Chicago: The University of Chicago Press, 1957), 394-395.

418 Ibid, 537-538.

419 Randy Alcorn, *Heaven,* (Carol Stream, Illinois: Tyndale House Publishers, Inc., 2004), 13, 15, 41-49.

420 Hugh Ross, *Navigating Genesis,* (Coving, CA: Reasons to Believe, 2014), 96-101.

by God's statement as being "very good."[421] Flesh and spirit are one. Heaven and earth are one. As far as this author can discern, the major outline of events detailed (not taking into view the debate concerning the Rapture and the Millennium) here falls into four significant actions by God. We have the second bodily or physical coming of our Lord Jesus Christ, known as "The Second Coming" by the Christian world. The resurrection of the dead and the embodiment of the new physical resurrection body granted to the righteous is the next major happening. The Judgment eventually takes place. Finally, the age known as the "eschaton", wherein heaven and earth become one, is accomplished. The unification, which ends all forms of separation (Romans 8:35-39), is finally achieved!

Another concept, which one can read between the lines of our text, is the comparison that is made to the ancient city of Babylon and its Biblical symbolism. It appears as if the "New Jerusalem" is being compared to the wicked Babylon. Babylon represents everything wicked, evil, and rebellious toward God. Babylon, along with the concept of Babel (which is another idea possibly behind the text), signifies all the rebellion of humanity toward God and our own concerted effort to construct the ultimate city based on our own design and for our own purposes. The giving, by God, of the New Jerusalem is just that – it is a gift. We do not build the city. God builds the city and presents it to us. Through the giving of the New Jerusalem, any remaining idea of evil Babylon is both judged and thrown on the ash heap of history! The New Jerusalem, which is the city of God, descends upon the planet. While images of the movie, "Independence Day",[422] might play in the minds of some, this descent is not some giant alien space ship bent on an ill intent and is wholly different than Babylon. Humanity cannot build the "city of God". Only God can construct and gift us with the perfect city. As a city, the new Jerusalem is fresh, clean, and clear of anything untoward. It is holy! Holy can mean "set apart" or distinct. Holy can also carry the

---

421   Genesis 1:31.
422   Roland Emmerich and Dean Devlin, *Independence Day*, motion picture, directed by Roland Emmerich (Los Angeles, CA: Centropolis Entertainment and 20th Century Fox, July 2, 1996).

idea of perfection.[423] The new Jerusalem is "perfect" according to God's purposes and design for its inhabitants.

One of the things I find interesting in Revelation 21 is the comment that the "sea" is no more. Over my career, I have noted how disturbing this is to some people who imagine an eternity of beach life! Rather than a reference to the newly transformed planet being void of oceans or large bodies of water, the concept advanced here appears to be symbolic in nature. It is my assertion that Revelation is highly symbolic and, perhaps, coded. While not in any way, shape, or form an expert on the book of Revelation, it is the opinion here that the book is highly symbolic and offers much deep meaning. This author has formed some educated opinions concerning the book, but leaves much of the debate, including the time-frame reference of the text, to the on-going examination and discussion by the scholarly community representing a wide variety of perspectives. Ultimately, there is only one perspective, meaning, and interpretation to the text. This author is hesitant to declare that anyone has completely discovered it! The meaning of the sea in context here has several possible meanings as advanced by various thinkers. The sea can represent a number of negatives in the ancient culture of the Bible. It can represent a symbol of separateness. In other words, the sea acts as a barrier keeping people apart. Once again, in my mind, the end of Romans 8 comes into view with the idea that there is no longer any separation from God or among God's people. The sea may represent, in antiquity, an alien and hostile environment, the concept of which is totally, and finally, dispatched by God. Apparently, another concept of the sea, in antiquity, represents it as a cauldron of evil and death. Out of the sea, according to the imagery of Revelation, comes evil personified. The good news, in this case, is that the source of evil in the world has been eliminated. The sea can be a symbol for the changefulness of the world. It can represent a maelstrom of the conflicting tides of issues and problems. If so, Revelation represents these as no more. I have

---

423   David B. Guralnik and Joseph H. Friend, eds., *Webster's New World Dictionary of the American Language, College Edition* (Cleveland and New York: The World Publishing Company, 1968) 693-694.

heard that the sea can represent the world of politics. The good news with Christ's eschaton is that the political, mercifully, is banished once and for all. It is our Lord who reigns and reigns completely. Everything political is now of a bygone era! The sea was also imagined as a canopy covering the vast subterranean cavern representing the place of confinement.[424] Known in antiquity as Hades, it was the place of the dead. Part of the good news prophecy of the book of Revelation is that Hades, like death, hell, sin, and Satan will be cast into the all-consuming Lake of Fire (Revelation 20:14).

Following human expulsion from Eden, the mention of, and the concept of, cities develops in Genesis.[425] What matters here is only what can be gleaned of the new Jerusalem itself. Much of the content, character, and description of this immense city is described in the verses following the text under consideration in this chapter. The new Jerusalem is both a new city and a holy city. It is the city of God. It is different and unlike any city that earth has ever known. As it is God's city, it is not our city. God is the architect, designer, engineer, and builder of the city. We are not! In reality, we have nothing to do with the city other than to inhabit it, enjoy it, and marvel at it. The city is all of God! The city comes down to us from God and cements the concept of heaven now on earth in a number of ways. The city is the final expression of God's grace to us. The city is a gift. It is the ultimate and central focus of the newly transformed planet. We must not miss the fact that it descends onto the planet. It comes from above. It is of the top down, and not of the bottom up. The city is the reverse of Babel.[426] It carries overtones of the Incarnation and Virgin Birth. The city is of the God who came down and tabernacles with us for a while.[427] This time, the tabernacling is final, permanent, and complete!

---

424   Rob Phillips, "The Sea No Longer Existed – Revelation 21:1," *Once Delivered* (November 1, 2016), https://oncedelivered.net/.../the-sea-no-longer-existed-revelation-21:1 (accessed April 16, 2019).
425   Genesis 4:17.
426   Genesis 11:1-9.
427   John 1:14.

Picking up the theme of the "with-me God" throughout the Bible, particularly in John 14, God does several significant things. Jesus returns for his bride; Corpus Christi – the Body of Christ, his church. Jesus also brings the "mansion" with him – the prepared place. The concept of the insula or courtyard is defined in its description meaning that our social and relational life will be totally that which is approved and defined by God in a most blessed state. Our eternal interaction, one with another, will reach both a secure and blessed state.

The security and blessedness we experience in the house and city of God is due to the fact that seven evils will no longer plague us. Seven evils will be no more! The sea, symbolically the source of evil, has been eliminated.[428] Death is no more.[429] Mourning the dead has ceased because death itself no longer plagues humanity.[430] Weeping due to decay, decline, and death has been terminated.[431] Pain, particularly that of separated love through death, has ceased.[432] The curse upon humanity has ended.[433] The terrors of this world, symbolized as night, are no more.[434] All these things, which are the debilitating effects of sin, are abolished forever and will no longer be found in the city on the planet.

What ends the text under scrutiny is a declaration of the finish. In 21:6 a grand pronouncement that the end of the sinful human era which began in Eden is over. With its end, the plagues recorded in the book of Revelation and everything else that is the scourge of humankind ends as well. All evil has been terminated forever! Satan, his minions, death, hell, sin, and sin's consequences are completely vanquished. Revelation 21:6 can also be a reference to the descent of the city with all its overflowing and effervescent blessings. The city of God has arrived! The reality of the "with-me God" is both permanent and secure. The story of paradise lost and found ends here. The story of the Bible is now complete. The story of the human grappling with God has now come to

---

428   Revelation 21:1.
429   Revelation 21:4.
430   Revelation 21:4.
431   Revelation 21:4.
432   Revelation 21:4.
433   Revelation 22:3.
434   Revelation 21:25; 22:5.

resolution. The story of Eden and its aftermath is over. God wins! We who belong to God win as well. Now a new and glorious story begins!

During my years at Pittsburgh Theological Seminary there was much discussion in the Church and Society curriculum, particularly in terms of Neo-orthodox theology, Liberation theology, and Process Theology, that humanity would actually evolve and advance, enabling us to construct the "City of God" ourselves. It seems to me that much of this notion developed, particularly in the United States, from the optimism following World War II with the way the U.S. government was able to mobilize and effectively conduct the war to its victorious completion. It was no small effort. In fact, it was an astounding effort! If the federal government could take on and complete such a monumental task, there was no telling what advancements "big government" could entertain and accomplish. This idea seems to have been translated into the former, and now struggling, mainline denominations. Denominational leadership seemed to me to believe, teach, and work toward the building of the city of God in cooperation with government policy and political action. Living through the administration of 12 Presidents, particularly the Johnson administration with its "Great Society" programs, how has this worked out, I might ask you? The human hubris, arrogance, and pride appears to me to have been blasphemous. To think that we could actually build the city of God here on earth through our own efforts, even if it is understood that we are cooperating with the Spirit of God to do so, appears to me at this time in my life to be complete folly. There is no cooperation with the Spirit of God on this matter because the Bible indicates that the city descends from heaven. The city is that of our God. The city is a gift of God. Those who advocate this alternative idea do so from a position that is totally alien to the Scriptures and miss the whole point of salvation history. We cannot save ourselves. Everything and all is a gift of God. We can do nothing without God. Apart from God nothing can be accomplished. The idea that we can construct the city of God is not, and has never been, part of God's plan. To endeavor to do so through human effort will not work. It has not worked. It will never work. Such efforts just continue to exacerbate the mess we have made of this world. It seems to me that the history of humankind, particularly of the 20th century, exemplifies this assertion. This is, of course, the sin of the tower of Babel. We all know the pronouncement of God on that subject many millennia ago. The city of God is God's city. It descends from above. It is given by God and reverses Babel. Through the gift of the transformation of the planet and the descent of the new Jerusalem, instead of casting people abroad, it brings people back into the fold again. Together we enjoy the community created by God fulfilling all the themes of goodness and completion to which the Bible testifies.

The description of the final consummation of things found in Revelation 20-22, have both their genesis and declaration of that which is to come in the encounter and embrace of Jesus and Mary Magdalene in Joseph's Garden on Resurrection Day morning. What is communicated in this startling event for Mary is nothing less than the beginning of the history of eternity. From this moment, the revelation and unfolding of forever, takes place. It is for Mary. It is for us. If Mary is the human representative of the redeemed Eve, God is communicating the beginning of the end which has no end. In the words of that great old resurrection hymn, "The strife is o'er, the battle done; The victory of life is won; The song of triumph has begun. Alleluia! The powers of death have done their worst, But Christ their legions hath dispersed: Let shouts of holy joy outburst! Alleluia!"[435]

---

435   Giovanni Pierluigi da Palestrina, *The Strife is O'er, The Battle Done.* Adapted by William H. Monk and translated by Francis Pott (Cologne, Germany, 1695).

24

Responding to The King of Terrors

"Dying with Jesus, by death reckoned mine; Living with Jesus a new life divine; Looking to Jesus till glory doth shine, Moment by moment, O Lord, I am thine."

(Daniel W. Whittle)

One of the strangest moments of my life occurred in late July of 2001. I was visiting an 89-year-old member of my congregation whom I came to love dearly. Her name was Margaret Evans Jacques. I visited her monthly. She became like an adopted grandmother to me. She lived at Longwood at Oakmont in Verona, PA. As was her habit, Margaret would linger outside her door and wave to her guests as they departed down a very long hallway to one of the two elevator stations. I always went to the furthest one down the hall. As I turned and waved to her one more time before boarding the elevator, I was hit like a blast from something akin to Rod Serling's "Twilight Zone". What I experienced was an overwhelming sensation that this would be the last time I would wave good-bye to her. I was encompassed by a most discomforting awareness that this would be my final visit with her. I was gripped with the premonition that this would be the last time I would see her alive. My soul during that short elevator ride was gripped by a sense of foreboding, the thought of which, I cared not to tarry upon. As I walked through the rest of the complex into the parking area and returned to Natrona Heights, I attempted to shake off this dread notion as a flight of the mind. A few days later, the call came that Margaret had been discovered dead in her apartment. She had died quickly and surely just as she desired. I instantly knew then that my premonition was, most likely, from the Holy Spirit. In an unusual way, perhaps, I found it comforting. It was comforting to me not only because Margaret died just as she had requested of God, but also because I knew that another entity was at play for a positive purpose. Margaret, for several years (particularly after the death of her husband, George, in 1995), wondered why God permitted her to live on. What was the continuing purpose of her life, she bemused? Her life, in my critique and evaluation, had great purpose in those six continuing years. She was, however, ready to depart and to be with the Lord. Margaret viewed death simply as the passage to a greater personal and corporate reality. She had no fear for her person and for that which might be beyond. She expressed total confidence in her Lord and Savior Jesus Christ to embrace her in her advent to the heavenly realm. The reality, in the face of death, for many people is more disconcerting!

Job 18:14 records one of Job's so-called friends, Bildad the Shuhite, reminding him that life's reality is one of calamity, terror, and death. Death appears to be described here as the "king of terrors"! It is common for many people to fear death. In the opinion of many, death is that great unknown. Josh McDowell writes: "Not only is it extremely difficult to imagine ceasing to exist, it is even terrifying. We are the center of our own universe. Our conscious existence is our own reference point. While we know in our minds that someday death will come, it is difficult for us to come to terms with this frightening reality."[436] McDowell suggests six reasons why we fear death.[437]

Death, according to McDowell, is both mysterious and unknown. For human beings, fearing that which is unknown is a natural defense mechanism response. Death is, of course, the great unknown. What may exist beyond death's veil can be characterized as life's greatest mystery. Once this realm is entered, there are no return visits by anyone to inform us about it. What is beyond death is something we cannot understand until we too experience it. At this point we fear that even any ability to do that will vanish as well![438]

McDowell notes that we must also face death alone. Death is a very personal individual event. It is a path that we travel alone. It is not something that we experience in the company of others. To each individual, whether the occasion of death is a solitary experience or one of mass exodus with many dying at the same time, the reality is that we go into what appears to be the dark night of death all by ourselves.[439]

Thirdly, McDowell indicates that death is the point in which we are separated from our loved ones. We all wonder, hope and long for the continuance of relationship on the other side of this life. The fact of the matter is that we cannot possibly know if relationship is even possible let alone if continuance occurs at all. Part of the dread notion of death is the questions as to if we will ever see and be with our loved ones again.[440]

McDowell suggests that a fourth reason we fear death is the extinction of our hopes and dreams. We fear that when we die our longings, desires, ideas, and hopes of accomplishment are vacated as well. In death our dreams may well die with us. In death, the work we failed to accomplish in life may vanish with us. We fear that the things we accomplished in life may come to an end as well, because we are no

---

436   Josh McDowell and Sean McDowell, *Evidence for the Resurrection* (Ventura, CA: Regal From Gospel Light, 2009), 57.
437   McDowell and McDowell, 57-58.
438   Ibid, 57-58.
439   Ibid, 58.
440   Ibid, 58.

longer present to see them through to a positive end or shepherd their continuance. In death our goals, plans, and dreams come to an abrupt termination, with no possibility of restoration or completion.[441]

Death also, according to McDowell, raises the most unsettling and anxiety producing notion that the only reality we experience is nothingness – annihilation. Is death the end of everything? Is eternal unconsciousness that which awaits us? There are many who fear such a prospect, though I have known those who hope that such is the case![442]

McDowell's final assertion is that death is unavoidable. I have read that the body is really designed, optimally, to last 160 years. With some brain and genetic re-engineering, the possibility has been asserted that people could live for several hundred years, even approaching or going beyond a millennium as suggested in the Bible, and Sumerian royal recordings. No matter how long we might be able to extend our lives, no one, ultimately, can escape the inevitability of death. Mortality is irreversible. Something, somehow, some time will do us in! If it is not disease and decline, it will be calamity, violence, warfare or the ravages of the natural world that will terminate our physical existence.[443]

The good news is that, from the perspective of the one revelation of God in the person of Jesus Christ, everything I shared with you from McDowell, and the commentary I added, can find rebuttal. There is an alternative perspective for each point, as McDowell is eager to advance.[444] God has provided us with one person who has experienced death and who has returned to tell us about it. This one person informs us to that which lies beyond. While much mystery remains, Jesus transforms our dread into that of expectation and wonder. Death was not the end of Jesus. His Resurrection demonstrates that it need not mark the end of us as well. In resurrecting from the dead, God has done for us that which we could never do for ourselves. Death has been conquered. Even if we find ourselves anxious concerning the process and circumstances surrounding our death, death itself need not be feared.

---

441   Ibid, 58.
442   Ibid, 58.
443   Ibid, 58.
444   Ibid, 58-67.

The Resurrection of Jesus provides hope that a loving God ultimately controls our person and destiny.[445] According to the New Testament, Jesus' Resurrection provides the assurance that believers will also find translation beyond death's curse and take on the experience of new life.

McDowell, who suggested in his book six reasons why we fear death, also responds to each point he makes and writes how the Resurrection can allay each one of those fears. According to McDowell, death may be mysterious and possess a quality of the unknown. Following the Resurrection of Jesus, however, we have secured some information about death that was previously unrecognized. The fact of the matter is that Jesus charted the course into and out of death. He went through it. He has been there and continues the interface between the reality of our world and the great circumstances of life beyond where we currently reside. The divine factor in the Bible is the promise that God will walk us through death's process, leading to a new and secure permanent life. Some aspects of the veil of secrecy covering death have been raised for us to see.[446]

A second assertion made by McDowell is the news that we do not have to face death alone. Though it may appear that such is still the case, Jesus, as our good shepherd is our traveling companion. He is our "paraclete" who comes along side of us to aid, assist, help, and accompany us throughout life's journey, including the ominous "valley of the shadow of death." Jesus does not abandon us as our translation from this life to the next plays out. As the "with-me God", God escorts us right to this life's "journey's end." In Jesus, God gave us the greatest gift of God's person. The focal point of this gift is a vital, personal, present, and powerful relationship with members of God's creation. God is present with us through our lives, come what may. God is also present with us in and through our passage from this life to the next. We do not journey alone.[447]

---

445 Ibid, 59.
446 Ibid, 64.
447 Ibid, 65.

McDowell also asserts that the Resurrection of Jesus calms our fears that we will not be permanently separated from our loved ones. Christ conquered death. One of the results of his conquest is that our affectionate and most valued relationships are carried forward, remain, and continue forever. Death, which is the Separation Factor, is overcome by the "Resurrection Factor".[448] Reunion awaits us in and through the person of Jesus Christ, the Door.[449] The greatest reunion passage in all the Bible is the long embrace that Mary Magdalene and Jesus share the morning of the Resurrection. Reunion with our loved ones is secured as we, one by one, are gathered into the intermediate heaven. Reunion with our loved ones occurs at what is known as the "second coming of Jesus Christ", wherein, in both time and space, God's people are collected and proceed to congregate forever. Death may separate us temporarily from our loved ones, but the resurrection that Christ secured and grants us reaps an eternal togetherness. Jesus, who is Lord of both the living and the dead (Romans 14:9), to my way of thinking, is the connecting factor between those on either side of life's physical demise. If as Paul writes in Romans 8:39 concerning the impossibility of ever being separated from the love of Christ, it appears to me to be a statement that both the living and those living after death are all under Jesus' umbrella of love. It is his love that is the "connecting factor" between those here and those there. Not only does our love for each other go on, but it is the person of Jesus who actively guarantees love's continuation and fulfillment. Jesus is the link that insures the reality of love's vitality and viability between worlds. Our relationships continue from life to life. They are also vitally transformed as well. As described in Revelation 21, all the garbage of this present life and world will be the circumstances of the past. Jealousy, vile competition, anger, resentment, suspicion, ill intentions, and hurts perpetrated will be among the ghosts of the past. We will be free to love and regard each other completely and with a transparency that knows no fear or restraint.[450]

---

448   Josh McDowell, *The Resurrection Factor* (San Bernardino, CA: Here's Life Publishers, Inc., 1981), 7-8.
449   John 10:7-10.
450   McDowell and McDowell, 65.

McDowell also believes that the Resurrection guarantees us a future which includes the fulfillment of all our hopes and dreams, as they are, of course, in God's will and free from sinful impulse. It appears that the motivating factor behind our dreams and desires in the life to come will be centered around our relationship with God. The dreams and desires we possessed in this life do not abandon us, but they are filtered and re-calibrated toward that which finds divine approval and heavenly fulfillment. The twin parables of the master and his stewards in Luke 19 and Matthew 25 appear to give clear application here. Our hopes and dreams grow out of the abilities God grants to us. We work toward their development in this life. In the resurrection we will be given both the assets and the time to develop them completely. We will be able to master ever new horizons. We will also be able to learn well those things that were closed to us in this life. The life to come is not a situation of idleness and boredom. The life to come is filled with responsibilities that will require and employ our talents, abilities, and creativity.[451]

A fifth assertion by McDowell challenges the question concerning the possibility of annihilation. The event of the Resurrection of Jesus, as both Josh and Sean McDowell, among many others, have labored to point out and define historical credence, may be the best attested fact in the history of antiquity. The evidence provided by Josh, Sean, and a host of others in the past 200 years, is overwhelming. Reviewing this great body of evidence in support of the historicity of the Resurrection is something this author believes that every Christian should pursue and master, not only for one's personal confidence in the faith, but as a basis for witness as well. Life after life is not based on some wishful thinking or a faith devoid of historical and literary evidence. The good news is that God has given us the information we need to construct a faith response that no one has ever been able to negate. Christ arose and lives and so shall we! This is the good news we embrace! Personally, I have found it to be unshakable![452]

---

451   Ibid, 65-66.
452   Ibid, 66.

While it is true that death is inevitable, save for those very few who have experienced or will experience instant translation, the inevitability of a complete and eternal demise is not. As McDowell notes, while we cannot escape death, we do not have to be in morbid fear of death. Death will certainly come! We go, however, through it with Christ at our side coming safely into the loving countenance of our loving heavenly Father. It is appropriate, therefore, that we invite God to come, according to God's will and purposes for us in this present life, to take us to be with God's person when what we are to accomplish and learn in this life has been fulfilled![453]

I once received a birthday card which featured Ziggy in a football uniform on the cover. The card stated, "The game of life is funny..." Opening and viewing inside the card, the statement continued, "by the time you finally know the score all you can do is drop back and punt!" Think about how prophetic and true this statement really is! Life reminds me in many ways of a close football game wherein one team is running out of time to achieve the goal-line and win. Everything is focused on the goal while constantly keeping a keen eye on the clock. How many times does the clock expire before the goal is, or can be, accomplished? Personally, I have set many goals in life. At my current age I am acutely aware, and have already begun to lament those things that I will not be able to secure or fulfill in my lifetime. What is encouraging is the thought that there awaits all eternity to pursue and fulfill a myriad of tasks and pursuits, either currently a part of my "bucket list" or the listings that develop in the future eschaton. Time, which waits for no one in this life, will be but an ally and asset in the next. What is critical for us to accomplish now is the surety that we secure a place in the age to come. God has made provision for our eternity. The provision God has made is through the work of God's son, the incarnate Jesus, the Christ. Jesus offers us an eternal gift. It is God's gift of himself, forever! It is through this gift that we are saved from death, hell, sin, and Satan, and are granted life that marvelously knows no end. God's gift is for you. Have you received it? Have you embraced it? Do you own it?

---

453   Ibid, 66.

Uncertainty in answering these questions hopefully will prompt you to reflect and evaluate your divine standing in life. If you desire a forever relationship with God, do not hesitate or delay embracing Jesus and the sacrifice he made to discharge your sin and grant to you the gift of eternal grace. Embrace the Christ as Mary Magdalene did on Easter morning nearly 2000 years ago. Hold onto the Christ dearly throughout all the trauma, perplexities, and sorrows of this life. Ultimately, it is not only the most important decision you will ever make, it is the only one that really matters in this life for its consequences are eternal!

25

Coping with Loss

"And I think I'm gonna miss you for a long, long time."

(Gary White/Linda Ronstadt)

Death is something, in terms of the pastoral ministry, with which I never got comfortable. During my career, I performed 530 funeral or memorial services. I also wrote 272 funeral homilies (sermons) in the attempt to personalize and make unique each service that I performed. I never wanted to get too carefree, cavalier, or unfeeling about death. I wanted to feel "the sting of death" paracleting with the loved ones who remained. I never wanted to engage services at the time of death in a perfunctory, static, and mechanical way. As a generalist in a specialized world of ministry, officiating services at the time of loss was one of my strengths. In fact, the final funeral service I officiated in my ministry at Natrona Heights Presbyterian Church was one in which the very senior (in terms of age) funeral director told me that it was the best one he had ever witnessed in his long career. With each funeral service performed, a part of me died as well. There were times that the sheer rapidity of death after death became so depressing and difficult to deal with emotionally. In dealing with the grief of others, I had to find ways to deal with my own grief as well. When one develops the type of deep relationships one can form in the pastoral ministry, it is like losing close family members on a continual basis. I will never forget the day I got the phone call from a dear woman named Ruth Sleighter concerning the unanticipated death of her last child. Ruth had already suffered through the death of her mother at age three (with her father giving her away to her aunt to raise), her marvelous husband, George, and two of their three children. Now her third child and only daughter, Sandy, had died attempting to recover from surgery. Sandy was a most delightful person, full of life and wit. She had the personal ability to make everyone in her presence happy. At the news of her demise, I wept bitterly. Ruth then said to me, "I called you to receive comfort, but now I find you need it more than I!" Ruth made it through these circumstances, not through any stoicism of her generation, but sharing the same secret known also to the apostle Paul (Philippians 4:12,13).

Many were the difficult circumstances surrounding numerous deaths, whether the cause was accident, long term disease, sudden mortality, the taking of one's own life, and the death of infants, toddlers, and children. There were people whose life was cut off whose impact, in terms of ministry, could not be replaced. They left the stage of life with the question floating in the air of what could have been! The death of many people, including the profound grief and questioning by those who remained, all etched an indelible mark on my person and soul. Perhaps the death that had the greatest impact on my life personally was that of Heather Ann Ehrman on June 26, 1996. She died tragically at the age of 19. Heather and her parents, Jeff and Karen, had united with NHPC on June 6, 1993. Almost instantly I became fast and lasting friends with Jeff and Karen. On June 25, I was in Trenton, New Jersey, with the Senior High Youth Group working with Habitat for Humanity. At the house we were rehabilitating, I received word that an important message was waiting for me at the East Trenton Habitat Center. I instantly thought, "I wonder who has died?" When we arrived back at the center for lunch I was ushered upstairs into the office area where I was instructed to call the number the secretary handed me. I dialed the number and was informed to call Jeff and Karen Ehrman. I was told by the church receptionist that Heather had been the victim of a tragic highway accident and was not going to survive her injuries. I called the Ehrmans and reached Jeff on the phone. He told me that the moving company work van in which Heather was a passenger, as a summer time employee while attending Thiel College, had been hit broadside by a garbage truck that had lost its brakes. Careening into an intersection, the large vehicle instantly killed the van driver, fatally injured Heather, and permanently injured the sole survivor. Jeff informed me of the circumstances from a Pittsburgh hospital as decisions were pending concerning Heather. I will never forget how ill and forlorn I felt following that phone call. I remember poignantly descending the stairway of the former church, plunging into a throng of youth group members and staff and informing them of Heather's demise. The rest of the day we worked in the house. I chipped and scraped old paint from window frames, working in absolute sorrow and wishing not only that things could be different, but that I could be physically present with Jeff and Karen during their ordeal. It all seemed so surreal! That night as I slept on the floor in the educational wing of the First Presbyterian Church of Pennington, New Jersey, who sponsored our mission trip, my mind was dominated by the situation and happenstance. I never fell asleep that night. There was too much sorrow and pain. It was the worst night of my life. It was also a night dominated by the Holy Spirit. All night my mind was filled with the thoughts of the Christ and the great salvation he wrought for us. I reflected mightily on the message of Jesus' resurrection, the intermediate heaven, and the translation that Heather was experiencing. I also formed the entire funeral service in my mind that night, picking out what I would say! By morning I was dominated by a mixture of both grief and hope. Due to medical and coroner circumstances, the funeral service was not held until the following morning after our scheduled return from New Jersey. The service was full of the Holy Spirit. As we got out of the vehicles at the cemetery and walked to the grave site, Jeff looked up at the sky and said to me, "Hey Cam, we've got a Penn State sky" (blue with white clouds – the colors of Penn State University of which we are fans). Karen looked at us and replied, "You two are weird!" as we all chuckled, breaking the tension of the stroll to the grave. It was at that moment I realized something very important in Jeff's communication about the sky. What he was really saying to me was not something flippant or an inconsequential obser-vation to break this somber moment. What Jeff was telling to me was the importance of "presence." Our God, who is revealed Biblically as the "with-me God", enlists God's own to be God's present "with-me agents" as "under-shepherds", who also walk along-side those in need through the gloomy valleys of this life. This "under-shepherding" or "paraclet-ing" testifies both to the presence of God in times of difficulty in life, but also to the caring of God as well. Through the physical presence of God's people, God communicates God's own spiritual presence with us. With God we are never alone. God never abandons us. The totality of it all testifies to and points us to the greater reality of life and the "ultimate hope of the ages." The greater reality of life is that there is life beyond this life. The terminal zone of the grave is not our destiny, fate, or complete end. The ultimate "hope of the ages", in the words of the late Walter Martin,[454] is that resurrection is fact, and we will be a part of God's coming new world – paradise restored! Heather, like countless others who have died "in Christ", will experience newness both in her personhood and physicality. The time is short until we will be in her presence again. "Presence"; eternal presence, is what the Resurrection of Jesus is all about. It is "presence" that was communicated to Mary Magdalene in her embrace on Easter morning, outside the tomb, in the arms of Jesus.

I find that "presence" is essential in terms of dealing with the loss of a loved one. When a friend, family member, companion, confidante, and a brother or sister in Christ dies, there is something also that dies

---

454   Walter Martin, *Essential Christianity* (Santa Ana, CA: Vision House, 1962), 89-101.

within and about us. A portion of our life has now ended. The deceased represented a part of our world which is also now over. The age of the individual matters not. The circumstances surrounding their demise may not matter as well. What does matter is that a huge hole or vacuum has been cut into our lives. Usually, such tears in the fabric of our lives cannot be mended nor replaced by something, or someone, new. In terms of my life and ministry, the untimely death of one significant member who was superbly talented and now retired hit me hard. He was planning to work with me as a volunteer to revolutionize the work of NHPC and relieve some of my duties. The plan was set. Everything was ready to go. Illness then raised its ugly head and the individual was dead just 4 weeks or so later. Besides the loss of a good brother in Christ and a friend, a void existed now in the ministry that forever remained vacant. What could have been has haunted me ever since. I remember those poignant conversational words of a member of the Kennedy administration when JFK was assassinated. One individual responded saying, "We will laugh again, but we will never be young again!"[455] How true! Grief is sobering. Mourning is not something that one can "get over", "move on", "get through", or "forget". The healing of a broken heart, in many cases, cannot be mended. If the possibility of healing does become a reality, the scars remain to testify to something that once was, and a person who was once here. Gathering and huddling with others must be a part of our coping mechanism. Sometimes "presence", having someone by our side to help us continue our life journey, is all that we might need. Often, however, we need the presence of people who can truly minister to us deeply and beyond all the clichés. More importantly, we need those brothers and sisters in Christ who can lovingly, without preaching to us and questioning our faith, help us deal with our questions concerning the realities of life and death, the rationale behind this life, and hold out the good hope of life to come. This is the reason this author thinks that it is important for members

---

455   Statements made by Mary McGrory and Senator Daniel Patrick Moynihan in reaction to the assassination of President John F. Kennedy awaiting Air Force One at Andrew's Airbase. Mary McGrory states to Moynihan, "O we will never laugh again!", to which Moynihan replied, "Heavens Mary, we'll laugh again. We'll just never be young again!"

of the Body of Christ to know their doctrine, and have a firm grasp on the apologetics of the Resurrection of Jesus Christ. My personal faith has its mooring in the intellectual. Like C. S. Lewis, Josh McDowell, Lee Strobel and many others before me, my faith is grounded in the literary, historical, and legal methodology for determining truth. I have shared this with many people during the time of death in my ministry. For Jeff and Karen Ehrman, the teachings of the Christ event and his resurrection have become the bedrock of their great expectation to be with their daughter again. As I have said many times, and the Ehrmans have echoed to others, "The person and work of Jesus has to be real because there is nothing else out there!" The loving, gracious, and Spirit-filled presence of God's people mightily prepared to minister at the time of death is indispensable. Presence matters. The right kind of "presence"is irreplaceable and, absolutely, invaluable. Presence helps us in the time of death to run toward God and not away from God as in imitation of Mary Magdalene.

While my second assertion will not make anyone else's "top ten" of coping mechanisms, the writings of many others, particularly from a Christian faith-based standpoint have been helpful to me in terms of dealing with death and dying. For me, the best book I ever read on the subject was C. S. Lewis' brief volume known as "A Grief Observed".[456] Lewis has always been an apologetic giant of mine in the faith and an intellect I greatly admire. The man was truly wise (few people are). The history of his late marriage, the demise of his wife, Joy, and his heartbrokenness following her death, as recorded in his journaling, have been most sobering and helpful to me personally and ministerially.

This leads me to a third assertion in dealing with the death of others. When an individual is faced with the great barren desert of loss and emptiness within and without, how does one deal with the void that has been created in one's life? How does one keep from being swallowed up in grief, sadness, and what appears to be permanent loss? The good news is that we are not a people without hope! Hope begins, for

---

456   C. S. Lewis, *A Grief Observed* (New York, NY: A Bantam Book published by arrangement with the Seabury Press, Inc., 1963), 1-89.

me, with my understanding of the Creator. Psalm 24:1 is one of the great stewardship passages in the Bible, "The earth is the Lord's and everything in it, the world, and all who live in it." God owns me. I am a possession of the Almighty God. That is good news! Even better news is that the character of our owner is one of benevolence and caring. God wishes us well. God wants good for us and not harm, including the solution to the ravages and barrenness of death. We also learn in the Creation narratives that we are created in God's very image. I think a significant part of the meaning of this Biblical assertion is that as God is, so are we! God is eternal. God created us to share in God's eternality. Relationships with God are meant to go on forever. To my way of thinking, it means that God wills God's own to survive the grave. There is more to life than just this life. Our God is an eternal God who desires and creates eternal relationships. It means that God wills God's own to go on. Hope exists. Hope is present in God's realm so that reunion is not only possible and likely, but a surety! Once again, that is super news for those who suffer the loss of another and grieve!

As noted previously, Paul employs the culture and language of his readers to paint the pictures he portrays of the faith and life in Christ. He employs both athletic and military imagery in his writings (particularly in Philippians). His view of life's journey as a race to achieve and secure the finishing line has always been a leading concept in my thought of the translation between this life and the next.[457] My grandmother died in the hospital in the presence of one of her relatives. The nurse's station was notified and through the action of the staff they resuscitated her. Upon my arrival to the hospital, I found her rather upset and angry that she had been revived. She made me promise that if she "went out" in my presence to "just let her go." She also made me promise to pray that she would die. She said to me, "I know where I am going, and I want to get there!" Praying for a loved one to die raises some potential issues and can cause some internal conflicts. My grandmother, I reasoned, who was once very energetic, athletic, and vibrant, was now a shell of her former self. I would never know her again, in this life, in the way

---

457   Philippians 3:12-14; 2 Timothy 4:7-8.

she once was. Her desire was to achieve that refusion of energy brought about by translation and the presence of the Christ. She knew it was time for her to cross that finishing line and go to Jesus. When her final decline and passage began on Easter Sunday, I honestly felt good for her and relieved. In Christ, I will experience my grandmother again. The vibrant and bright woman I knew will be restored. In Jesus she still is! With Jesus I do not have to worry about her anymore. She is safe and secure. While she will not come back to me, she becomes a forerunner of the great reunion and gathering the family will one day experience.[458] That thought is most encouraging! I have always thought that separation, while difficult, can be bearable as long as we are ultimately together again! Those who have gone before us in Christ are a part of the great ingathering that eventually brings all of God's people together, forever. I find something very uplifting and optimistic when thinking about it and viewing those who depart our presence in this way. The life of the resurrection is much about anticipation. While "anticipation is making us wait", the expectations of what is to come heightens our reception of this reality when we finally receive it!

Like the case of my grandmother, another possible coping mechanism at the time of death is to feel positive about the prayers answered and wishes granted to our departed loved ones. In my family we have a major tendency to die on holidays: Christmas, Thanksgiving, New Year's Day, Easter, and even Halloween (we have yet to have anyone die on Labor Day as my mother is oft to point out). My father was the family member who went to be with the Lord on Thanksgiving. Prior to getting together for the holiday meal, my mother called to tell me that she could not wake up my father. I covered the four-mile distance between the manse and the house within a few moments. Walking into the bedroom I could tell that he had expired. Seeing him lying there, I remembered what he had told me as a boy. He said to me, "I want to die in my sleep, in my own bed, and in my own house." As I looked down upon his lifeless body I said to him, "Well Dad, you got your wish and God answered your prayer." I smiled and strangely felt good

---

458   2 Samuel 12:23.

for him! He had lived to be 81 1/2, which is the second oldest person in his direct family line. He had lived a nearly 22-year retirement. He had accomplished much, and now would unite with the growing family throng in the intermediate heaven. In terms of the eternal state, how could one not feel good?

It is important to also know, from the divine perspective at the time of death, that we are loved. God has given us a stupendous demonstration of that love in the Christ event. A part of which is dramatically demonstrated for us in the reunion of Jesus and Mary Magdalene. God loves us so much that God became one of us to accompany us through the events of this life including the isolation and barrenness of death. God laid aside, in Jesus, God's immunity to pain (a critical factor in the thought of the late John Stott)[459] and did something definitive about our circumstances. The historical fact of his resurrection means that there is life beyond this life. With God, there is no termination. In Jesus, God has delivered a major pronouncement that the eternity promised in the Creation is reaffirmed in our recreation. God's promise and intention are kept!

It is also good news that "the love goes on", which is a significant statement at the end of the movie, "Ghost"![460] Ultimately for those in Christ, there is no final and complete separation from our loved ones. We all are, as I like to say, under Christ's big umbrella of love. This includes both those living presently on earth, and those living presently in the intermediate heaven. It is the love and person of the Christ that keeps us connected so that our love for each other spans the dimensions of time and space. Two of the best words in the Bible are "en Christos" which means "in Christ". To be "in Christ" is to imbibe and be saturated in the love of the personal Jesus who expresses God's most important attribute and self-designation (other than holiness) – love! God is always love! As I often like to say to people, "those who have died still are! We do not have to refer to them in the past tense. They are well and very much alive with God, and we will be together with them

---

459   John R. W. Stott, *The Cross of Christ* (Downers Grove, Illinois: InterVarsity Press, 1986), 335.
460   *Ghost*, directed by Jerry Zucker, Paramount Pictures, July 13, 1990, final scene.

again!" The brief separation, from the perspective of Godly reality, can be lonely and painful, but it is not the final statement on the issue! All that ultimately matters, is that we will be together again. God will fulfill God's assertion that such reunion and togetherness will be the case. Those who have gone before us have been gathered in before us. As stated above, we will go to them, and never, ever, be separated again!

All of what has been mentioned above, when dealing with death and the grave, indicates that we who remain must not focus on the deceased, but upon our Lord God and Savior. The Bible tells us to fix our minds and eyes on God who is the author and finisher of our faith (Hebrews 3:1 and Hebrews 12:2). God is our "finisher" in that God gets us to God's desired completion; the promise of a perfected life that lasts for eternity. The only hope we have of ever being in the presence of our loved ones again is through the Lord. The way then is clear! We must latch on and cling to God! We must never retreat from God, as well!

None of what has been written above negates the fact that grieving is real and that it is perfectly alright to grieve. There is much that we can learn from Jesus at the death of Lazarus.[461] Jesus did not deny or try to mask his pain. At the tomb of Lazarus, the Greek indicates that he wailed dramatically.[462] The possibilities as to why he cried so bitterly are numerous. Certainly, I believe for Jesus, anger played a role in his tearful expression. Here again the reason for Jesus' anger at that moment are probably multiple. Feelings of anger concerning death are legitimate. We were not created to die. Death, while it may be strange to say this, is unnatural. We have a right to be angry at the ill circumstances of this world and our lot in life. If Jesus did not lock his grief away expressing his sorrow and anger to the Father and to those around him, why should we not be expressive as well? Jesus expressed his grief. He appears to be angry about death and the pain it causes. The good news is that Jesus did something definitive about it, putting it away forever. His encounter with Mary Magdalene is the first expression he makes of the new reality, and that which he has accomplished.

---

461 John 11:1-44.
462 John 11:33-38.

Another positive expression that one can make when coping with loss is to count one's blessings. When a loved one dies, it may be difficult to focus on anything positive. We need to remind ourselves of the good things that came to us in our lives through the deceased. We need to remind ourselves of the good things we still have. We need to remind ourselves of the good things that will yet to be! Listing our blessings mentally, on screen or paper can be helpful. Contemplating the future and the important life lessons the deceased may have taught us can also assist us as we journey through life. As in mountaineering, our memories of the deceased can become markers that help guide our way and reveal the path ahead. Doing these things may not fill the void created in your life, but they can remind you that your life goes on and you need to live it, in Christ, triumphantly making the best of every situation and opportunity.

Becoming action oriented in the face of grief is also a good coping mechanism. At Christ's Resurrection, as his embrace with Mary Magdalene continued, he broke it off putting her person into action. He gave her an assignment to fulfill. He gave her something important to do. He assigned her to tell the story of her encounter and the resurrection to others. Reflecting on the life story of our deceased loved ones may prove valuable. Recording the life and times of the individual as a testimony to their person and faith in Christ can be instructive for the reader. This can also be a fitting memorial of lessons learned and guidance offered from the individual's life for future generations of the family. For the writer, it can also be a positive expression to help one deal with one's grief!

When dealing with grief, we need to remember that God has created each one of God's own for a purpose. Each life, of the believer, has purpose. Our lives have meaning. There are good things that God would like you to do and accomplish in your life. These good things can have an eternal impact. They are not insignificant or unimportant. I am one who does think that those in heaven view and have an awareness of the events on earth. This includes the circumstances of those who remain. It is my opinion that those who go to be with the

Lord do know what is happening on earth and, to some degree, with those they knew on earth. This is not a cause for sadness and sorrow to them. They already know the end of things. They are also in agreement with God about them. In knowing the end of our earthly endeavors, our departed friends and loved ones can still smile and be optimistic even amid misfortune and if bad things befall us. They know that in Jesus, the end will be good. As in the creation story, the end will be "very good", indeed! It is my habit to usually comment at the end of a funeral or memorial service to think of the departed as very much alive. They are now living life in a way much more than we live it now. We can still gift them. We can still give them a special gift. The best thing we can do in memory of our loved ones comes through the way we live our lives and the things we do in love for Jesus and the kingdom of our Lord and Christ. The best memorial we can possibly give to those who have departed is to witness and rejoice from heaven in that which we experience in personal growth, spiritual growth, and accomplishment. As I like to say, "Really give them something great to cheer about!"

One additional, the thirteenth assertion in terms of coping with a loss is some practical advice to individuals and families following the death of a loved one, particularly a spouse. One of the things I find very problematic among people when coping with death is to avoid irrevocable decisions for months, perhaps even a year, after a loved one has died. I have experienced too many people and families (particularly the children of an aged parent) make decisions that turned out to be not good or helpful following death. The rule is simple. Do not do anything right away that you cannot undo! Many people clean things out, give things away, or junk material too fast and then regret forfeiting certain items. Also, I find that people relocate too rapidly after the death of a loved one. Much of the time it is regretted. Do not rush! Take your time with life decisions until clarity and rationality rule. Too much is done on emotion and what is perceived as convenience. Often the convenience does not benefit the person for whom the decisions are made.

It is the hope of this author that the compendium of things shared above have provided some help and comfort when thinking about the reality of the death of a loved one. When it comes to grief there are some things we can control and there are some things with which we cannot! One cannot control whether one grieves. One can make the decision not to let grief control you. The decisions people make on managing or coping with the death of a loved one can determine both the value and the quality of one's life experiences in response to the loss moving forward. Christians are uniquely positioned to refrain from being consumed at the time of death with bitterness, unrequited sorrow, misery, and being enslaved by unhelpful obsessions. Our life experiences have taught us that time does not heal all wounds. In fact, some wounds fester and become greater, never to disappear. This is not only true of physical injuries, but emotional ones as well. Fortunately, members of the Body of Christ have a powerful healer as a friend. As Jesus Christ renewed the joy of Mary Magdalene on Resurrection Day morning, so our Jesus promises to renew our joy as well. The assertion of renewal is more than a promise, it is an eternal fact!

26

The Mary Magdalene Moment

"They say there's a place where dreams have all gone. They never said where, but I think I know. It's miles through the night just over the dawn on the road that will take me home... Love waits for me 'round the bend. Leads me endlessly on. Surely sorrows shall find their end and all our troubles will be gone. And I'll know what I've lost and all that I've won when this road finally take me home. I'm going home! I'm going home! I'm going home!"

(Mary Fahl, Byron Isaacs, Djam Karet, and Glenn Patscha/Mary Fahl)

Whether or not the opinions of this writer on the Biblical symbolism of Mary Magdalene, as presented in this book, are valid or not, all that ultimately matters is the experience I call the "Mary Magdalene Moment". The "Mary Magdalene Moment" reminds me a great deal of the story that James Clayton Dobson, Jr. shared on the death of his friend, the late great basketball player, "Pistol Pete" Maravich (1947-1988). Following the death of Maravich, which Dobson witnessed, he communicated with his son, Ryan, a poignant message. James told his son that one day he would hear of his father's death. On that day there would be only one thing that would matter to James. He told his son that it mattered not how high he rose on the career, social, financial, educational, and professional ladder. On that day it would not matter all the awards he had won and the success he had had thus far in life. James said to his son that on the day his father died, all that would matter to him is that Ryan would one day, "Be there!" All that would matter to James Dobson was that one day in the future, his son would "Just be there", joining his father in a glad reunion in heaven and the eschaton.[463] Dobson is correct. All of life ultimately boils down to this one acquisition. Whether an individual has a theological bent more toward free will or predestination in terms of the reality of justification and salvation, everyone should desire to be embraced by Christ immediately following one's earthly demise. This embrace is what I call the "Mary Magdalene Moment" as Jesus first shared with Mary outside the sepulcher. Regardless of whether Mary Magdalene is the "second Eve", the "New Testament Eve", the figurative "Bride of Christ", and perhaps shares some of this with Mary, the mother of Jesus, all that really matters is for the reader to share in a similar embrace with our Savior. In that pinnacle moment during the Easter morning sunrise, seven stupendous and momentous happenings, all wrapped up into one, occurred to Mary Magdalene. In that one moment, she took possession of seven fantastic things: she was rescued; redeemed; regenerated; raised; rejuvenated; restored; and imbibed realized hope. Mary Magdalene represents the symbol of the redeemed Eve, whose relationship with God has been returned to that which it was meant to be. The redemption that re-elevates Eve also reanimates Eve's children, beginning with Mary Magdalene. If, in this great encounter on Easter morning in Joseph's garden, Mary Magdalene represents and stands for the deliverance of fallen humanity, then this is the moment we must all desire – to be embraced by the Christ, the door or gate (John 10:7-10) to eternity!

---

463   This story was experienced on a radio broadcast of Focus on the Family many decades ago.

There are moments in the Bible that hint to an ongoing and greater reality. In the Old Testament we have the incident with Saul and the witch of Endor in 1 Samuel 28. In the witch's conjuring, the spirit of the deceased judge and prophet Samuel appears and engages King Saul in conversation, affirming what Samuel had previously spoken to him about his coming doom. While this passage is controversial, this author believes that it truly was the deceased spirit of Samuel who appeared before the witch and Saul. What we must recognize here, and not lose sight of, is the Biblical assertion that life goes on – that we "still are" – possessing personality, identity, consciousness, memory, and spirit. The same is true in the New Testament with the appearance of Elijah and Moses on the Mount of Transfiguration (Matthew 17, Mark 9, and Luke 9). This could also be said to be true of the resurrection of Lazarus in John 11, though in a different way.

The focal point of this ongoing and greater reality is all wrapped up in Jesus who is, John 8:12 & John 9:5, the light of the world. Jesus talks a great deal about light (Matthew 5:14-16, Mark 4:21, Luke 8:16, John 1:4-9; John 12:35, 46). He is the light to which his own are drawn. In the light of the rising sun on Easter morning, Jesus' appearance to Mary Magdalene is the real "son-rise", shining a light for her to advance, embrace, and imbibe! As God did with Adam and Eve in Eden and desired to continue to do so, save for their sin, Jesus invites Mary Magdalene to walk with him in the light of a new, forever reality. Mary Magdalene advanced and embraced the light. Christ holds out the same invitation for us to follow in her wake as well! The light of Christ in his Resurrection discloses a new reality. What was hidden is now revealed! What was concealed is now open! The light of the Resurrection is opportunity. Mary Magdalene took advantage of the opportunity afforded her by Jesus. The central drama of her life was played out in Joseph's garden, and she chose wisely!

Some of my favorite stories in the Bible concern the moment of choice. In the account of the patriarch Jacob in Genesis 32 and 33, the deceiver is about to discover grace. On five occasions in his life, Jacob has practiced or been subject to deception (Genesis 25:27-34; 27:1ff;

29:25; 30:37ff; 31:20). Jacob is one of the most despicable and deplorable characters in the Bible. The good news for Jacob, and for us by extension, is that God does not "throw in the towel" when it comes to destroying Jacob's self-sufficiency and working to re-mold his character. The coming of Jacob's brother Esau to meet him becomes a moment of crisis for Jacob. Years earlier, Jacob had deceived Esau out of his birthright, and now Jacob feared that Esau was coming to him to get his revenge. The story reveals that the approach of this confrontation brings to a head the personal and internal battling Jacob's conniving had reaped. It is against God, not Esau or Laban (Jacob's father-in-law), with whom Jacob has been struggling all his life. Jacob discovers that he must embrace God and hold on to God for "dear life". Jacob is humbled. His pride is chastened. His self-sufficiency is purged. His person is re-directed toward God and he discovers that his only security in life originates in his relationship with God. In the interplay in these chapters with God and his brother Esau, Jacob discovers grace. Grace is the only remedy for the lifetime of sin and cheating he has committed. Instead of meeting Jacob with the sword of judgment, Esau runs to embrace his brother, throws his arms around him, and continually kisses him as the two of them weep. This is a classic story of reconciliation which Dr. Ken Bailey noted, late in his career, as one with parallels to the prodigal younger son in Luke 15.[464] When the curtain descends on this story the conclusion of the matter has been determined. The conclusion is the triumph of grace, reconciliation, relationship, and life.

There are two other stories in the Bible that are very much theatre oriented (possessing the appearance of a play), wherein the curtain descends before a decision is rendered, leaving the audience wondering what choice will ultimately be made. The purpose of this is, of course, to stimulate and encourage the audience to think about the decision and hopefully to choose wisely. The first of these is the drama in the book of Jonah. As Jonah contends with Nineveh's repentance in chapters 3 and 4, we discover that Jonah is rather upset with the success of his mission.

---

464   Kenneth E. Bailey, *Jacob and the Prodigal* (Downers Grove, Illinois: InterVarsity Press, 2003), 121-194.

Here we have the depiction of a prophet whose work is remarkably successful, and he laments about it to the point of despondency, severe depression, and a desire for life termination. He would rather see Nineveh, Israel's arch-enemy, totally destroyed in judgment, including all women, children, and animals, than celebrate the greatest mass repentance in human history. God deals with Jonah's anger, disgust at the outcome, and his lack of understanding of God's grace. Before we know if Jonah repents, changes his mind, and what choice he finally makes the curtain descends and we are left seemingly in the world of unknowing. The ending is really for the audience to make. What decision or outcome would we design or choose? The choice is up to us! If what we believe to know about the subject matter of Jonah, its purpose, and the reality of history, there is little doubt as to the choice Jonah makes.

In another significant drama, this time in the New Testament, the curtain descends before a choice is seemingly rendered. The parables of the lost in Luke 15 are normally understood as three-fold, a trilogy. In actuality, there are four parables depicted here. The third parable is that of the lost younger son. The fourth parable is that of the lost older son. As the late Ken Bailey teaches, the eldest son, the one who stayed home and performed his duties on the estate, is also equally lost. In these teaching stories, the Father is portrayed as violating custom and culture, reaching out in grace to secure the love of his sons. His actions "of the costly demonstration of unexpected love", as Ken Bailey terms it,[465] prove fruitful with the prodigal younger son. Do they prove to be as fruitful with the prodigal elder son? While the younger son experiences a life of renewed love and fellowship with his father, the elder son moves into a position of open hostility toward his father. As the eldest son, he is the master of the ceremonial feast celebrating his younger brother's return and restoration. By refusing to enter the house and take charge as host, he places himself in open rebellion to his father for all the guests to see. For a second time that day, the father humbles himself by leaving the house to reason with one of his sons. The father avoids

---

465   Kenneth E. Bailey, *Finding the Lost: Cultural Keys to Luke 15* (St. Louis, MO: Concordia Publishing House, 1992), 152-153.

engaging with his eldest son the many arguments he could employ and expresses only an outpouring of love. At this point in the story, the curtain descends. The end is missing. The teaching story is left incomplete. The drama is left hanging in midair! It is the purpose of Jesus to terminate the story in this way. The story, however, is far from over. Jesus omits the ending on purpose. He confronts the audience with a choice. Will the audience embrace the "costly demonstration of unexpected love" the Father has granted and to which Jesus will secure, or will they gravitate toward an alternative ending? Will they opt, as the elder son might opt for in the story, to pick up a stick and in great anger attack and beat his father? Jesus leaves the story incomplete. The audience, in the coming days, will have to make that very decision about "God and His Christ" themselves. What will they choose? We know what they chose! For the most part they picked up the stick and beat Jesus nearly senseless. The cross is the ending of this story of invitation.[466]

The cross, however, represents both a rejection of Jesus by the many, and an open invitation of grace to come and embrace his person and the new life opportunity he openly grants to those who decide to approach and share in his goodness. The person of Jesus demands of us the making of a decision. The Christ event demands of us the selection of a choice. What choice will we make? What decision will we render? What will we determine to do? This is the "Mary Magdalene Moment"! Mary Magdalene made her choice when she saw Jesus standing there! She ran to him and embraced him as her own! She zealously accepted the invitation to come and share the joy and celebration of what "once was lost and now is found".

Jesus sets up the "Mary Magdalene Moment". I always enjoyed the motto of producer Roone Arledge's 1961-1998 ABC sports show, "Wide World of Sports" hosted for many years by Jim McKay; "The thrill of victory and the agony of defeat." In many ways, this motto reminds me of many of the circumstances swirling around Jesus Christ and his passion. Jesus, in his crucifixion and resurrection, as I like to say, "snatches victory from the jaws of defeat and life from the jaws of death."

---

466   Ibid, 163-192.

Christ's mission becomes a dramatic rescue operation, snatching those imperiled from complete demise. The "Mary Magdalene Moment" is the first indication humanity has of the success of the operation. She is the first person to witness, experience, and comprehend God's new eternal reality. In the fields of science, medicine, and exploration humanity remembers and celebrates those who were first. During my life that list includes Yuri Gagarin, John Glenn, Frank Borman, Neal Armstrong, Alan Shepard, and Jim Lovell in terms of space exploration. As spectacular as Neal Armstrong and Buzz Aldrin's moon landing is a human cosmic first, Mary Magdalene is party to a human eternal first, making this moment the most significant step taken in the history of humankind. As she takes a step and advances toward Jesus, her footprints in the garden are more significant than the footprints pressed on the moon! When Jesus reveals himself to Mary and the two of them embrace, this is the most important event, encounter, happening, and act in human history. This is truly "Independence Day"! This is VDHS Day – Victory over "death, hell, and sin." Unlike the celebrations that occurred after Yorktown, Appomattox, VE Day, and VJ Day, the realization of this cosmic triumph, which is quietly shared by two, creates ripples of recognition that move out in concentric circles to the whole world, becoming a sweeping tsunami of gigantic proportions that will be eternally celebrated and never forgotten on the consciousness of the redeemed. As Jesus enhanced the party at Cana in Galilee, so the celebration of this triumph will never fade, but only gain in its glorious character and expression as eternity marches onward. What is a whisper in the garden on Easter morning becomes a triumphal shout that reverberates through the eons. What is a simple, solitary, short, and silent instance shared by two thunders out and down through the ages. The "silent morning" is no "silent spring." God's life now rules eternal as the "Mary Magdalene Moment" is played out over and over billions of times in the individual welcoming of God's own from the prospects of death to life everlasting.

A replay of sorts of the "Mary Magdalene Moment" is something that is in our future. For those in the church triumphant, it is part of each person's glorious past. For the living, the "Mary Magdalene Moment" informs us about our future. In fact, it instills in us confidence to move forward in life with optimism and without the dread and fear of our demise and that of others. At the entrance of our grave, as we move out from our own tomb, Jesus awaits the emptying. He waits to embrace us and welcome us to the new life he has so graciously given us. He speaks our name. We recognize our Savior. We move toward our first "up close and personal" encounter with our Lord. Arms are opened. We embrace. Jesus welcomes us to eternal life and the intermediate heaven with the surety of the eschaton to come. We personally receive the embrace of life. We share in the embrace of eternity. The risen Son is the rising sun of our new life! The very moment Mary Magdalene recognizes Jesus and runs to embrace him, the horrors and the terrors she has witnessed and experienced of the past and any frightening prospects of the future are terminated. Instead, she is charged with a new expectation and certainty. The expectation of life eternal and a forever loving and joyful relationship with God and God's own fills and emanates from her being forever. As it is with Mary, so it will be with us who follow in her wake! Death and the grave no longer need be the end of our own personal life story. The "Mary Magdalene Moment" truly illustrates the statement of the late Paul Harvey; "And now, the rest of the story!" The good news is that "the rest of the story" – our story, yours and mine - is an eternal one!

As the reader considers all of that which is advanced in this book, only one vital question remains. This question reminds me of two of the great hymns of the church: Newton's "Amazing Grace" and the song which echoed throughout each one of Billy Graham's crusades, "Just as I Am." Casting the debates concerning theological particulars aside, the most important question we must answer in our lives is "Who is the person of Jesus Christ?" If we arrive at the same conclusion as C.S. Lewis, another question immediately confronts us as it did him; "Will I then personally accept Jesus as my Savior and Lord?" To put it in terms of Mary Magdalene, will we depart the tomb which confines us, run toward him, and embrace him? Newton's hymn is his confession of great personal guilt and sin which he had perpetrated in his life, and his complete and utter need for grace. Through the appearance of the offer of Christ's grace, the one who was "lost" is now "found", and the one who was "blind" now possesses a new vision. No hymn is more poignant concerning the "Mary Magdalene Moment" than Charlotte Elliott's text, "Just As I Am." As I wrap up the writing of this tome, this hymn, with its 5 verses, seems a proper and fit summary with which to end:

Just as I am, without one plea But that Thy blood was shed for me, And that Thou bidd'st me come to Thee, O Lamb of God, I come! I come!

Just as I am, and waiting not To rid my soul of one dark blot, To Thee whose blood can cleanse each spot, O Lamb of God, I come! I come!

Just as I am, tho tossed about With many a conflict, many a doubt, Fightings and fears within, without, O Lamb of God, I come! I come!

Just as I am, poor, wretched, blind – Sight, riches, healing of the mind, Yes, all I need in Thee to find – O Lamb of God, I come! I come!

Just as I am, Thou wilt receive, Wilt welcome, pardon, cleanse, relieve;` Because Thy promise I believe, O Lamb of God, I come! I come![467]

---

467   Charlotte Elliott wrote the poem *Just as I Am, Without One Plea* in 1835. It first appeared in the Christian Remembrance the same year. The original melody, "Woodworth" was written by William B. Bradbury in 1835, and was published in his *Third book of Psalmody* in 1849. Thomas Hastings adapted Bradbury's tune for Elliott's poem. The song as it is written here comes from "The Hymnbook" published by the former Presbyterian Church United States, the former United Presbyterian Church United Stated of American, and the Reformed Church in America. The copyright is by John Ribble, 1955.

About the Author

Robert Cameron Malcolm IV

is a 1977 graduate of Westminster College, New Wilmington, PA, with a Master of Divinity Degree from Pittsburgh Theological Seminary In 1981. He served Natrona Heights Presbyterian Church for 30 years as their pastor and youth group leader after pastoring and leading the youth ministry at the First Presbyterian Church of Bentleyville, PA. During his career, Cam led a vibrant youth group and counseling ministry. Cam has a keen interest in Christian apologetics, religious movements, and Biblical studies. As a retired pastor, he resides in Natrona Heights, PA with his wife, Laurie, and his son, Cameron, where he continues to serve his Lord and Savior through a new endeavor of authorship and writing.

Bibliography

Abarim Publications. "The Name Magdalene in the Bible: Etymology and Meaning of the Name Magdalene." *Abraim Publications.com* (November 21, 2017), www. abarim-publications.com/Meaning/Magdalene.html (accessed April 8, 2019).

Alcorn, Randy. *Heaven.* Carol Stream, Illinois: Tyndale House Publishers, Inc., 2004.

Archer, Gleason L. *Encyclopedia of Bible Difficulties.* Grand Rapids, MI: Zondervan Publishing House, 1982.

Archer, Gleason L., Jr. *A Survey of the Old Testament: Introduction.* Chicago: Moody Press, 1985.

Aulen, Gustaf, *Christus Victor: An Historical Study of the Three Main Types of the Idea of Atonement.* Translated by A. G. Hebert. New York: MacMillan Publishing Co., Inc., 1977.

Bailey, Kenneth E. "Burial Customs." *Oxford Biblical Studies Online.* www. oxfordbiblicalstudies.com (accessed April 5, 2019).

Bailey, Kenneth E. "Leadership in the New Testament." Lectures presented at Pittsburgh Theological Seminary, Pittsburgh, PA., June 8-12, 1998.

Bailey, Kenneth E. *Finding the Lost: Cultural Keys to Luke 15.* St. Louis, MO: Concordia Publishing House, 1992.

Bailey, Kenneth E. *Jacob & the Prodigal: How Jesus Retold Israel's Story.* Downers Grove, Illinois: InterVarsity Press, 2003.

Bailey, Kenneth E. *Jesus Through Middle Eastern Eyes: Cultural Studies in the Gospels.* Downers Grove, Illinois: InterVarsity Press, 2008.

Bailey, Kenneth E. *Open Hearts in Bethlehem: A Christmas Drama.* Downers Grove, Illinois: InterVaristy Press, 2013.

Bailey, Kenneth E. *Poet & Peasant & Through Peasant Eyes: A Literary-Cultural Approach to the Parables in Luke.* Grand Rapids, Michigan: Wm. B. Eerdmans Publishing Co., 1983.

Bailey, Kenneth E. *The Cross and the Prodigal.* St. Louis, Missouri: Concordia Publishing House, 1973.

Barclay, William. *The Gospel of John.* Vol. 1 of *The Daily Study Bible Series.* Philadelphia: The Westminster Press, 1956.

Barclay, William. *The Gospel of John.* Vol. 2 of *The Daily Study Bible Series.* Philadelphia: The Westminster Press, 1956.

Barclay, William. *The Gospel of Luke.* The Daily Study Bible Series. Philadelphia: The Westminster Press, 1956.

Barclay, William. *The Gospel of Matthew.* Vol. 1 of *The Daily Study Bible Series.* Philadelphia: The Westminster Press, 1958.

Barker, William P. *Everyone in the Bible.* Westwood, NJ: Fleming H. Revell Company, 1966.

Barnes, Albert. "Barnes' Notes on the New Testament, Commentary on Isaiah 7:14." *Studylight.org verse-by-verse Bible Commentary* (2001-2019). https:https://www.studylgiht.org/commentaries/bnb/Isaiah-7.html.1870 (accessed April 23, 2019).

Bauer, Walter. *A Greek-English Lexicon of the New Testament and Other Early Christian Literature.* Translated by W. F. Arndt and F. W. Gingrich. Chicago: The University of Chicago Press, 1957.

Berkhof, L. *Systematic Theology.* Grand Rapids, Michigan: Wm. B. Eerdmans Publishing Co., 1977.

BibleStudy.org. "Meaning of Numbers in the Bible: The Number 40." www.biblestudy.org/bibleref/meaning-of-numbers-in-bible (accessed April 5, 2019).

Bowie, Walter Russell. *The Book of Genesis, Exposition.* Vol. 1 of *The Interpreter's Bible: A Commentary in Twelve Volumes.* Edited by George Arthur Buttrick. Nashville: Abingdon, 1982.

Bowie, Walter Russell. *The Gospel According to St. Luke, Exposition Chs. 1-6.* Vol. 8 of *The Interpreter's Bible: A Commentary in Twelve Volumes.* Edited by George

Arthur Buttrick. Nashville: Abingdon, 1982.

Buttrick, George A. *The Gospel According to St. Matthew, Exposition.* Vol. 7 of *The Interpreter's Bible: A Commentary in Twelve Volumes.* Nashville: Abingdon, 1980.

Buttrick, George Arthur. *The Gospel According to St. Luke, Exposition Chs. 13-18.* Vol. 8 of *The Interpreter's Bible: A Commentary in Twelve Volumes.* Nashville: Abingdon, 1982.

Campolo, Tony. *The Kingdom of God is a Party: God's Radical Plan for His Family.* Dallas, Texas: Word Publishers, 1990.

Campolo, Tony. *Who Switched the Price Tags?* Dallas, Texas: Word Publishing, 1986.

Cann, Rebecca L., Mark Stoneking, and Allan Wilson. "Mitochondrial DNA and Human Evolution." *Nature* (January 1987).

Chaffey, Tim. "Christ's Resurrection-Four Accounts, One Reality:Biblical Authority." *Answers Magazine* (April 5, 2015), https://answersingenesis.org/jesus-christ/ resurrection/christs... (accessed April 5, 2019).

Cheney, Johnston M. *The Life of Christ in Stereo: The Four Gospels Combined as One.* Portland, Oregon: Western Baptist Seminary Press. 1969.

Christianity Stack Exchange. "Why is Mary Magdalene the Patron Saint of Hairdressers: Theory 2: Actual Hairdresser." (2017). Christianity.stackexchange. com/questions/33729 (accessed April 8, 2019).

Clark, W. K. Lowther, ed. *Concise Bible Commentary.* Aylesbury and London SPCK: Hazell, Watson, and Viney LTD, 1952.

Cockrell, E. and Carmen Puscas. "Ancient Jewish Wedding Customs and Jesus Christ, His Bride, the Church." *Rapture Bible Truth* (2014). https://www. rapturebibletruth.com/ancient-Jewish-wedding-customs (accessed April 15, 2019).

Collins, Ace. *Stories Behind the Best-Loved Songs of Christmas.* Grand Rapids, MI: Zondervan, 2001.

Compelling Truth. "Do the Gospel Resurrection Accounts Contradict Each Other?" Got Questions Ministries. (2011-2019). https://www.compellingtruth.org/ resurrection-account.html. (accessed May 3, 2019).

Crabtree, Vexen. "Christian Adoptionism and the Baptism of Jesus Christ: Centuries of Belief Before the Trinity. *The Human Truth Foundation* (January 11, 2011) www.vexan.co.uk/religion/christianity-adoptionism.html (accessed April 1, 2019).

Dobson, James. *Focus on the Family* broadcast. Date unknown.

Ehrman, Bart. D. *How Jesus Became God: The Exaltation of a Jewish Preacher from*

Galilee. New York, NY: Harper Collins, 2014.

Elliot, Charlotte. *Just as I am, Without One Plea.* Edited by John Ribble. Richmond, Philadelphia, New York, 1955.

Emmerich, Roland and Dean Devlin. *Independence Day,* directed by Roland Emmerich, Los Angelos: Centropolis Entertainment and 20th Century Fox, 1996.

Fahl, Mary, Byron Isaccs and Glenn Patscha. *Going Home.* Performed by Mary Fahl. "The Other Side of Time." 2003.

Ferguson, Sinclair B., and David F. Wright, and J.I. Packer, eds. *New Dictionary of Theology.* Downers Grove, Illinois, InterVarsity Press, 1988.

Fleming, Kenneth C. *God's Voice in the Stars: Zodiac Signs and Bible Truth.* Neptune, NJ: Loizeaux Brothers, Inc., 1981.

Frank, Pat. *Hold Back the Night.* Philadelphia: Lippincott, 1952.

Gascoigne, Mike. "Virgin Birth, Jewish Adoption and Genealogy of Yeshua." *Anno Mundi Books* (1997 and updated December 1999.) www.annomundi.com/bible/virgin-birth.htm. (accessed April 1, 2019).

Geisler, Norman L. *The Roots of Evil.* Dallas Texas: Probe Ministries International & Grand Rapids, MI: Zondervan Publishing House, 1978.

Geldenhuys, Norval. *The Gospel According to Luke.* The New International Commentary on the New Testament. Grand Rapids, Michigan: Wm. B. Eerdmans Publishing Co., 1979.

Gerstner, John H. "Jonathan Edwards and God." *Tenth: An Evangelical Quarterly.* Vol. 10, No. 1. Philadelphia: Philadelphia Conference on Reformed Theology and Tenth Presbyterian Church, UPCUSA. (January 1980): 2-71.

Gerstner, John. "Historical Studies: Jonathan Edwards." Classroom course lectures at Pittsburgh Theological Seminary, Pittsburgh, PA, 1979-1980.

Ghost. Directed by Jerry Zucker. Paramount Pictures, July 13, 1990.

Gilmour, S. MacLean. *The Gospel According to St. Luke, Exegesis.* Vol. 8 of *The Interpreter's Bible: A Commentary in Twelve Volumes.* Edited by George Arthur Buttrick. Nashville: Abingdon, 1982.

Gossip, Arthur John. *The Gospel According to St. John, Exposition.* Vol. 8 of *The Interpreter's Bible: A Commentary in Twelve Volumes.* Edited by George Arthur Buttrick. Nashville: Abingdon, 1982.

Guralnik, David B. and Joseph H. Friend, eds. *Webster's New World Dictionary of the American Language, College Edition.* Cleveland and New York: The World Publishing Company, 1968.

Habermas, Gary R. and Michael R, Licona. *The Case for the Resurrection of Jesus.*

Grand Rapids, MI: Kregel Publications, 2004.

Hengel, Martin. *Crucifixion: In the Ancient World and the Folly of the Message of the Cross.* Translated by John Bowden. Philadelphia, PA: Fortress Press, 1977.

Holl, Adolf. *Jesus in Bad Company.* Translated by Simon King. New York: Holt, Rinehart and Winston, 1972.

Hopkins, Joseph. "John." Classroom course lecture at Westminster College, New Wilmington, PA. January 1974.

Hopkins, Joseph. "Old Testament Studies." Classroom course lectures at Westminster College, New Wilmington, PA, 1973-1974.

Horvath, Anthony. "Evidence of Jewish Guards at Jesus' Tomb." *SntJohnny.com* (2013) https://www/scribed.com/book/194951629 (accessed February 5, 2018).

Horvath, Anthony. "Pilate Puts Jesus on Trial, The Jews put Pilate on Trial." *SntJohnny.com* (2013) https://www/scribed.com/book/194951629 (accessed February 5, 2018).

Horvath, Anthony. "The Discipline of the Roman Soldier." *SntJohnny.com* (2013) https://www.scribed.com/book/194951629 (accessed February 5, 2018).

Horvath, Anthony. "The Romans and Jews So (un)Happy Together." *SntJohnny.com* (2013) https://www/scribed.com/book/194951629 (accessed February 5, 2018).

Horvath, Anthony. "Were They Roman Guards of Jewish Guards?" *SntJohnny.com* (2013) https://www.scribed.com/book/194951629 (accessed February 5, 2018).

Horvath, Anthony. "How Many Guards at Jesus' Tomb?" *SntJohnny.com* (April 6, 2019). https://scribed.com/book/194951629/How-Many-Guards-at-the-Tomb (accessed February 5, 2018).

Houdmann, S. Michael. "What is the Meaning of the Parable of the Ten Virgins?" *Got Questions Ministries* (February 14, 2019) https//www'gotquestions.org/parables-ten-virgins.html (accessed April 15, 2019).

Howard, Wilbert F. *The Gospel According to St. John, Exegesis.* Vol. 8 of *The Interpreter's Bible: A Commentary in Twelve Volumes.* Edited by George Arthur Buttrick. Nashville: Abingdon, 1982.

Hunt, Dave. *The Cult Explosion.* Eugene, Oregon: Harvest House Publishers, 1980.

Jackson, Wayne. "Crushing the Serpent's Head: The Meaning of Genesis 3:15." *Christian Courier* (2019). www.christiancourier.com/articles/1571-crushing-the-serpents-head-the-meaning-of-genesis-3-15 (accessed April 22, 2019).

Johnson, Sherman E. *The Gospel According to St. Matthew, Exegesis.* Vol. 7 of *The Interpreter's Bible: A Commentary in Twelve Volumes.* Edited by George Arthur Buttrick. Nashville: Abingdon, 1980.

Johnson, Sherman E. *The Gospel According to St. Matthew: Introduction and Exegesis.* Vol 7 of *The Interpreter's Bible: A Commentary in Twelve Volumes.* Edited by George A. Buttrick. Nashville, Tennessee: Abingdon, 1980.

Josephus, Flavius. *The Works of Flavius Josephus: Comprising the Antiquities of the Jews; A History of the Jewish Wars; and Life of Flavius Josephus, Written by Himself.* Translated by William Whiston. Philadelphia: David McKay, Publisher, 1910.

Jones, David Hugh, ed. *The Hymnbook.* Philadelphia, PA: John Ribble for the Presbyterian Church in the United States, The United Presbyterian Church in the USA, and the Reformed Church in America, 1955.

Jukes, Andrew. *The Names of God in Holy Scripture.* Grand Rapids, Michigan: Kregel Publications, 1986.

Kelley, Robert E. "Luke". Lecture series presented at Pittsburgh Theological Seminary, Pittsburgh, PA, 1979.

Kennedy, D. James. *Knowing the Whole Truth: Basic Christianity and what it Means in Your Life.* Old Tappan, New Jersey: Fleming H. Revell Company, 1985.

Kittel, Gerhard. *Theological Dictionary of the New Testment.* Vol 7. Edited by Gerhard Friedrich. Tranlated by Geoffrey W. Bromoiley. Grand Rapids, Michigan: Wm. B. Eerdmans Publishing Company, 1971.

Knox, John. *The Gospel According to St. Luke, Exposition Chs. 7-12.* Vol. 8 of *The Interpreter's Bible: A Commentary in Twelve Volumes.* Edited by George Arthur Buttrick. Nashville: Abingdon, 1982.

Leman, Derek. "Yeshua In Context: The Life and Times of Yeshua (Jesus) the Messiah, Jewish Names in Galilee and Judea." *Yeshua in Context* (March 29, 2011), YeshuainContext.com (accessed April 18. 2019).

Lewis, C. S. *A Grief Observed.* New York: Seabury Press Inc., and Bantam Books, 1976.

Lewis, C. S. *Mere Christianity.* New York: MacMillan Publishing Co., Inc., 1952.

Little, Paul E. *Know What You Believe.* Wheaton, Illinois: Victor Books, 1970.

Little, Paul E. *Know Who You Believe: The Magnificent Connection.* Colorado Springs, Colorado: Victor, 2003.

Little, Paul E. *Know Why You Believe.* Downers Grove, Illinois: InterVarsity Press, 1968.

Logusz, Michael O. *With Musket & Tomahawk: The Saratoga Campaign and Wilderness War of 1777.* Havertown, PA: Casemate Publishers, 2010.

Machen, J. Greshman. *The Virgin Birth of Christ.* Grand Rapids, Michigan: Baker Book House, 1982.

Marsh, John. *Saint John.* The Pelican New Testament Commentaries, Harmondsworth, Middlesex, England: Penguin Books Ltd., 1968.

Marshall, Alfred. *The Interlinear Greek-English New Testament.* NY: The Iversen-Norman Associates, 1976.

Martin, Walter. *Essential Christianity.* Santa Ana, CA: Vision House, 1980.

McBirnie, William Steuart. *The Search for the Twelve Apostles.* Wheaton, Illinois: Tyndale House Publishers, 1978.

McDowell, Josh and Sean McDowell. *Evidence for the Resurrection: What it Means for Your Relationship with God.* Ventura, CA: Regal Books, 2009.

McDowell, Josh. "No, The Positive Answer." Video lecture published January 22, 2010.

McDowell, Josh. *More Than a Carpenter.* Wheaton, Illinois: Tyndale House Publishers, 1977.

McDowell, Josh. *The Resurrection Factor.* San Bernardino, CA: Here's Life Publishers, Inc., 1981.

Mikkelson, David. "Fact Check: God Rest Ye Merry Gentleman." *Snopes Media Group Inc.* (December 5, 2013). https://www.snopes.com/fact-check/god-rest-ye-merry-gentlemen (accessed April 16, 2019).

Miller, J. Keith. *Sin: Overcoming the Ultimate Deadly Addiction.* San Francisco, CA: Harper & Row, Publishers, 1987.

Miller, Madeleine S. and J. Lane. *The New Harper's Bible Dictionary.* New York: Harper & Row, Publishers, 1973.

Montgomery, John Warwick. *History and Christianity: A Vigorous, Convincing Presentation of the Evidence for a Historical Jesus.* Minneapolis, Minnesota: Bethany House Publishers, 1965.

Morris, Leon. *The Gospel According to John.* The New International Commentary on the New Testament. Grand Rapids, Michigan: Wm. B. Eerdmans Publishing Co., 1979.

Morris, Leon. *The Gospel According to St. Luke.* The Tyndale New Testament Commentaries. Grand Rapids, Michigan: Wm. B. Eerdmans Publishing Co., 1979.

O'Reilly, Bill, and Martin Dugard. *Killing Jesus.* New York, NY: Henry Holt and Company, LLC, 2013.

Ott, Stanley. *The Vibrant Church: A People Building Plan for Congregational Health.* Ventura, California: Regal Books, 1989.

Palestrina, Giovanni Pierluigi da. *The Strife is o'er, The Battle Done.* Adapted by William H. Monk and translated by Francis Pott, Cologne, Germany, 1695.

Papondrea, James L. *The Earliest Christologies: Five Images of Christ in the Postapostolic Age.* Downers Grove, Illinois: InterVarsity Press, 2016.

Pfeiffer, Charles F. and Everett F. Harrison, eds. *The Wycliffe Bible Commentary.* Chicago: Moody Press, 1962.

Phillips, Rob, "The Sea No Longer Existed-Revelation 21:1." *Once Delivered* (November 1, 2016), https://oncedelivered.net/.../the-sea-no-longer-existed-revelation-21:1 (accessed April 16, 2019).

Pope, Charles. "What Were Typical Homes Like in Jesus' Time?" *Community in Mission.* Word Press (March 21, 2017). Blog.adw.org/2017/03houses-like-time-Jesus (accessed April 15, 2019).

Rattenbury, John. "A Living Architecture: Frank Lloyd Wright and Taliesin Architects." *AZ Quotes: Frank Lloyd Wright Quotes* (October 31, 2000). https://www.azquotes.com/author/15963-Frank_Lloyd_Wright (accessed April 9, 2019).

Robinson, John A. T. "The New Testament Dating Game." *Time.* March 21, 1977.

Ross, Hugh, Kenneth Samples, and Mark Clark. *Lights in the Sky & Little Green Men: A Rational Christian Look at UFO's and Extraterrestrials.* Colorado Springs, Colorado: NavPress, 2002.

Ross, Hugh, *Navigating Genesis: A Scientist's Journey through Genesis 1-11.* Covina, CA: Reasons to Believe Press, 2014.

Ross, Hugh. *Why the Universe is the Way it is.* Grand Rapids, Michigan: Baker Books, 2008.

Scherer, Paul. *The Gospel According to St. Luke, Exposition Chs. 19-24.* Vol. 8 of *The Interpreter's Bible: A Commentary in Twelve Volumes.* Edited by George Arthur Buttrick. Nashville: Abingdon, 1982.

Scripture Backdrops: Relevant Historical Insights into Scripture. "Jerusalem at Passover." Bible History On-Line. https://www/bible-history.com (accessed April 5, 2019).

Seekins, Frank T. *A Mighty Warrior: The Hebrew-Biblical View of a Woman.* Phoenix, AZ: Living Word Pictures, Inc., 2004.

Simon, Paul. *Bridge Over Troubled Waters,* performed by Paul Simon and Arthur Garfunkel. Columbia Hall of Fame Recording, 1970.

Simpson, Cuthbert A. *The Book of Genesis, Exegesis.* Vol. 1 of *The Interpreter's Bible: A Commentary in Twelve Volumes.* Edited by George Arthur Buttrick. Nashville: Abingdon, 1982.

Sproul, R. C. *The Holiness of God,* Wheaton, Illinois: Tyndale House Publishers, Inc. 1985.

Sproul, R. C. *The Last Days According to Jesus: When Did Jesus Say He Would Return.* Grand Rapids, MI: Baker Books, 2003.

Stott, John R. W. *The Cross of Christ.* Downers Grove, Illinois: InterVaristy Press, 1986.

Tasker, R. V. G. *The Gospel According to St. John.* The Tyndale New Testament Commentaries. Grand Rapids, Michigan: Wm. B. Eerdmans Publishing Co., 1980.

Tasker, R. V. G. *The Gospel According to St. Matthew.* The Tyndale New Testament Commentaries. Grand Rapids, Michigan: Wm. B. Eerdmans Publishing Co., 1977.

The Chronicles of Narnia – The Lion, The Witch, and the Wardrobe, directed by Andrew Adamson, Walt Disney Pictures and Walden Media, 2006.

The Lost Books of the Bible. New York: Bell Publishing Co., 1979.

Thinkexist.com. "Quotations", www.thinkexist.com (accessed April 9, 2019).

Turner, Ryan. "Does the Gospel of Peter Belong in the New Testament?" *Christian Apologetics Research Ministry.* https://www.carm.org. (accessed April 4, 2019).

Webber, Andrew Lloyd and Tim Rice. *Jesus Christ Superstar.* London, England: Leeds Music Ltd., 1970.

Weintraub, Stanley. *11 Days in December: Christmas at the Bulge, 1944.* New York, NY: NAL Caliber, published by New American Library, a division of Penguin Group, 2006.

White, John Wesley. *Re-entry.* Grand Rapids, Michigan: Zondervan Publishing House, 1970.

Wikipedia. "First Jewish-Roman War," military.wikia.com/wiki/First Jewish-Roman War (accessed April 4, 2019).

Wikipedia. "Jewish-Roman Wars," https://en.wikipedia.org/wiki/jewish-romanwars (accessed April 4, 2019).

Wikipedia. "Mary Magdalene," https://en.wikipedia.org/wiki/Mary_Magdalene (accessed April 8, 2019).

Wikipedia. "Pope Telesphorus." Wikimedia Foundation, Inc. (September 28, 2018), https://en.wikipedia.org/wiki/Pope_Telesphorus (accessed April 16, 2019).

Wildolive. "Jewish Wedding Customs and Their Place in Jesus' Teachings." (February 16, 2013). www.wildolive.co.uk/weddings.htm (accessed April 15, 2019).

Wilson, Ralph F. "Burial in Joseph's Tomb." *Jesus Walk Bible Study Series 107* (2019), http://www.jesuswalk.com (accessed April 5, 2019).

Winward, Stephen. *A Guide to the Prophets.* Atlanta, GA: John Knox Press, 1977.

Yancey, Philip. *Disappointment with God: Three Questions No One Asks Aloud.* Grand Rapids, MI: Zondervan Publishing House, 1988.

Yosef, Uri. "The Seed of a Woman: A Kernal of Deception – Gen. 3:15." *The Ancient Path* (November 20, 2011), Noahide-ancient-path.co.uk/index.php/Judaism-articles/2011/the-seed-of-a-woman-a-kernal-of-deception-genesis-315/ (accessed April 22, 2019).

WA